W9-AFT-679

Gramley Library
Salem Academy and College
Winston-Salem, N.C. 27108

English L2 Reading

Getting to the Bottom

❧

ESL and Applied Linguistics Professional Series
Eli Hinkel, Series Editor

Birch • *English L2 Reading: Getting to the Bottom*

Hinkel • *Second Language Writers' Text: Linguistic and Rhetorical Features*

Hinkel/Fotos, Eds. • *New Perspectives on Grammar Teaching in Second Language Classrooms*

English L2 Reading

Getting to the Bottom

Barbara M. Birch
California State University–Fresno

LAWRENCE ERLBAUM ASSOCIATES, PUBLISHERS
2002   Mahwah, New Jersey   London

Gramley Library
Salem Academy and College
Winston-Salem, N.C. 27108

Copyright © 2002 by Lawrence Erlbaum Associates, Inc.
All rights reserved. No part of this book may be reproduced
in any form, by photostat, microform, retrieval system, or
any other means, without prior written permission of the
publisher.

Lawrence Erlbaum Associates, Inc., Publishers
10 Industrial Avenue
Mahwah, NJ 07430

Cover design by Kathryn Houghtaling Lacey

Library of Congress Cataloging-in-Publication Data

Birch, Barbara M.
English L2 reading : getting to the bottom / Barbara M. Birch.
    p. cm.
    Includes bibliographical references and index.
ISBN 0-8058-3899-6 (alk. paper)
1. English language—Study and teaching—Foreign speakers.
    2. Second language acquisition. 3. Reading comprehension.
    I. Title. II. Series.
PE1128.A2 B497   2002
428'.0071—dc21   2001058366
                                                          CIP

Books published by Lawrence Erlbaum Associates are printed
on acid-free paper, and their bindings are chosen for strength
and durability.

Printed in the United States of America
10 9 8 7 6 5 4 3 2 1

To Jim, Elena, Susan, and Hannah

Contents

Preface

An ideology is more than just a theory or a practice. It is a complex body of interrelated concepts, opinions, and assumptions about an area of culture. Different ideologies are the foundations for different social positions. Nowhere is this truer than in education and in education, nowhere is this truer than in the area of reading research and methodology. One ideology has dominated second language reading for quite a while. This ideology, usually called "whole language," has many ideas and practices that have stood the test of time in research and in the classroom. Many English as a Second Language (ESL) and English as a Foreign Language (EFL) readers benefit greatly from this instruction, which generally takes a top-down view of reading, because students learn to take full advantage of their cognitive abilities to comprehend the text.

This book strongly supports the whole language ideology in general. The materials are exciting and interesting and the methods are inviting and creative. In the hands of an expert teacher, students learn useful reading and vocabulary acquisition strategies. They learn about the importance of cultural knowledge and the characteristics of textual discourse, such as coherence and cohesion. Students learn to enjoy and appreciate reading and writing.

However, in recent years whole language has been characterized as incomplete, in that it seems to de-emphasize certain aspects of reading. A complete, balanced reading ideology (a "truly whole" language ideology) should be big enough to embrace all reading theories and practices. In particular, it should be able to accommodate those researchers and teachers who find that attention to the details of language can also help students learn to read better. This book takes the position that supplementing whole language with a bottom-up focus can strengthen our approach, making it truly holistic.

In fact, research into native English reading processes has, in recent decades, included both the top and the bottom of the reading process; that is, higher level cognitive knowledge and abilities have been examined, but so have low-level linguistic knowledge and abilities. This is producing a more accurate and well-rounded view of reading and how English-speaking children become successful readers. High level reading and general learning strategies have fortunately been topics of research in the English as a second or foreign language field as well, to the benefit of teachers and learners alike. We now know more about English as a Second or Foreign Language (L2) reading than ever before. However, research interest in low-level linguistic knowledge and processing strategies has lagged somewhat behind interest in the top level strategies. I hope this book stimulates more ESL and EFL reading researchers to join those who are exploring this relatively uncharted "ocean" with vigor, persistence, and imagination.

In general terms, this book is intended for all ESL and EFL practitioners interested in or involved in teaching reading. It is relevant to those who are teaching illiterate people to read in English or to those whose students already know how to read in their native language. Taking a fairly theory neutral information-processing perspective for the sake of the organization and presentation of complex material, the book is relevant to reading researchers, curriculum designers, and materials writers. It is for teachers-in-training as well.

Chapter 1 introduces several of the organizing threads to be followed throughout the book. The metaphor of the psycholinguistic guessing game has been a common one since the 1970s, but in the chapter, reading is described as an interactive (top-down and bottom-up) process; this model will be expanded on in each subsequent chapter. The psycholinguistic guessing game metaphor is critiqued and a new metaphor is suggested: that the reading process is an expert decision-making system based on a knowledge base (world and language) and high- and low-level processing strategies. Early developmental stages of native English reading are described in this chapter and are applied to ESL and EFL learners in later chapters.

In chapter 2, after a discussion of various common writing systems in the world and their differences, I make a case that the second language reading literature generally disregards the importance of the first language (L1) writing system. Chapter 3 questions the idea that low-level reading processes in L1 and L2 are the same and begins another organizing thread: that knowledge and processing strategies develop in response to L1, that they might transfer negatively to L2, and that strategies optimal for reading English may not develop without direct instruction. This point is further illustrated by four sample case histories that are followed throughout the remaining chapters: MariCarmen, a Spanish reader; Despina, a Greek reader; Mohammed, an Arabic reader; and Ho, a Chinese reader.

Chapter 4 asks about the relation between pronunciation and reading, starting with a look at English consonant and vowel sounds and some contrasts with other languages and a discussion of some important concepts in linguistics. The idea that pronunciation and reading are directly related is discarded in favor of the idea that accurate listening comprehension is more directly related to reading. From this chapter on, each chapter contains a section entitled "Spotlight on Teaching," which gives some ideas about how the main concepts can be presented to ESL and EFL students, and practiced. In chapter 4, perception and discrimination activities that lead to phonemic awareness are the focus.

Chapter 5 argues in favor of a reunderstanding of the common idea that readers just sample the text. This chapter begins with a look at the concept of the grapheme (as opposed to "letter") and a discussion of English graphemes. Summarizing research that shows that readers read fairly carefully and don't just sample the text, the chapter goes on to discuss expert graphic identification strategies in English and, in the "Spotlight on Teaching," suggests that teachers use direct instruction in grapheme-to-phoneme correspondences to help ESL and EFL learners.

Chapter 6 disputes an idea that is pervasive within the whole of the English-speaking culture throughout the world: that English spelling is chaotic. When carried to the classroom, this idea often means that teachers don't teach about our writing system because they believe that the system is so complex students cannot grasp it or take advantage of it. If they do teach it, it is often with the negative idea that it doesn't make any sense. In fact, our English writing does have a system.

Chapter 7 describes several approaches to phonics instruction in English L1. I outline the strategies that native English-speaking readers develop to handle English vowels, because the correspondence between grapheme and phoneme is not predictable. Recent research from L1 English reading shows that children run through different processing strategies until they ultimately settle on the best strategies for English: the use of onsets and rimes and analogy to known spelling patterns. This is an example of cognitive restructuring of knowledge and suggests methodologies that are quite different from traditional views of "phonics," which should be discarded once and for all.

Chapter 8 revisits the theme that English spelling is systematic if you know what to look for. The chapter examines morphological processes in English, morphology in other languages, phonological processes in English words triggered by derivational changes (as in sane and sanity), and spelling difficulties that stem from them. English writing again is shown to follow fairly consistent morphophonemic spelling rules. There is evidence that readers use different processing strategies to deal with morphological information in reading L1 and L2. Implications for ESL and EFL pedagogy are presented in "Spotlight on Teaching."

Chapter 9 addresses an assumption that teachers sometimes take for granted: that skipping words you don't know is a good strategy for the ESL and EFL reader. This chapter is an exploration of word learning and word recognition, suggesting that the only way that readers can build up an ample mental lexicon in L2 is if they take responsibility for their learning and habitually use the best vocabulary acquisition strategies we know. This is the only way for the mental lexicon and semantic memory to grow and for the reader to improve in automaticity. Chapter 10 is an epilogue that summarizes the book.

In general, this book fits within the growing emphasis on accuracy of form (along with meaning and use) as an important component of communication. In writing this book, I hope to empower teachers to become better able to address specific student needs while maintaining their whole language methodology. I hope to stimulate interest among reading researchers in the study of low-level reading strategies. Although this book is focused exclusively on English reading instruction for the non-native speaker, it can be of interest to anyone interested in second language reading instruction.

ACKNOWLEDGMENTS

I would like to acknowledge the volume's plucky and intrepid reviewers, whose perceptive comments have made this manuscript what it is today. I have been very happy to work with Eli Hinkel and Naomi Silverman, whom I hope one day to meet in person. I am also indebted to all of my colleagues in the Department of Linguistics at California State University–Fresno for their encouragement and help and for providing me with the opportunity to teach Linguistics and Reading, which was where this manuscript began 10 years ago. I must also thank those students of Linguistics 132 and graduate students who read earlier versions, gave insightful feedback, and helped me pilot materials. I am grateful for a sabbatical in 1998, during which I edited an earlier draft of this book and began the process of finding a publisher.

—*Barbara M. Birch*

Chapter 1

The Expert Decision Maker

Prereading questions—Before you read, think, and discuss the following:

1. How do people read? What happens in your mind when you are reading?
2. Do you remember learning to read as a child? Was it a positive or negative experience?
3. Do you enjoy reading now? Why or why not?
4. What do you have to read? What do you like to read? How are these reading experiences different for you?
5. If you are a nonnative speaker of English, do you like to read English as well as your native language? Why or why not?
6. What problems do you have with reading? What is the cause of the problems?

Study Guide questions—Write answers to these questions during and after reading the chapter:

1. What are the metaphors that help us understand the reading process?
2. Explain the components of Figure 1.1.
3. Explain the components of Figure 1.2.
4. What are the developmental stages in reading?
5. What special considerations make English reading difficult for English as a Second Language (ESL) and English as a Foreign Language (EFL) learners?

For many of us, when we sit down to read something, our eyes move across and down the page and we understand the message that the text contains without apparent effort. Such an unconscious process seems simple, but in fact, like many other mental activities we do, reading is complex when examined in all its detail. It is complicated because it involves a great deal of precise knowledge which must be acquired or learned and many processing strategies which must be practiced until they are automatic.

The knowledge and processing strategies for reading can be modeled through the use of a metaphor; that is, we can create a model of a hypothetical information processor in which the different parts and procedures illustrate the different skills of reading and their interaction. The metaphor or model is a pedagogical tool, a convenient fiction, a mere analogy, that permits explanation of some of the complexities of reading in a systematic way. It provides a coherent framework on which to arrange the linguistic information that expert readers need to acquire and that teachers need to know. It serves as the organizational infrastructure of this book.

A very simplified model of the reading process (Adams, 1990; Crowder & Wagner, 1992; Underwood & Batt, 1996) would include storage for general and specific knowledge in long-term memory. The knowledge is organized into memory structures like images, networks, schemas, and frames, which are discussed in later chapters. The knowledge base alone is not sufficient for reading because it cannot interact directly with the text without some kind of processing mechanism. The processing component consists of a variety of strategies that the reader has acquired or learned. The strategies allow the reader to take the text as a source of information and, drawing on the knowledge base as another source, make sense of what is on the printed page. The processing strategies can be optionally consciously or unconsciously applied; that is, they can operate automatically beneath the level of our awareness or they can kick in selectively because of our attention to something we perceive.

The top of the reading process model contains cultural and world knowledge and generalized cognitive processing strategies that construct a meaning for big pieces of text like sentences, paragraphs, or stories. Using these high-level processing strategies, the reader makes predictions about what the text is going to be like, inferences about the motivations of the characters, decisions about how certain events are related in the reading, and the like. The bottom of the model contains precise bits of knowledge about language, writing, and processing strategies that permit our minds to turn squiggles on the page into meaningful symbols. Such a model might look like Fig. 1.1.

In this model of the reading process, the processing strategies work together in parallel, that is, at the same time, with access to the knowledge base to permit the reader to construct ideas and meaning from the printed text. When someone is reading, they need both the information flowing upward from the bottom to the top and the information flowing downward

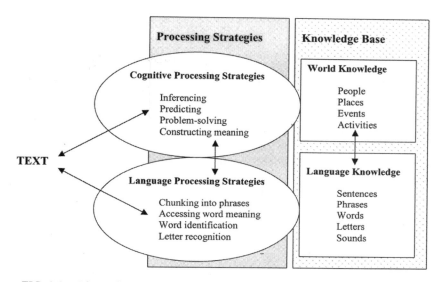

FIG. 1.1   A hypothetical model of the reading process with some sample processing strategies and types of knowledge.

from the top to the bottom to understand the meaning successfully. For example, our perception and recognition of letters lead to our recognition of words, from which we construct meanings. In the other direction, contextual information, inferences, and world knowledge can influence the processing strategies at lower levels. World knowledge can affect our expectations about words and meaning, which can allow us to recognize some words faster than others or understand some meanings faster than others. (See Aebersold & Field, 1997; Day & Bamford, 1998; Urquhart & Weir, 1998; and other recent reading theory texts for similar views.)

Although researchers now know that information flows in both directions while we are reading, there is still some debate among teachers and teacher–trainers about which is the most important in successful reading. Some emphasize the top-down flow of information, sometimes to the neglect of the bottom levels of processing. For example, Coady (1979) said, "The teacher should always put primary emphasis in reading instruction on comprehension strategies ... too much emphasis on concrete process strategies such as letter–sound correspondences can leave the student with a poor priority of strategies" (p. 11). This point of view is generally associated with an approach called whole language instruction. Others place more importance on bottom-up flow of information, to the detriment of comprehension of meaning and world knowledge. This is most often called the "phonics" approach to reading.

In this book, a balanced or integrated approach is adopted; neither direction of information flow is more important than the other because the successful reader must be adept at both bottom-up and top-down processing (Nunes, 1999). Instead of focusing on bottom-up processing to the exclusion of top-down or vice versa, the balanced approach, which emphasizes the interactive nature of reading, is chosen. Indeed, reading is interactive in three ways:

- The different processing strategies, both top and bottom, along with the knowledge base, interact with each other to accomplish the reading.
- The reader's mind interacts with the written text so that the reader can understand the message.
- The reader interacts indirectly with the writer of the text across time and space because it is the writer who is communicating information to the reader, but it is the reader who must grasp the information from the writer.

After describing an interactive approach to reading (much like the one advocated here) in Carrell, Devine, and Eskey (1988), Eskey said, "Despite the emergence of interactive models, I am concerned that much of the second language reading literature continues to exhibit a strongly top-down bias." In a footnote, he noted the preponderance of research into top-down reading, concluding, "This research has resulted in many useful insights, but the lack of attention to decoding problems has, I think, produced a somewhat distorted picture of the true range of problems second language readers face" (p. 95). He went on to say the following:

> In practical terms, my concern is thus to keep the language in the teaching of second language reading. That may not sound very controversial, but I think that in promoting higher-level strategies—like predicting from context or the use of schemata and other kinds of background knowledge—some researchers have been sending a message to teachers that the teaching of reading to second language readers is mostly just a matter of providing them with the right background knowledge for any texts they must read, and encouraging them to make full use of that knowledge in decoding those texts. Though that is certainly important, it is also, I think, potentially misleading as a total approach.... We must not, I believe, lose sight of the fact that language is a major problem in second language reading, and that even educated guessing at meaning is not a substitute for accurate decoding. (p. 97)

Eskey's observation is still true today. Many recent texts on second language reading recognize the importance of the bottom of the reading processing model, but their attention remains firmly on the top (Aebersold & Field, 1997; Day & Bamford, 1998; and others). Wallace (1992), for example, after a very brief discussion of bottom-up processing in reading, said the following:

Eskey (1988) for instance, claims that second language readers need to attend more to "bottom-up" features than do first language readers. Eskey's view is based on the incontrovertible fact that the former will have weaker linguistic competence than the latter and will therefore have less ability to draw on the range of cues—both within and external to the text—which are available to readers in a first language. One response to this situation would be, not to encourage different reader strategies for second language readers, but to ensure that text, context, and reading task give maximum support to the second language learner's current linguistic and schematic knowledge. (pp. 42–43)

Wallace is correct in advocating maximum support for ESL and EFL readers' higher-level processing to supplement deficiencies at the lower level with language. This has been the foundation of second language reading instruction for many years, and should not be discarded. However, teachers can, in addition, help students acquire different, more efficient, bottom-up reading strategies, if they know what to do. That is why, in this book, we focus on the bottom part of the reading model, which we might imagine to look like Fig. 1.2.

Phonological strategies allow us to recognize the sounds of our language as we hear speech. As we will see, phonological information is used in some word recognition strategies especially in languages which use an alphabet for writing. Orthographic strategies allow us to recognize the letter shapes of our alphabet (often called *decoding*), and match them with the sounds of our language, forming a visual and auditory image of a word (often called *recoding*) in our mind. Lexical strategies are the processing strategies we use to recognize words and access word meaning. For frequent words, it is possible that we use a decoded visual image with a direct connection to meaning. For less frequent words we may use a recoded visual and auditory image to recognize the word through sound first and then access the meaning secondarily. Lexical strategies also help us to deal with unknown words. Syntactic strategies help us to unconsciously arrange the recognized words accurately and quickly into phrases and sentences, so that the meaning can be constructed at the top of the reading process. The different strategies each do their own specialized work in coordination with the others so that we can read successfully. Each of these sections of the model (except for syntactic strategies which are omitted from this treatment for space limitations) are discussed in detail in later chapters.

The interactive model described here is complex and somewhat different from another metaphor that has helped us to understand reading: reading is a "psycholinguistic guessing game." This metaphor (Eskey, 1979, p. 69) has become commonplace for describing second language reading since Goodman coined it in 1967 and is still in use today (Underwood & Batt, 1996, pp. 78–79). Bernhardt, 1991, puts it the following way:

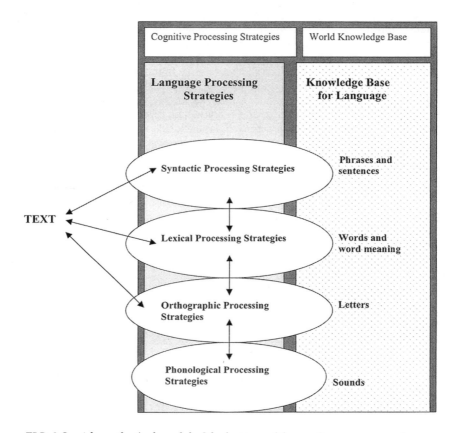

FIG. 1.2   A hypothetical model of the bottom of the reading processor, showing how processing strategies mediate between language knowledge and the
text to create a basic understanding of the text.

One of the major findings in this examination of the literature is the dominance of the psycholinguistic model exemplified by the writings of Goodman
(1968) and Smith (1971). It is remarkable that an area of disciplined inquiry
such as reading in a second language could be so dominated by one con-
ceptual framework. There may be two explanations for this phenomenon. It
may be that academicians in this field have agreed that the psycholinguistic
framework provides the most viable explanation of reading as a second language. Another is that there is a basic lack of awareness and perception of
the capabilities of models other than those of Goodman (1968) and Smith
(1971) to explain second language reading phenomena. Since unanimity is
rare in any academic area, the latter explanation is more convincing. (p. 22)

In spite of its longevity, the "psycholinguistic guessing game" metaphor has certain limitations. One problem with it is that it oversimplifies many people's idea of the reading process, something that Goodman (1967, 1968) never intended. Guessing is a complex cognitive process of weighing the importance of different information to come up with the best answer; it is not like flipping a coin. Although much of this processing is unconscious, it is not easy, and correct guessing relies on having reasonably correct information with which to work. Another consequence of the metaphor is that instruction about sounds and letters is sometimes neglected because, as teachers have been overheard to say, "readers are just guessing anyway."

I suggest another metaphor for understanding reading based on the interactive model discussed earlier. Our model of the reading process is actually an expert decision-making system, a highly sophisticated computing system that allows good readers to make split-second decisions about what they are reading in such an effortless and unconscious way that they do not realize they are doing anything special. It is only in this very specialized sense that reading is a guessing game.

There are two reasons why it's time to discard the "reading-as-a-psycholinguistic-guessing-game" metaphor, especially for ESL and EFL learners. Many learners learn to read English without much direct instruction in decoding or recoding the letters. They learn unconsciously by themselves the relation between letters and sounds and can successfully generalize this information to apply it to new words with which they are confronted. However, not all ESL and EFL learners become expert readers; they don't seem to catch on to the relation between letters and sounds, or they are unable to extend their knowledge to words that they haven't seen before. Some ESL and EFL readers seem to get stuck in an early stage of reading development and they need direct intervention to move on. Some readers advance as far as they can with top-down reading strategies and then can go no further.

At the same time that teachers have noticed that not all ESL and EFL learners learn to read without direct instruction in decoding and recoding, researchers have become aware of the great complexity of the reading process, even at the lowest levels. They have learned that phonological knowledge is crucial for fluent alphabetic reading with comprehension although we are not consciously aware of it. They have learned that processing strategies are language-dependent, that is, they differ from writing system to writing system. They have learned that such processing strategies can transfer from first language (L1) to second language (L2), and thus have positive or negative consequences for readers.

Teachers and teacher–trainers should begin to think of reading as an expert decision-making system such as Medsker and Liebowitz (1994) describe. An expert system is an artificial intelligence application designed to emulate the abilities of a human expert. (I appreciate the irony of using a computer model which is designed to emulate human processing as a metaphor for understanding human processing.) An expert system is a computer program which can do symbolic processing well, based on a large number of facts and several hundred rules or heuristics. Heuristics are rules learned either directly (i.e., through instruction) or indirectly (i.e., through experience), that guide the expert decision maker to its decisions. Expert systems are appropriate when there is consensus on the proper solution or decision, but when decisions sometimes need to be based on incomplete or uncertain information and when incorrect or nonoptimal results can be tolerated.

In reading, decoding and recoding is the processing of written symbols with strategies based on facts, patterns, and heuristics. There is consensus about the proper outcome in low-level processing because we agree (barring dialect differences) on the relation between the written symbols and what they represent: letters and sounds, sequences of letters and sequences of sounds, written words and spoken words, and so on. In higher-level processing of texts, there is also general consensus on what specific passages are supposed to mean, but they can be subject to individual interpretation at times. For example, in poetry, we may agree that certain words have a particular meaning or we may think that the words are being used in an individual way. The overall meaning of the poem may be accepted by many, but individual readers may also find different meanings.

In addition, in reading, incorrect outcomes, like misread letters or misinterpreted words, can be tolerated in specific tasks because there is quite a bit of redundancy in reading. Words and meanings are repeated several times, so the reader has ample chance to correct an incorrect outcome. Also, in reading, the reader's eye can travel backward on the page, going back to check earlier outcomes if there is some conflicting information that the reader detects. The information that the reader has is often incomplete or uncertain; certainly this is true in reading a stranger's handwriting, but it is also true in reading anything that might have errors, incompleteness, or ambiguities.

THE DEVELOPMENT OF LOW-LEVEL READING

The interactive model of the reading process and the metaphor of the expert decision-making system both suggest that there are important bits of linguistic knowledge and different strategies which must be developed for a reader to become expert at reading an alphabetic system. Chall (1983) is still the best (and the original) source for the five general developmental steps in learning to read English. Chall's first stage of reading, Stage 0, actually describes the optimal prereaders who can name and recognize the letters of the alphabet and write their own names. They can hold a book right side up and pretend to read it by remembering the words and looking at the pictures. They can use clues in the pictures to guess what the story is. If prereaders pretend to read a book without knowing how to read, they are relying on top level abilities to get the information from the book: memory, guessing from context, and knowledge of the world. For this reason, Chall suggested that optimal prereaders seem to be using a top-down reading style.

Stage 1 is the beginning of reading, when readers begin to learn to decode and recode the written marks on the page and associate them with sounds, syllables, and words. Stage 1 readers learn the alphabetic principle, that the letters on the page "mean" the sounds of the language. They are preoccupied with learning the lower level skills of orthographic and phonological processing and this preoccupation is seen in beginning readers' preference for reading out loud. They are linking the written symbols (letters) with the spoken symbols (sounds) and this linkage must become automatic for fluent silent reading to develop. As orthographic and phonological processing strategies become more automatic, they do not become less important, but they do become less perceptible. The strategies become so inaccessible to perception that we do not always realize that we are doing them when we are reading.

In Stage 2, successful readers' abilities to decode and recode the written medium improve substantially. Automatic, fluent, and mainly unconscious bottom-up processing gives these readers the needed time to do more and better top-down processing of the written material, using context and world knowledge to make inferences about the reading material and to improve comprehension. We are beginning to understand how this automaticity and fluency is achieved in successful readers, and this will be a topic for later chapters. In Stage 2, however, some readers begin to lose momentum; they must be motivated to read extensively and abundantly with texts at their independent reading level. If for some reason this does not take place (e.g., if they are forced to read texts that are too difficult or unmotivating), readers often cease to improve their reading skill because they stop practicing. At this stage and the next, top-down comprehension processes can supplement deficient bottom-up decoding and recoding processes, but readers who cannot process English text automatically will face a handicap if they need to do extensive reading. A vicious cycle can develop. Poor readers avoid reading and lack of reading practice means they do not improve.

During Stage 3, reading joins other learning methods: tasting, touching, listening, and watching. Readers begin to be able to use reading as a tool to acquire knowledge. Stage 3 readers are occupied with learning new vocabulary, which encodes the information they are learning, so it is vital that reading material at this stage begin with the knowledge that learners have already acquired to establish a supportive framework for further learning. Vocabulary enrichment strategies are important for the reader at this stage. Top-down processing becomes especially important because readers must learn to look for facts, concepts, and points of view. Readers begin to use critical analysis while reading, but this ability becomes even more crucial in Stages 4 and 5, when reading becomes a primary method of learning. Advanced readers must read ever more complex texts and must comprehend subtle nuances of meaning. They must be skillful at analysis, criticism, synthesis, and detecting secondary meanings. Throughout their lives, people continue to improve their abilities to read as long as they read challenging and thought-provoking materials.

If these stages are normal for English speakers learning their alphabetic writing, we might wonder how many of our ESL and EFL students go through the early developmental stages that lead to later expert reading. Learning to read in English is harder for L2 learners than for English L1 prereaders because of interference from their L1. The languages of the world have different writing systems and each reader's knowledge base contains, at first, only that knowledge that is relevant to his or her own language and writing system. It is logical to think that exposure to any given writing system will cause L1 readers to develop different low-level reading strategies to deal with the exigencies of their writing systems. These L1 strategies, when the reader begins to learn to read English, may transfer to the L2. It is true that transfer may facilitate reading in the L2, but it is equally true that it might interfere.

Besides problems associated with interference and transfer, L2 readers may not develop the low-level processing strategies that native English speakers develop, so that they may not read English in the most efficient way. They may not be able to progress from the early developmental stages to later, more advanced stages. For students to advance in reading abilities, some may need direct instruction in the low-level processing strategies for English. Even students in advanced ESL and EFL reading classes may benefit from remediation so that their expert low-level decision-making capacity becomes automatic and fast. For English teachers to provide instructional support and remediation, they must know about how expert readers read in English, what linguistic knowledge they have, and what processing strategies work best. They must know something about what linguistic knowledge and processing strategies ESL and EFL students have developed for their L1. In the next chapter, we begin with a look at the different L1 writing systems of the world.

DISCUSSION QUESTIONS

1. Go over the model of the top and bottom of the reading processor in Fig. 1.1. In your opinion, what special problems in each area do English as a second and foreign language readers face in dealing with English texts?

2. Moats (1995) argued that many reading teachers lack enough knowledge to teach English grammar, word structure, and writing explicitly. Do you know what these words mean? Take this quiz now and then when you finish reading the book to see if your answers have changed:

   • Logogram.
   • Transparent orthography.

- Phoneme.
- Phone.
- Grapheme.
- Morphology.
- Derivation.
- Inflection.
- Onset.
- Rime.
- Tense vowel.
- Morphophonemic writing.

Gramley Library
Salem Academy and College
Winston-Salem, N.C. 27108

Chapter 2

Writing Systems

Prereading questions—Before you read, think, and discuss the following:

1. What other writing systems do you know about?
2. Which of these representations of a number is more efficient to use in solving math problems: one or 1? Why?
3. If you were to devise a writing system for a language used in a science fiction movie (like Vulcan), which characteristics would it have?

Study Guide questions—Write answers to these questions during and after you read the chapter:

1. How did writing develop in general?
2. What are the three main types of writing in the world today? Define them.
3. Does each of specific writing systems for languages described fit into one of these types exactly? For example, is Chinese writing purely logographic? Is Japanese writing purely syllabic? Is English writing purely alphabetic?
4. What is the difference between transparent and opaque writing systems?
5. How has English writing become opaque? What are the chances of spelling reform?
6. For whom is opacity a problem? Why?

Our prehistoric ancestors dr(·v pictures of hunting activities on the walls and ceilings of the caves they inhabited. When modern humans find these pictures, they have a fairly good idea what they depict because they represent an object or event directly and not symbolically. Because they represent their meaning directly, cave drawings cannot be considered true writing. In a similar fashion, airports and train stations use standardized signs precisely because they are independent of specific languages. The stick figures used to symbolize restrooms or the crossed knife and fork for restaurants can be understood by those travelers who have acquired a certain global culture, no matter what language they speak. Similarly, on the Internet, a shorthand sign :-) is used to express an emotion directly because words cannot always convey the right tone. These signs cannot be considered true writing either, because true writing is symbolic and indirect.

A true writing system uses a written symbol to represent a unit of language and not an object, event, or emotion directly. All true writing systems were great advances in human technology. We are not used to thinking of writing as a technology, but in fact, it is. Technology is defined as the following:

> ... general term for the processes by which human beings fashion tools and machines to increase their control and understanding of the material environment.... Innovations [in technology] tend to transform traditional cultural systems, frequently with unexpected social consequences. Thus, technology can be conceived of as both a creative and a destructive process. Merritt (1999).

Writing is a tool which increases human control of communication and knowledge. It is creative in so many ways, but it also tends to be destructive of oral traditions relying on memory.

Over time, three types of writing technology have developed: logographic, syllabic, and alphabetic. Each technology is based on segmenting individual words from the flow of speech and representing them somehow in a more permanent manner on stone, clay, or paper. Segmentation is not necessarily easy or intuitive, and that is why people can make funny confusions when they write down spoken phrases, such as "pullet surprises" for "Pulitzer prizes." The written symbols in each of the three writing systems represent different linguistic units, although it is probably safe to say that most writing systems use more than one type of symbol. The different writing systems are summarized in Fig. 2.0.

LOGOGRAPHIC SYSTEMS

In logographic writing systems, one symbol represents the concept or meaning of an individual word or part of a word. Although the symbol can be read out loud with the sounds of the word represented by its meaning, a

Technological Basis	Script Name	Region of Use
Meaning-based		
Logographic	Sinograms	China,Taiwan
	Kanji	Japan
	Hanzza	Korea
	Arabic Numbers	World
	Math operations	World
Syllable-based		
Syllabary	Kana	Japan
Alphabetic-syllabary	Hangul	Korea
Phoneme-based		
Consonantal Alphabet	Arabic, Hebrew	Middle East/Africa
Roman Alphabet		Europe, Americas
Transparent	Spanish, Finnish	
Opaque	English	
Cyrillic	Russian, Serbian	Eastern Europe
Greek	Greek	Greece

FIG. 2.0   Summary of some writing systems.

logographic writing system is largely independent of any spoken language. We can understand the characteristics of logograms by looking at those with which we are most familiar. English writing uses certain logograms: 1, 2, 3, (and all numerical writing), !, #, $, and so on. These symbols do not really have a pronunciation (as the artist Prince found out when he tried to change his name to a logogram). Instead of a pronunciation, most logograms have a name. The term "dollar sign" is the name of $, not the pronunciation of $. The term "question mark" is the name of ?, not the pronunciation of ?. When reading these logograms, we understand the meaning of them without accessing the name. (Unfortunately, the logogram selected by Prince did not have such a name, so people didn't know what to call him and his symbol never became commonplace enough for people to understand by a direct link to meaning. Recently, he has reclaimed the use of his real name, with its pronunciation and written form.)

A standardized largely logographic system of approximately 60,000 sinograms (and still growing) is used to represent Cantonese, Mandarin, and the other languages and dialects we group as Chinese. The reason the system is still growing is that each time a new word is invented or borrowed, a completely new symbol must be invented as well to represent the word in writing. However, according to Mair (1996), only 6,600 sinograms are sufficient to convey most meanings in most texts. The script reflects the properties of Classical Chinese well, but it corresponds poorly to the contemporary vernacular languages and regional varieties of Chinese. Because of the poor correspondence, "each character is a distinct entity and must be stored as a separate unit in memories or fonts" (p. 200).

Chinese characters are more accurately called sinograms (and not logograms) because they are not completely logographic. Eighty-one percent of the Chinese sinograms consist of a combination of a *radical*, one of two hundred or so symbols representing an element of meaning, and a *phonetic complement*, which indicates the sound by means of an analogy. Henderson (1982) gave a useful explanation: "[i]t is as if we represented corn by means of a complex sign combining a semantic pointer to cereal crops and a phonological cue: rhymes with 'horn'" (p. 17). Chinese people are said to use the shape of the sinograms as gestures in the air as they speak, to disambiguate speech, so in some ways the gestural use of sinograms may resemble a sign language. Aebersold and Field (1997) noted that Chinese characters are used not only for communication, but also for artistic expression.

According to Mair (1996), Chinese writing has been standardized and therefore largely unchanging since approximately 200 BCE, but the spoken language has changed quite a bit since that time. Therefore, there is considerable difference between the way the words are actually pronounced and the written phonetic complements that are supposed to help the reader. He said the following:

> ... neither the semantic nor the phonetic components of the sinograms provide an exact indication of meaning or sound, but only give a vague approximation.... Readers must guess or memorize the appropriate sound of the phonetic complement for each character in which it occurs; they must also associate the graph with a word that they already know. Only then can they arrive at the meaning of the sinogram in question. (pp. 201–202).

Some phonetic complements have more than one pronunciation, and even more confusing for the reader, hundreds of sinograms may represent different meanings but the same sound because Chinese has many homophonous words. Also, Chinese writing does not represent grammatical markings that change in different contexts, such as tense markers on

Sample of Modern Mandarin Chinese

1. Chinese:	我	時常	記	起
2. Transliteration:	wǒ	shícháng	jì	qǐ
3. Transcription:	uo	ṣr ʂaŋ	ɉi	ʂü
4. Gloss:	I	frequently	remember	rise

1.	你	對	我	的	鼓勵,
2.	nǐ	duì	wǒ	de	gǔlì
3.	ni	duei	uo	də	guli
4.	you	toward	I/me	(Possessive)	encourage

1.	我	想	無論	生活	給予
2.	wǒ	xiǎng	wúlùn	shēnghuó	jǐyǔ
3.	uo	ɕiaŋ	u lun	ṣəŋ xuə	ɉi ü
4.	I	think/feel	no matter what	life	render/bestow

1.	我	們	多少	磨難,
2.	wǒ	men	duōshǎo	mónàn
3.	uo	mən	duə ṣau	mo nan
4.	I	(Plural)	how much	hardship/tribulation

1.	我	們	都	應該	勇敢	的
2.	wǒ	men	dōu	yīnggāi	yǒnggǎn	de
3.	uo	mən	dəu	iŋ gai	ioŋ gan	də
4.	I	(Plural)	all	must	brave/courage	(Possesive)

1.	去	面對。
2.	qù	miànduì
3.	ʂü	mian duei
4.	go	face/confront

'I often remember the encouragement you gave me, and I feel that no matter what hardships life bestows upon us, we all must have the courage to confront them.'

FIG. 2.1   Sample of Chinese writing. Personal letter (translated by Charles Ettner).

verbs. According to Tseng and Hung (1981), Chinese children, in learning to read, learn to associate each spoken syllable or word with a particular syntactically unchanging character of a designated meaning. (However, in the People's Republic of China, there is a "romanized" alphabetic system called *pinyin* which also has many uses, so some Chinese readers have become familiar with alphabetic writing.)

The Chinese logographic system is also part of Japanese culture, both historically and in contemporary writing. The Japanese borrowed Chinese writing by way of Korea in a form of writing that is still in use: *kanji*. (I have seen Japanese students and Chinese students communicate ideas in logographic writing that they could not communicate in their beginning English.) The kanji system is complex in Japanese; it is not a simple one-to-one correspondence between symbol and meaning. According to Smith (1996), there are two ways to read each kanji symbol. One represents the pronunciation in Chinese at the time it was borrowed and the other is with a Japanese word or morpheme that corresponds to the meaning. Approximately 25% of the 2,000 kanji in use have phonological clues to their pronunciation in Chinese. Kanji symbols encode content words: nouns, verb stems, adjective stems, and some adverbs.

SYLLABIC WRITING SYSTEMS

Japanese also has a syllabic writing system. In syllabic writing systems, one symbol represents a consonant–vowel sequence or a consonant–vowel–consonant sequence of sounds. Each symbol is a unified whole; it cannot be broken down into smaller parts to represent the individual consonants and vowels. Once individual spoken words are segmented from the flow of speech, they can be broken up into syllables in a way that seems quite intuitive because they have beats or rhythms. Then the sound of each syllable can be represented with a written symbol and the conglomerate represents the word in written form. Syllabic writing is very sensible for a language like Japanese, in which there are relatively few different syllables which make up the words. Think about the Japanese words and names that you know and you can see that they are made up of the same syllables used over and over in different combinations.

Japanese writing has two syllabaries, one called *katakana* which is used for foreign loan words and one called *hiragana* for grammatical formatives, although both are complete systems which can represent everything in the spoken language. There are 47 symbols in Kana. The Kana systems seem easy for children to learn because Morton and Sasanuma (1984) reported that most children have learned it by age 6 when they enter elementary school. There also appear to be few reading problems caused by dyslexia with Japanese writing. Syllable structure is stable over time, so syllabic writing maintains its connection to the sound system well. In Japanese writing the kanji and the kana are blended together, and to top it all off, words can be written in *romanji*, an alphabetic system used for names, signs, and acronyms. Smith (1996) called Japanese writing "a complexly organized, multi-scriptal (or multi-orthographic) system" (p. 213).

Korean is a language with more complex syllable structures than Japanese: V, VC, CV, CVC, and CVCC. Korea developed a syllabic writing system derived from Chinese characters, called *Hangul*, in the year 1444. It is

1. Japanese	:	現在	大学の		独自性や	ユニークさが
2. Transliteration	:	genzai	daigaku-no		dokujisei-ya	yunikusa-ga
3. Gloss	:	today	university-Gen		originality-and	unique-Nom

1. Japanese	:	就職	環境と		共に	大学	選択の	大きな
2. Transliteration	:	syushoku	kankyo-to		tomo-ni	daigaku	sentaku-no	ookina
3. Gloss	:	job	environment-and		with	university	choice-Gen	big

1. Japanese	:	ウェートを	占める	中で	次	から	次
2. Transliteration	:	ueito-wo	shimeru	naka-de	tsugi	kara	tsugi
3. Gloss	:	weight-Acc	hold	within	next	from	next

1. Japanese	:	へと	新	企画を	打ち出し	大きな
2. Transliteration	:	eto	shin	kikaku-wo	uchidashi	ookina
3. Gloss	:	to	new	plan-Acc	create	big

1. Japanese	:	注目を	集めている	大学が	ある
2. Transliteration	:	chuumoku-wo	atsumeteiru	university-ga	aru
3. Gloss	:	attention-Acc	getting	university-Nom	exist

"Today there are universities that are gaining much attention because they are hammering out new [recruitment] plans one after another in response to applicants giving greater weight in university selection to the university's originality and uniqueness, as well as to the employment situation."

FIG. 2.2   Sample of Japanese writing. Kanda (2000), translation by Dr. Raymond Weitzman with Eiji Koyama.

one of the few cultures in the world which commemorates the origin of its writing system with a special holiday. Hangul is complicated but very systematic; its basis is 24 alphabetic symbols, which in different combinations (called syllabographs), represent the syllables of the language. Each symbol begins with a consonant symbol; the vowel symbols are added to it. King (1996) suggested that "the simplicity of its graphic elements promotes learnability, while its syllabic organization enhances efficiency in processing and reading" (p. 220). Korean writing also makes use of Chinese characters in writing; they are called *Hanzza*.

ALPHABETIC WRITING SYSTEMS

In alphabetic writing, such as English uses, generally one symbol represents one sound, either a consonant or a vowel. The same alphabet itself may be used to write a number of languages with only minor adaptations, so the representation of writing in each case is related to spoken words of the language. That is, unlike logographic systems, which are largely independent of any spoken language, English writing is uniquely related to the English language, French writing to the French language, and so on. Thus, an advantage of alphabetic writing is that a small number of symbols (around 26) can be used to represent all of the words of the language. A disadvantage is that the reader must know the language to read the writing system. There are a number of different alphabets in use today: the Roman, as in English, the Greek, and the Cyrillic, used in many of the Slavic languages.

In many ways, alphabetic writing was a very complex technological development in human culture. First of all, as in all writing systems, someone had to get the idea that the flow of speech could be segmented into words, but then someone had to realize that spoken words can be segmented into individual consonant and vowel sounds. There is no inherent rhythmic sep-

Hangul (Korean)

1. 나는   여자들이   직장을 다니는   게   싫다.
2. nanun   yercatuli   cikcangul taninun   ke   silhta.
3. I-nom   woman-plural-nom work-obj go-nom   thing-nom   dislike.
4. 'I dislike that women go to work'

1. 물론 좋은 면도 있지만,   나는   젠틀맨도   아닌데
2. mulon cohun myunto issciman   nanun   centlmanto   aninte
3. surely good aspect is-even-though I –nom gentleman   not
4. 'surely there is a good aspect, but even though I am not a gentleman'

1. 여자들이   고생을   하면서   직장을 다니는   모습을
2. yercatuli   kosangul   hamyunse cikcangul taninun mosupul
3. woman-plural-Nom suffer-obj do-while   work-obj go to   feature(picture)-
                                                              obj
4. 'the picture that women go to work with suffering'

1. 그리   편안한   마음으로   보는   편은   아니다.
2. kuri   pyunanhan   maumuro   bonun   pyunun   anita.
3. so   easy   mind-with   look at rather   not-predicate verb
4. 'I feel rather uneasy looking at'

Translation:
'I dislike that women go to work. Surely there is a good aspect, but even though I am not a gentleman, I feel rather uneasy looking at the picture that women go to work with suffering.'

FIG. 2.3 Sample of Korean writing. Park (1998), translation by Su Min Hong.

aration between the various sounds in the words within the rapid flow of speech, in the way that there is with the syllable. Studies with illiterate people show that neither adults nor children find it easy to segment words into the individual sounds (Morais et al., 1979). It doesn't seem to be an ability that people are born with, but rather an ability which must be acquired, either as a precursor to, or even as a result of, reading with an alphabetic script. We'll come back to this issue of segmentation later, when we discuss phonemic awareness.

The originators of alphabetic writing had discovered the alphabetic principle: that one abstract symbol can be made to stand for one sound of a language, and that the symbols can be written together to stand for a word (Byrne, 1998). The relation between the symbol and the sound is arbitrary and conventional. In other words, there is no inherent reason why the mark s stands for the /s/ sound or the mark o often stands for the sound /o/. As English speakers and writers, we agree to represent the sounds in one way and not another. By convention, we all write (mostly) the same way. Spelling errors naturally break this convention. One important point about the alphabetic principle is that, just as its original invention was crucial, so is its acquisition by each child or adult who learns to read an alphabetic language. In fact, this is the first step in reading: that the prereader understand that the squiggles and marks on the page are not random but that they are a consistent system of representation in which each letter stands for a sound and writing the letters in one particular order together in a line means writing a spoken word composed of a sequence of sounds.

Some modern alphabets consist mainly of consonantal representation, with the writing of vowels fragmentary and incomplete; Hebrew and Arabic are examples of mainly consonantal representation. Modern Hebrew has 22 consonant letters which have remained largely the same since antiquity (Goerwitz, 1996). At present, Modern Hebrew can represent vowels only partially through diacritics, marks which occur along with the consonants, but even this use is inconsistent (Levin, Ravid, & Rapaport, 1999).

Standard Arabic has 28 consonant letters which are in a one-to-one relation with the Arabic consonants and some of the vowels (Bauer, 1996). As with Hebrew, there is a set of diacritics to indicate vowels, but they are of specialized usage, not normal usage. In reading Standard Arabic, the lack of vowel letters produces ambiguity. It is not always possible to determine what the word is or what part of speech it is from the writing without using syntactic context. Standard Arabic writing is a kind of lingua franca, a common language which unites the Muslim world, but it is not like any of the regional modern varieties of spoken Arabic. Thus, in order to read Standard Arabic, one must learn it in school.

For many languages, the alphabetic writing system represents both the consonant and vowel sounds of the language with fair regularity; for these languages, the connection between the writing system and the sound system is *transparent*. Although it is probably safe to say that no alphabetic writing

SAMPLE OF MODERN HEBREW

1. Hebrew	המדף	מן	החפץ	את	הרים	יואל ←
2. Transliteration	PDMH	NM	CPXH	T?	MYRH	L?WY ←
3. Transcription	fadam-ah	nim	cefex-ah	te	mireh	leoy ←
4. Gloss	the-shelf	from	the-object	ACC	raised.he	Joel

1.	המתווך	כאבו	עיניו	מקרוב	בו	והתבונן
2.	KWWTMH	WB?K	WYNY?	BWRQM	WB	NNWBTHW
3.	xevatem-ah	u-vaak	vane	vorak-im	o-b	nenobtih-ev
4.	the-agent	hurt.they	eyes.his	from-near	in-it	and-examined.he

1.	כן	ועל	שאלתו	את	שמע	לא	שיואל	חשב
2.	NK	LʕW	WTL?Š	T?	ʕMŠ	?L	L?WYŠ	BŠX
3.	nek	la-ev	o-taleeš	te	amaš	ol	leoy-eš	vašax
4.	so	and-on	question-his	ACC	heard.he	not	that-Joel	thought.he

1.	הבית	מאחורי	להציץ	נלך	עליה	חזר
2.	TYBH	YRWX?M	CYCHL	KLN	HYLʕ	RZX
3.	tiyab-ah	eroxa-em	cicah-el	xelen	ah-ela	razax
4.	the-house	from-behind	to-peak	let's.go	on-her	returned.he

1.	לענות	יואל	מהר	לא	החלי ט	שכבר	למרות
2.	TWNʕL	L?WY	RHM	?L	TYLXH	RBKŠ	TWRML
3.	tona-al	leoy	reham	ol	tilxeh	ravk-eš	tomral
4.	to-answer	Joel	fast	not	decided.he	that-already	despite

1.	תשובותיו	את	להשהות	היה	רגיל
2.	WYTWBWŠT	T?	TWHŠHL	HYH	LYGR
3.	va-tovušt	te	to?šah-el	ayah	ligar
4.	answers-his	ACC	to-dally	was.he	accustomed

'Joel raised the object from the shelf and examined it up close. His eyes hurt. The agent thought that Joel had not heard his question and, therefore, repeated it: "Why don't we take a look behind the house?" Although he had already decided, Joel did not answer quickly. He was accustomed to deliberating before answering...'

—Oz 1989:5

FIG. 2.4   Sample of Hebrew writing. Oz (1989), translation by Dr. Jack Zeldis.

system is completely regular, Spanish, German, Serbo–Croatian, and Greek tend toward transparency. German inconsistencies appear to occur mainly in consonant representations.

You have probably heard that English spelling violates the alphabetic principle in that there are fewer letters than needed to represent the sounds of English. Some letters are not needed: c, q, and x could be substituted by other letters: s, k, or ks. In addition, some letters stand for more than one sound (e.g., letter c can be pronounced /k/ or /s/ depending on the word: **cat** or **city**); some sounds are represented by more than one letter (e.g., the sound /k/ can be written as **c** or **k**: **cat** or **kin**); or some letters represent no apparent sound at all (e.g., **g** in the word **sign**). There is, in addition, little pattern in the way that the vowel letters correspond to vowel sounds. English spelling is often considered chaotic or inconsistent. In general, writing systems in which the correlation between letter and sound is not consistent are called *opaque*. Other writing systems which tend toward opacity are Russian and French. Opinions vary but these are generally considered less opaque or more transparent than English. How did the English writing system get so opaque? The earliest writing system used in English was the runic alphabet, but with the Christianization of the English the Anglo–Saxon alphabet was adapted from Roman letters in the late 6th century by missionaries from Ireland (Millward, 1996). The correspondence between letter and sound was very transparent at that time, but English orthography (rules or conventions for using letters to spell words) became complicated over time. There are problems stemming from the history of writing in English, from our propensity for borrowing words from other languages, and from the sound changes which have occurred in English over time. In fact, by the time of Middle English (1100–1600), there was a great diversity in the way that words were spelled, reflecting the great diversity of regional dialects of English. There were few conventions in the way that words were spelled from place to place within England. Writers wrote words however they were pronounced in that area (Millward, 1996).

When England was conquered by the Norman French, French writers introduced some French writing conventions. They wrote words like **right** with a **gh**, where in Old English it had been **riht**. Furthermore, the /h/ ceased to be pronounced at all by the late 15th century, leaving us with two "silent" letters in words like **right**, **night**, and so on. English scholars who admired classical languages tried to improve English spelling by tracing words back to their origins and revealing the origins in the spelling: **comptroller**, **debt**, or **sovereign**. The English word **island** never had an **s**; it was added to make it more Latin-like. Samuel Johnson's 1775 dictionary standardized and conventionalized many of the illogical spellings of his day (Taylor & Taylor, 1983).

Throughout the history of English, there has been a tendency to borrow foreign words. As a result, English has an abundance of loan words from other languages. Sometimes the spelling has been changed to reflect an English pronunciation (e.g., **vamoose** and **savvy** from Spanish **vamos** and **sabe**), but sometimes borrowed words are spelled the same as they are in the original language (e.g., Spanish **tortilla** [tortiya] or **marijuana** [mɛɾihwana]), causing more exceptions to English spelling conventions (ll ⟹ [y] and j ⟹ [h]).

Alphabetic systems, because they are linked to sound systems, have one big disadvantage. Phonological systems in a language usually undergo changes over time. The problem is that systematic pronunciation changes cannot easily be reflected in an alphabetic writing system which has become standardized in a culture. Once a writing system becomes standardized, it is extremely difficult to change because people resist any change to the system that is familiar to them. Phonological changes that have occurred over the centuries in the spoken language are not reflected in our writing system.

It may seem like these problems are overwhelming and that we should advocate a spelling reform which would bring English writing more in line with English speech sounds. However, there are some advantages to the system as it stands right now. For one thing, we said earlier that spelling was agreed on by convention a couple of centuries ago. Thus, we already have an abundance of literature and printed books which use this system and might be inaccessible if the writing system were to change. We said earlier that writing systems were instances of technology and when technology changes, it makes earlier forms obsolete and unusable. For instance, few people nowadays have record players and there is quite an industry in reissuing "classic" rock and roll hits in CD form so that people can still enjoy them. If our writing system were to change, current books, computer files, and the like might become obsolete or at least as inaccessible as Chaucer's writing is to most of us today.

Furthermore, although there are some small differences in spelling across the globe, the English writing system, for all of its complexities, is a convention among English speakers throughout the world. It doesn't represent any standard variety of English better than any other. If English spelling were to be made more transparent, it is unclear which spoken variety would be chosen to represent accurately: Standard British English (whatever that is), Standard American English (whatever that is), Standard Australian English (whatever that is), or any other. Spelling reform could have other consequences. There is some indication that having different spellings for homophonous words (words that sound the same) may aid in reading the words without ambiguity: pair and pare, night and knight. Furthermore, preserving the spelling between a root word and word derived from it may be helpful in showing the meaning relation between the two although the pronunciation is different: **sane, sanity; innate, nation, nationality; telegraph, telegraphy**. We discuss this topic further later.

In fact, English writing is complex but efficient enough for a reader who already knows how to read in English. In other words, once you know how to read, once you get into the system, the fact that English writing doesn't match the sound exactly ceases to be a problem for reading, although it continues to be a problem in spelling and writing. Readers, as they gain expertise in reading, develop processing strategies that allow them to make the best of their writing system. The main challenge to break into that system then is for two learner populations: beginning English-speaking readers and beginning ESL or EFL students. Much has been written about the former; our concern in this book is the latter.

Differences in L2 writing systems have not been given much attention in ESL and EFL reading. Wallace (1992) reflected a commonly held idea:

> ... the languages themselves may be so different in the way they represent meaning in their written form that there is, arguably, no generalization from the first to the target language.... [But] ... [i]f we turn to consider the ways in which different writing systems convey meaning, it has been argued, for example by Goodman (1984) that, while the contexts and functions of written language vary, reading as a process is unitary. Reading is a unitary process both because it cannot be adequately broken down into separate skills and because we draw on similar processing strategies in the reading of all languages, even where the writing systems are very different. Buck (1979), for example, argues that the process of deriving meaning from written or printed symbols is similar across languages and across contexts. And Cummins and Swain (1986) talk of a Common Underlying Proficiency in language development whereby literacy is generalizable from the first to a second language. (pp. 22–23)

Similar points of view about transfer from L1 reading to L2 reading can be found in Coady (1979), Alderson and Urquhart (1984), and Day and Bamford (1998). More recent research supports the idea that reading can be broken down into separate skills or strategies that, in the ideal situation, all work together so smoothly that they become one. The operant words in the previous quote are "similar" and "generalizable." The process of deriving meaning from writing is probably similar in some ways, but it doesn't follow that the knowledge base and low-level processing strategies are identical. Although a readers' L1 literacy is generalizable to L2, it is possible that the transfer may be either positive or negative.

We have seen that languages represent different linguistic units in writing: meaning, syllables, or phonetic segments, consonants or vowels, features of phonetic segments, or more likely, a combination of these. In addition, languages are spaced differently in a variety of directions on a page: vertically or horizontally, and with or without spacing in between "words." The number of symbols needed to represent a language in writing can vary greatly. The methods that schools and teachers use to teach children those symbols vary from country to country. Languages differ in whether syntactic changes to words are represented in the writing. Alphabetic writing systems differ in how "transparent" they are; that is, how accurately they represent the sounds of the language. It is reasonable to think that the knowledge stored in the knowledge base as a source for reading is different for each L1 writing system and that the low-level processing strategies that mediate between the text and the higher-level processes are different. We will discuss this topic in the next chapter.

DISCUSSION QUESTIONS

1. This is a common visual discrimination task. Identify which of these letter sequences is different from the other two and then verbalize the mental and visual process that you used to identify the different one:

i.	a.	βατ	b.	βατ	c.	γατ
ii.	a.	κατ	b.	κιτ	c.	κιτ
iii	a.	μαπ	b.	ναπ	c.	μαπ
iv.	a.	ενεραλιζατιο	b.	ενεραλιζατιο	c.	εμεραλιζατιο

Which one was the easiest to discriminate? Which one was the hardest? Why do you think that you got these results? Do you get the same results for these?

i.	a.	♌♋◆	b.	♌♋◆	c.	♑♋◆
ii.	a.	②♋♌⓪	b.	②⓪⓪	c.	②⓪⓪
iii	a.	‼✔🚗	b.	●✔🚗	c.	‼✔🚗
iv.	a.	♑♏■♏□♋●♓ ⌘♋◆♓□	b.	♑♏■♏□♋●♓ ⌘♋◆♓□	c.	♏○♏□♋●♓♒ ♋◆♓□

2. This quote comes from Tseng and Hung (1981):

> Miller ... has pointed out the importance of notational design in the history of mathematics. In Miller's words (1957) "In order to study the interaction of thought and symbol it is not necessary to travel with Whorf to the Zuni Indians; the language of mathematics is rich with excellent examples. Why are Arabic numbers so superior to Roman?" (p. 238)

In that spirit, compare these different representations of the same meaning concept (the number seven):

7   seven   vii

Which type of writing does each correspond to? (If 7 and vii are both logographic, what is the difference between them?) What are the advantages and disadvantages of each type of number? Do you agree that the history of mathematics has been affected by the type of notations developed? Could mathematics have advanced without the logogram like 7?

Could language and culture be similarly affected by the writing systems that evolved in different civilizations?

Chapter 3

Low-Level Transfer of Reading Strategies

Prereading questions—Before you read, think, and discuss the following:

1. If you are a nonnative speaker of English, tell the class about the writing system in your native language. Tell the class about your experiences learning English, especially learning to read. How well do you feel you read now? What would improve your reading?
2. If you are a native speaker of English, find an English learner to interview. Ask them the aforementioned questions. Present your information to the class.
3. If you are a native English speaker and have studied another language, what problems did you have with reading it silently? What problems did you have if you tried to read it out loud?
4. If you have studied a language with a different writing system, what problems did you have learning to read it?
5. Do you hear sounds in your head when you are reading words? Or do you have a sense of pronouncing words even though you are reading silently? If so, do you think that it slows down your reading? Is it a disadvantage to read slowly?

Study Guide questions—Answer these questions during or after reading the chapter:

1. What evidence is there that different writing systems require different knowledge and processing strategies?
2. What are the four different ways that logograms could be read?
3. What low-level strategy might develop in readers of consonantal scripts?
4. What low-level strategy might readers of transparent scripts be using?
5. Do processing strategies transfer if the L1 and the L2 are very different? If they are similar?
6. Will preference for different processing strategies transfer?
7. What is the significance of the evidence about Japanese readers' preference for a meaning-based strategy for unpronounceable (to them) words with regard to their acquisition of English?

Given the differences in writing systems in the world, it is not surprising that learning to read a new script can be problematic for the language learner. When thinking about our ESL and EFL students, we find there are really two preliminary issues:

- Do the demands of reading different writing systems cause readers to develop different knowledge and different low-level reading strategies when they are learning to read in their native language?
- If so, do these strategies transfer from L1 to L2?

If readers acquire different knowledge and develop different processing strategies, then we must consider whether they transfer to L2. If they don't transfer, there will be no facilitation but also no interference in L2. If they do transfer, there could be either facilitation or interference. We might expect facilitation if the writing systems are similar in L1 and L2, but how similar do they need to be for facilitation to take place? Is interference in fact more likely even if a learner is moving from a transparent alphabetic L1 to an opaque alphabetic L2 such as English? These concerns lead us to the possibility that many beginning English-learning readers who are already literate in their native language may need direct instruction in the strategies that expert English readers form to read English most efficiently.

Let us try to answer the first question. In the last chapter we saw that languages differ in their writing systems and we concluded that it is reasonable to think that these differences can result in the development of different low-level processing strategies. There is some evidence that this is so. Taylor and Olson (1995) reported the following humorous anecdote:

> Procter and Gamble have a well-known advertisement for laundry detergent, which shows a pile of dirty clothes on the left, a box of Tide in the middle, and clean folded clothes on the right. The ad worked very well in North America and Europe. But in Arabia, sales of P & G products dropped. Why? Arabic readers viewed the ad from right to left, associating the Tide not with the clean folded clothes but with the dirty ones on the left! (p. 13)

There have been a number of research studies of the question, and many show that participants use different word recognition strategies depending on their L1 orthography (Chikamatsu, 1996). Each writing system provides the mind with different tasks to perform, so the mind responds by developing different strategies to work with the different input. One question that researchers have tried to answer is whether logograms (Chinese sinograms, Japanese Kanji, or Korean Kanzza) can be read by visually associating the symbol directly with the meaning stored in memory without any reference to the sound of the word. That is, the written symbol would be decoded and recognized without any recoding into sound. It is a complicated question because there are actually four possible orthographic and lexical processing strategies. In the first, the logographic symbol is decoded, recognized, and associated with a word meaning directly, which is then used to access the sound of the word in recoding. In the second, the symbol is decoded and recoded with sound first, and the visual and auditory image is used to access the meaning of the word. In the third, the symbol is decoded and associated simultaneously with both the meaning and the sound. In the fourth, the logogram is associated only with meaning and not with sound at all.

Some researchers have found some evidence that reading logograms is more like processing pictures than reading (Henderson, 1982). Morton and Sasanuma (1984) also generally concluded that, for Japanese writing, although the Kana are read phonetically, the Kanji are read visually, that is, like a picture. To them, there seems to be "a strong *dissociation* between the processes involved in reading the two scripts" (p. 40). However, Leong and Tamaoka (1995) argued that both visual and phonetic processing can occur in accessing difficult Kanji with phonetic elements. Sakuma, Sasanuma, Tatsumi, and Masaki (1998) concluded that Kanji characters were processed both orthographically and phonologically.

Koda (1995) explained how logograms are read in a way that unifies these apparently conflicting results. In Koda's opinion, all writing systems are recoded into phonological information in reading because studies show that short-term memory is better for phonological material than for visual material. However, alphabetic writing is recoded to a phonological representation prior to or at the time that the word is accessed in memory. Logographic writing is converted to phonology only after the word is accessed because that is the time that phonological information becomes available to the reader. It is, in fact, impossible to pronounce an unknown sinogram; the phonetic cues are not enough. In simpler terms, logograms are accessed through the meaning of the word first, and only afterward does the sound of the word become available to the reader, so that means that logograms are read as in number 1 in Fig. 3.1. (In contrast, only the most frequent of words written in alphabetic scripts may be accessed with a direct connection between the decoded visual image of the word and the meaning of the word, as in number 1 in Fig. 3.1. Less frequent words written in alphabets are decoded and recoded into a visual and auditory image, then the meaning becomes available to the reader, as in number 2 or possibly number 3 in Fig. 3.1.) Logograms can also be read without access to sound, as in mental math calculations, where thinking of the name of the word only slows down and complicates the process. This is shown in number 4 in Fig. 3.1.

This evidence supports the claim that readers use different processing strategies to handle logograms (a meaning-based strategy) and alphabetic words (a sound-based strategy). There is some evidence that syllabic writing is processed differently also. Kang and Simpson (1996) found, in comparing Korean grade-school readers with English speaking grade-school readers, that word recognition processes for Korean sixth-grade readers were different from those found for English-speaking sixth graders. Also, there may be some variation in the way the differing alphabetic systems are processed. The demands of those scripts that represent consonants primarily may produce different reader strategies from those writing systems that encode both consonants and vowels.

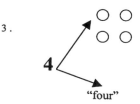

"four"

"four"

Reader associates logogram with meaning first, then with the sound of the word. Sinograms are probably read this way. This is a meaning-based visual strategy.

Reader associates logogram with meaning and sound simultaneously. Sinograms are probably NOT read this way.

"four"

Reader associates logogram with sound first, then meaning. Sinograms are probably NOT read this way.

Reader associates logogram only with meaning. Sinograms (like numbers) may be able to be read this way. This is also a meaning-based visual strategy.

FIG. 3.1   Summary of four ways logograms could be read.

Shimron and Sivan (1994) studied English and Hebrew bilingual graduate students and faculty reading texts translated into Hebrew and English. The English native speakers read the English texts significantly faster than the native Hebrew speakers read the same texts in their Hebrew version. Ben-Dror, Frost, and Bentin (1995) found that Hebrew speakers, when given a task to segment complete words into their component sounds (e.g., "kite" into /k/ /ay/ /t/), segmented words into sounds differently from English speakers for both Hebrew and English words. The variation was attributed to differences in the way that writing systems represent phonological information. Ryan and Meara (1991) found that Arabic readers reading English confuse words that have similar consonant structures. Their hypothesis was that because of the orthography of Arabic, readers tend to rely heavily on the consonants when attempting to recognize English words, as in Fig. 3.2. This is a partial alphabetic strategy that is not very effective for English because of our nu-

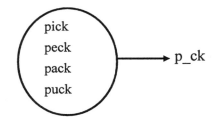

Arabic or Hebrew readers might use a partial alphabetic strategy.

FIG. 3.2   Hypothetical strategy used by readers of consonantal L1s.

merous words that are differentiated merely by vowel, our extensive use of vowel spellings, and overall complicated writing system.

Alphabetic languages tend to be read with phonological recoding, meaning that the words are read by associating sounds with the letters. This makes sense because that is the best way to take advantage of the information writing systems provide. It is possible, however, that the demands of dealing with an opaque script such as English might cause English readers to develop different strategies from readers of transparent scripts. Oney, Peters, and Katz (1997) suggested, from their research with readers of Turkish (transparent) and English (partly opaque), that readers become less dependent on phonological processing with experience and that this reduction is more rapid for readers of opaque orthographies. Naeslund and Schneider (1996) found differences in the emergence in phonological processing skills among beginning readers of German when compared to beginning readers of English. One reason for this, they offer, is the differences between German writing (generally transparent) and English writing (partly opaque). Chitiri and Willows (1994) reported on a study of Greek and English monolingual readers in which they concluded that the reading process is not uniform across languages and that readers are influenced by orthography. There is reason to think that readers with an L1 transparent script may develop a transparent fully alphabetic strategy, one in which each letter or syllable is read and recoded directly into its predictable sound. This strategy, shown in Fig. 3.3, also is not effective for English, be-

$$\text{price} \longleftrightarrow \begin{array}{ccccc} \text{p} & \text{r} & \text{i} & \text{c} & \text{e} \\ \updownarrow & \updownarrow & \updownarrow & \updownarrow & \updownarrow \\ \text{/p/} & \text{/r/} & \text{/i/} & \text{/s/} & \text{/e/} \end{array}$$

Readers of Greek, Spanish, and other languages with transparent writing systems might develop a fully alphabetic strategy with reliance on syllable structure.

FIG. 3.3   Hypothetical strategy used by readers of transparent L1s.

cause English writing is opaque. Readers of transparent alphabets like German or Greek also rely heavily on the syllable as a unit (Nunes, 1999). This is probably less useful as a strategy for English. In a later chapter, we'll discuss the best strategies for decoding English writing.

Thus, the evidence is that yes, readers do develop different strategies to cope with differing orthographies: a visual meaning-based strategy, a partial alphabetic strategy, and a fully alphabetic strategy.

Now we come to the question of transfer, interference, and facilitation. There is evidence that in some cases, no transfer occurs if L1 and L2 are very different. Abu-Rabia (1997) reported that although syntactic and working memory skills show a significant correlation between Hebrew and English skills for Hebrew–English bilingual children, phonological and orthographic tasks showed no such positive correlation. Instead, they concluded that some language-dependent features do not transfer from one language to another.

There is evidence of transfer and facilitation if the L1 and L2 writing systems are similar. Muljani, Koda, and Moates (1998) studied English word recognition in Indonesian and Chinese students of English to find out whether the alphabetic writing system of Indonesia would facilitate reading in English when compared to Chinese writing. Their results suggested that there was some positive transfer from the L1 reading processor to the L2 when both the L1 and the L2 were alphabetic systems. There was no positive transfer from Chinese to English reading because those systems are so different. Thus, L1 knowledge of the alphabet aided the Indonesian students, but L1 knowledge of sinograms did not aid reading alphabetic writing.

Preference for different processing strategies also transfers sometimes. Chikamatsu (1996) studied American and Chinese learners of Japanese, using Japanese Kana because it would be a different writing system for both learners. Kana is syllabic; the American learners would have learned an alphabetic system and the Chinese learners a logographic script of sinograms. Chikamatsu found that Chinese individuals relied more on the visual information in L2 Kana words than did the American individuals and that American individuals utilized the phonological information in Kana more than did Chinese individuals. The conclusion was that there are different strategies involved in reading different orthographies and that these strategies transfer to L2 word recognition. The Chinese readers transferred their preference for a meaning-based visual processing strategy. The English L1 students transferred their sound-based strategy.

Similarly, Koda (1995) studied Japanese, Arabic, Spanish, and English readers of English and found that symbols that had no phonological cues and unpronounceable words interfered less with the Japanese readers than with the alphabetic readers. It is well-established that unpronounceable words interfere with English reading because of the difficulty they pose for phonological recoding. If you are a native speaker of English, you may have stumbled over unpronounceable foreign names in the novel

War and Peace, for example. You may have tried to process them without recoding into phonology, by remembering the appearance of the name and associating it with a certain character, which would mean a more direct visual and meaning connection. Or you may have tried a laborious alphabetic strategy of sounding out the names and remembering them by sound. Which did you choose, a visual meaning-based strategy or a sound-based strategy?

However, unpronounceable words did not cause difficulty for the Japanese readers, Koda (1995) concluded, because they treated the problem words as they did Kanji. They did not try to pronounce them, they tried to remember them visually. In a footnote, Koda (1995) reported that Japanese ninth graders extended the same strategies they had developed to deal with unfamiliar Kanji to guess the meaning of unfamiliar words in English. Also, ESL reading comprehension among Japanese college students was unaffected by the unpronounceability of English words, suggesting a strategy of relying little on phonological information in the letter representation. The strategy these Japanese students were applying to unknown English words was visual and meaning-based, discarding the very strengths of the alphabetic writing system with its cues to sound. The short-term strategy of treating unfamiliar words as logograms may assist these ESL and EFL readers at first, but over time, it is more efficient to be able to decode unknown words and assign a pronunciation to them.

Thus, the answer to both questions from the beginning of the chapter is that people do develop different low-level decoding strategies in response to different L1 scripts, and the strategies do transfer from L1 to L2. Facilitation can occur if the knowledge and processing strategies are similar in L1 and L2, but L2 readers may rely on their L1 strategies even when the L2 is different, which may cause interference or at least inefficiency in reading.

How can we understand what this means to students who need to learn to read the more or less opaque English script? We have seen that in general, ESL and EFL students bring with them different types and amounts of prior knowledge and strategies from their L1 literacy. We can discuss these differences by referring to hypothetical case studies of four typical ESL and EFL reading students: MariCarmen, Despina, Mohammed, and Ho. What these students have in common is that they have all learned to read their own L1 script accurately and quickly. They are all now in the process of becoming good readers of English as an L2.

Many students enter ESL or EFL classes having already learned an alphabetic script to read and write their native language or for another language that they have learned. These students can transfer quite a bit of this knowledge directly from that experience into their English learning experience. There are two types of students within this category: those who have learned a script a lot like English (e.g., Spanish speakers, Italian speakers, German speakers, etc.) and those who have learned an alphabetic script unlike English (e.g., Russian speakers, Greek speakers, etc.).

For those students coming from languages with a Roman script, it is reasonable that there will be positive transfer or facilitation; in other words, much transferred information from L1 to L2 would aid these ESL learners in beginning to read English. For example, readers would know that reading goes from left to right across the page. They would know the alphabetic principle and they would recognize letter shapes and fonts. However, many languages have a more transparent writing system than English does; the letter-to-sound correspondences are more regular. So students who have learned such a transparent system may experience some negative transfer of their reading strategies when they begin to experience the more opaque English writing. It is possible that they need to develop additional strategies to cope with the opacity of English writing.

MARICARMEN

MariCarmen is a 12-year-old student from Mexico who has been studying English for a year. Because Spanish uses the same alphabet as English, she is catching on fairly quickly to English reading and writing. Much of what she already knows about reading would help her in the new task of reading English For MariCarmen to begin reading in English, she needs to learn the few English letters or letter combinations which are not used in Spanish (i.e., k, x) or which are used in English associated with a very different sound (i.e., g, h, j, ll, rr, th). She needs to recognize English sounds. (We'll see later why she doesn't need to pronounce them perfectly.) She needs to begin learning English vocabulary and phrases orally, and for a while, she needs to read and write very simple selections which replicate the words she knows orally. MariCarmen also needs to learn how to deal with the "opacity" of English writing: that English letters represent sounds with less regularity than Spanish. This will be the topic of later chapters.

DESPINA

Students who speak languages which use alphabets other than the Roman alphabet may find the early stages of reading development more problematic because they need to learn to recognize new letter shapes quickly and efficiently. These students must also learn to recognize the new sounds of English. The associations between the new letters and new sounds take a while to become automatic, as in Chall's (1983) reading stages 1 and 2 (described in chap. 1), so that bottom-up reading can occur with fluency. Until this happens, these students must spend most of their attention on the bottom levels of the reading processor and have less attention to spare for the higher levels. It is unfair for the reading teacher to require a great deal of comprehension from students in these stages.

Despina is 14 and has recently traveled with her family from Greece to the United States. She is in eighth grade at a middle school. Her language arts teacher is Ms. Gordon and her ESL teacher is Ms. Crabtree. Despina knows only a few words of spoken English although she studied English for several years in school before coming to the United States. Despina's native language is Greek, which she knows how to read and write well. Greek is written with an alphabet, but it is very different from the English alphabet. Like MariCarmen's, much of Despina's reading abilities would transfer directly and positively to the task of reading English. Despina's knowledge of the world is similar to MariCarmen's and similar to that of any American 14-year-old. She knows how to hold a book and how to read left to right across the page. Despina's knowledge of sounds derives from her experience with her native language, and it would transfer with some modification to English. Where Despina differs greatly from MariCarmen, however, is in her lack of knowledge of English letters. There is little overlap between the Greek alphabet and the English one.

For Despina to become a good reader of English, she must learn to recognize English sounds quickly and accurately. She must read and write English selections which do not contain words that are unfamiliar to her. The crucial thing for Despina to learn, however, is the English alphabet: the letter shapes in various fonts and the correspondence between the letters and the sounds of English. In addition, Greek, like Spanish, has a more transparent connection between writing and sound, so Despina may need to acquire some new procedures and mechanisms for coping with English writing system opacity.

MOHAMMED

In many ways, Mohammed, from Egypt, is like Despina. His writing system is alphabetic, but it uses different symbols. It is also consonantal. Thus, Mohammed must learn the same things that Despina must learn, but he must also learn to look at vowels and process them efficiently. However, Mohammed also presents some additional challenges because his eyes are trained to process writing in the opposite direction from English. Furthermore, standard Arabic writing is very different from spoken Arabic. In fact, some consider written Arabic and spoken Arabic to be different dialects entirely and as a result, it is very difficult to learn to read and write. There is a lot of illiteracy in the Arab world, and this is considered one reason why. So, Arabic writing is opaque (in consonants), but in a different way from the way that English writing is opaque (in vowels). The strategies that Mohammed may have developed to deal with the opacity of Arabic may not be useful for reading English, but I know of no research on this topic.

HO

Some Chinese L1 ESL and EFL students are not very familiar with alphabetic writing at all until they try to learn English or another alphabetic language. If the processing of sinograms or Kanji is different from the processing of an alphabet, those ESL and EFL readers whose L1 is Chinese, Japanese, or Korean may try a strategy of memorizing the English written words as unitary wholes like sinograms or Kanji that may or may not also involve some kind of memory for the pronunciation of the word. (In fact, some beginning English-speaking children try this also as a strategy, but they usually don't become proficient readers using it. They must develop an alphabetic strategy.) Chinese L1 students may use their prodigious memories to learn English words as if they were whole entities and unreduceable to letters and sounds. In other words, they try to read English words without any modification to the reading processor they have already acquired through reading Chinese. The situation for the Japanese and Korean reader is somewhat different because of the multi-orthographic nature of Japanese and Korean writing, but research cited earlier suggests that they use a visual and meaning-based strategy for unknown words. The transparency of the Japanese and Korean syllabic systems may also affect the development of reading strategies for English.

Ho is a Taiwanese student who has come to study at an American university. He can speak and listen well, but reading and writing are a problem for him. Ho takes so long to decide what the word is in English that by the time he has come to a decision, he has lost track of what the sentence means. If he can't recognize a word as a whole and summon up a meaning, he can't sound it out. When Ho has an assignment to read, he looks up each word he is not sure of in his English–Chinese dictionary and writes the Chinese symbol for the word in the line above the word. This takes him forever, but at the end, he can read the English passage as if it were Chinese because it is Chinese. When he rereads the passage to review, he looks only at the Chinese writing. His slow and laborious reading is having a serious impact on his success in college.

For teachers to help students like MariCarmen, Despina, Mohammed, and Ho acquire efficient bottom-up processing, they must first understand that L1 and L2 low-level reading processes are never quite the same. Aebersold and Field (1997) said the following:

The differences between the writing systems and rhetorical structures of the native language and the target language may be another factor in L2/FL reading. Orthographic systems vary widely, and some systems include strong aesthetic elements—for example, Chinese calligraphy is not only a communication tool but is also one of the most highly respected arts in that culture. *Readers who use basically the same alphabet or writing systems in their L1 as they are learning to use in the L2/Fl will have less to learn and be able to begin reading faster.* Conversely readers switching from a system with a limited number of symbols to a system with abundance characters will need more time to become proficient.... It is prudent to keep in mind Haynes's (1989:iii) argument that mastery of the L2 writing system "is both harder and more important to L2 reading success than existing theory and research would suggest." (emphasis added; p. 28)

A similar but more complexly worded point is made in Geva (1999):

> ... At the same time, the acquisition of literacy skills may be also propelled by language specific processing requirements at the phonological, orthographic or morphosyntactic levels. In the latter analysis, underlying cognitive resources are tapped differentially, to the degree demanded by the orthographic or linguistic characteristics of L1 and L2.... Considerations of orthographic complexity refine our understanding of L2 literacy skills development. For example, Hebrew and Persian word recognition and decoding are associated with less steep developmental trajectories than those associated with parallel development in English. (pp. 360–361)

The fact for teachers to recognize is that no other writing system is like English; therefore positive transfer or facilitation from L1 will be either limited or nonexistent, but negative transfer may be great. Teachers who overlook this fact may not have a realistic view of the reading task for their students, even at an advanced stage. Their expectations may be unrealistic, and worse, they may not know how to assist their students beyond supplying background knowledge and activating schemas. They may not know how to begin helping their students improve their reading speed and automaticity. One surprising place for teachers to begin is with their students' listening comprehension. We turn to that topic next.

DISCUSSION QUESTIONS

The Chinese linguist Wang (1973) observed the following: "To a Chinese the character for 'horse' means **horse** with no mediation through the sound /ma/. The image is so vivid that one can almost sense an abstract figure galloping across the page." Which representation from Figure 3.0 does this quote agree with? Which representation, if any, seems to indicate the way that you recognize and understand the word "horse" in English?

Chapter 4

Listening Skills in Reading

Prereading questions—Before you read, think, and discuss the following:

1. Say the words **pat** and **bat**. What is the difference in the pronunciation of these two words?
2. Say the words **peat** and **pat**. What is the difference in the pronunciation of these two words?
3. Can you sing the sequence tttttttttt? Can you sing the sequence mmmmmmmm? Can you sing the sequence aaaaaaaa? Why can you sing (or hum) the latter two sequences and not the first?
4. Why do we have accents when we try to speak another language?

Study Guide questions—Answer these during or after reading the chapter:

1. What property do all voiceless sounds have in common? What property do voiced sounds have in common?
2. What is the difference between oral sounds and nasal sounds?
3. Using the diagram of the mouth and your own mouth, go over the place and manner that these consonant sounds are produced: /p/, /tʃ/, /f/, /ð/, /ŋ/, and /l/.
4. Make the vowels [iy] and [uw]. What is the difference in how they are made?
5. Define the following terms: phone, phoneme, allophone, and minimal pair.
6. Do you pronounce the names Don and Dawn the same? What vowel sounds do you have in these two words?
7. What is phonemic awareness? How can it be developed?
8. What are the suprasegmental features of English? How are they important to the nonnative speaker?
9. Why does pronunciation not matter in silent reading?

In some ways it makes sense to believe that phonological processing in reading is linked to the reader's ability to pronounce words accurately (Freeman & Freeman, 1999; Hatch, 1979), but Wallace (1992) quite rightly argued against the idea:

> "Phonics," as the method is popularly called, involves the ability to match up letters (or "graphemes") to some kind of sound representation. It tends to be assumed that phonic skill is displayed by the ability to read aloud with a "good"—that is native-like, standard English—pronunciation. (p. 54)

Wallace is more properly referring to phonemic or graphemic awareness, the ability to match letters and sounds. (Phonics is a teaching methodology.) However, she is correct in disconnecting reading and pronunciation, and here's why: The fact is that phonological processing in reading is more heavily dependent on accurate perception and recognition of sounds in listening, than it is on the production of sounds in speech (Bradley & Bryant, 1983). Therefore, accurate pronunciation of the sounds of English is largely irrelevant to reading. This chapter explores the issue further.

Studies show that infants can discriminate (perceive the difference) between different sounds from birth and that the innate ability to discriminate is applied to the sounds of the language that surrounds them. As infants begin to comprehend and later to produce their own language, they lose their ability to discriminate between sounds that are irrelevant to their own language. For example, infants discriminate between many sounds that are not used in English but they lose this ability as their knowledge of English sounds develops and as they gain the ability to understand the speech that is directed at them and the speech that goes on around them. They usually master the comprehension of spoken language before they can produce all of the sounds of English accurately. Slowly they begin to be able to produce the sounds with accuracy, although many children's production of difficult sounds like /r/, /y/, and /l/ can be delayed until the age of 6 or 7.

Speakers of other languages also lose the ability to discriminate between sounds that do not occur in their native language, but if the ESL and EFL instruction that they receive has a strong oral and aural focus, they, too, will master the discrimination of English sounds, although completely accurate production of English sounds can be challenging and may, in fact, never occur. Accurate pronunciation seems to be highly correlated with the age of acquisition; the earlier in life English is acquired, the more accurate the pronunciation of the speaker. Luckily for our students, accurate silent reading is more dependent on accurate discrimination of sounds rather than accurate production of sounds. I know of no evidence that the ability to develop accurate aural discrimination in an L2 diminishes with age unless hearing becomes impaired.

However, discrimination of English sounds, especially vowels, can be problematic for ESL and EFL learners because most languages have fewer vowels than does English. A common vowel system in the languages of the world has five spoken vowels, roughly those in Bach, bait, beat, boat, and boot. Another common vowel system has three vowels, those in Bach, beat, and boot. Although there is quite a bit of dialect variation even in so-called Standard English, English is thought to have 12 vowels. There are also some consonant sounds in English that can cause discrimination difficulties because they are uncommon: the initial sounds in **th**is, **th**in, **sh**ip, **ch**ip, **g**enre, **j**et, and the final sound in si**ng**.

For accurate listening comprehension and reading, the learner's knowledge base must contain an inventory of English sounds, each sound in the form of a generalized mental image learned from a number of different experiences with the sound in different contexts (Baddeley, Gathercole, & Papagno, 1998). Learners need not be able to verbalize or describe the difference between two sounds, but they need to be able to discriminate two sounds. In addition, learners don't need to be able to pronounce sounds perfectly. In silent reading of familiar words, only the abstract mental image of a sound may be used in recoding. It is in oral reading that pronunciation becomes relevant. Articulation of sounds is also important in reading and learning new words, as we shall see in later chapters.

In English, we have hypothesized that for most words, the squiggles on the page (A. in Fig. 4.1) are identified as letters (decoding), and matched with the abstract mental images of English sounds stored in memory (recoding), as in B. in Fig. 4.1. This creates a visual and aural image of the word which then undergoes lexical processing to identify the correct meaning, as in C. The more accurately and quickly this can happen, the better for the reader. Phonological processing (recoding) can probably stop right here in the quickest and most efficient silent reading of familiar words.

However, there are three other possibilities for reading, and each possibility involves slightly more processing work. In the first type of reading (D. in Fig. 4.2), readers proceed to summon up a memory of the physical sounds in the word they are reading. They have the sensation of hearing the words in their heads. In the second type of reading (as in E. in Fig. 4.2), readers proceed even further to activate the motor commands to the mouth that are associated with the sound, so that the reader has the sensation of saying the words, but nothing is audible. This is called *subvocalizing*. Fast readers sometimes use these as techniques to slow down their reading so as to comprehend better, but in general, they are less efficient than pure and simple activation of the abstract mental image because they require more

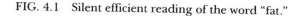

FIG. 4.1   Silent efficient reading of the word "fat."

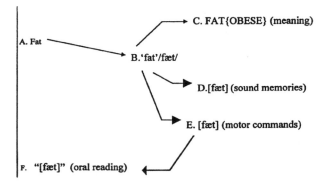

FIG. 4.2   Other types of less efficient reading follow: hearing the words mentally (D), subvocalizing (E/F), and reading out loud (F).

processing effort and attention. Subvocalizing may be important to learn new words, however (Baddeley et al., 1998).

The third alternative way of reading is oral reading, in which the motor commands to the mouth are actually realized and the read words are pronounced audibly, as in F. in Fig. 4.2. This requires quite a bit of processing work, effort, and attention, especially for careful pronunciation. Many ESL and EFL students find oral reading difficult and stressful because they must process the squiggles into letters, match the letters with abstract mental images of sounds, activate the right motor commands to the mouth, and put those motor commands into effect with the most accurate pronunciation. Is it any wonder that comprehension of orally read material suffers? Another problem is that the way the word looks is more likely to affect the pronunciation of the word, which, for English, is sometimes counterproductive because the pronunciation is distorted. There are some occasions in which oral reading is useful as a pedagogical tool, for instance, in learning new vocabulary, but it is not useful either for testing pronunciation or for testing reading comprehension. We turn our attention now to an elaboration of the inventory of English sounds.

Phonetics is the study of the sounds of the flow of speech. Although it seems like we perceive individual sounds as we hear them, the flow of speech is actually continuous. The sounds are not really discrete segments, but we learn to discriminate discrete sounds in the flow of speech as we acquire a language. If we hear speech in a foreign language that we do not understand, at first we cannot segment the speech into words, and we often cannot even segment the speech into discrete sounds because we have lost the ability to discriminate between sounds that are not in our native language. As we acquire knowledge of the L2, we acquire the ability to segment the flow into separate words and sounds because our phonological and lexical processing strategies can draw upon knowledge about sounds and words stored in the knowledge base.

One of the strategies that we use to distinguish sounds in the flow of speech is to notice certain invariant properties of each sound. Thus, every time we hear a [d], although it might be different from speaker to speaker or from environment to environment, we can recognize it as /d/. (Linguists use square brackets to "write" sounds as they are actually produced in speech and slanted lines around symbols for abstract mental images of sounds, so that we keep them separate in our thinking and we know that we are not talking about ordinary written letters.) When we hear someone with an accent, we can understand their speech as long as they more or less pronounce the main invariant properties of the sounds (or at least substitute a sound with some similar acoustic properties). The speech of each individual is unique. It's called a *voiceprint*. The pitch of a person's voice depends on the length of his or her vocal tract. That is why small children have very high-pitched voices. The resonance in the vocal tract depends on the shape of it, so that will also vary from individual to individual. Yet, these individual variations in speech and accent do not stop us from understanding because the invariant properties of the sound are maintained no matter who is speaking.

It is possible that the invariant properties that linguists use to classify English sounds are similar to the unconscious and informal knowledge that is stored abstractly in the reader's knowledge database to be accessible in processing both spoken and written language. We also need knowledge of the sounds of English for our discussion of letter-to-sound correspondences in the next chapters.

ENGLISH CONSONANTS

We describe consonants based on the way the sound is produced and the place that the sound is made in the mouth, as shown in Fig. 4.3. To make most of the sounds in human language, the airstream has to pass through the trachea and the glottis, the opening between the vocal folds. *Voiceless* sounds are those that pass through the glottis unobstructed by the vocal folds, so they do not vibrate. Voiceless sounds are /p/, /t/, and /k/, and others. *Voiced* sounds are produced when the airstream causes the vocal folds to vibrate because they are pulled together and obstruct the airstream. Voiced sounds are /b/, /d/, and /g/, and others. The voiced and voiceless distinction accounts for the difference in the first sound of following word pairs: **fat** and **vat**, **sit** and **zit**. If you say these words carefully and focus on the sounds and how you are producing them, you will note that each pair is identical except for the vibration or lack of vibration in the first sound. All sounds are either voiced or voiceless.

If the uvula is closed, the airstream passes through the mouth. Those sounds are called *oral*. If the uvula is open and if the airstream is stopped somewhere in the mouth, the airstream passes through the nasal cavity and

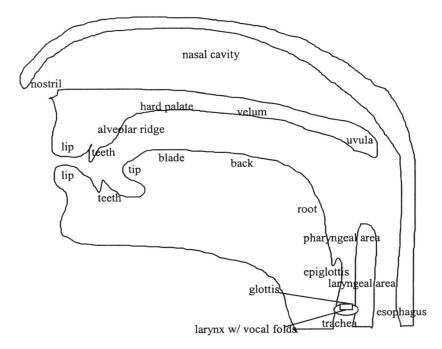

FIG. 4.3   The vocal tract.

out the nose; those sounds are called *nasal*. All sounds are either oral or nasal. Nasal sounds are /m/, /n/, and /ŋ/. They are voiced and nasal. Oral sounds are /b/, /p/, /t/, /k/, /l/, /r/, and others. Thus, all sounds can be divided according to their manner of articulation (how they are made) into voiced or voiceless, oral or nasal. Consonants have other distinguishing manners of articulation also.

In Fig. 4.4, we see a chart of the English consonants. The place of articulation is across the top, the manner is down the left side. We'll talk about manner first. Going from the top to the bottom of the chart, the manner goes from maximal obstruction of the air flow to minimal obstruction, or a mere shaping of the vocal tract. In other words, in making a *stop*, the air flow is stopped completely at some point in the mouth. Air pressure is built up and then released. In an *affricate*, the air flow is stopped briefly to build up a little pressure, but then quickly released with a small force of air that passes through the mouth which is shaped to produce friction. *Fricatives* are produced by bringing two parts of the mouth very close together, making a small channel for the air to go through. When the air goes through the small channel, a lot of friction is produced in the airstream. Stops have maximal

	bilabial	labiodental	interdental	alveolar	palatal	velar	glottal
stops vl	p		p	t		k	
v	b			d		g	?
affricates vl					tʃ		
v					dʒ		
fricatives vl		f	θ	s	ʃ		h
v		v	ð	z	ʒ		
nasals vl							
v	m			n		ŋ	
liquids vl							
v				l	r		
glides vl							
v	w				y		

FIG. 4.4 The Consonant Inventory.

obstruction or stoppage; affricates have maximal obstruction and then constriction; fricatives have a continuous airflow that is highly constricted.

Recall that *nasals* are produced by allowing most of the air to flow through the nasal cavity, but a little air goes through the mouth, where it is stopped by the two lips for /m/, by the tongue tip and the alveolar ridge for /n/, and by the back of the tongue and the velum for /ŋ/. *Liquids* are produced by bringing two parts of the mouth very close together so that they may even be touching, but the channel that the air goes through is large and no friction is produced. Instead, a kind of resonance or musicality is produced by the shape of the tongue and mouth. *Glides* are like liquids, but the shape of the mouth is different. The continuum of "aperture," or opening, as I call it, explains why liquids and glides are similar to vowels. As we shall see, vowels also are produced more by mouth shape than by stopping or constricting the air flow.

Across the top of Figure 4.4 are some terms that refer to the parts of the mouth that are involved in producing the sound. *Bilabial* refers to sounds produced by the two lips; *labiodental* means that the lower lip and the upper teeth are involved. *Interdental* sounds are produced with the tongue tip between the two sets of teeth. *Alveolar* sounds are produced with the tip of the tongue on the alveolar ridge, the bony part just behind the upper teeth. *Palatal* sounds are produced at or near the hard palate with the blade of the tongue and *velar* sounds are produced at or near the velum with the back of the tongue. *Glottal* sounds are produced in the pharyngeal or laryngeal areas. Besides the glottal fricative, there is also a glottal stop, written with the symbol **?** (a question mark without the dot at the bottom). It is a sound which has no correspondence with any letter in the alphabet; it is the sound at the beginning of each syllable in the word **uh–uh**. If you say this word, you will sense a closing, a build up of air pressure, and an opening in the glottis before the vowel sound. Although the glottal stop is not a contrasting meaningful sound in most dialects of English, I include it on the chart for completeness.

As you read through the descriptions of the individual consonants in Fig. 4.5, make each sound and focus on what you are doing to verify the place and manner of articulation.

Phonetic or Phonemic Symbol	Description	Example words
p	voiceless bilabial stop	pig, dipper, lip
b	voiced bilabial stop	big, fiber, rib
t	voiceless alveolar stop	tick, fatty, fat
d	voiced alveolar stop	dig, laddie, lid
k	voiceless velar stop	kid, sicker, snack
g	voiced velar stop	get, digger, dig
tʃ	voiceless palatal affricate	chick, kitchen, birch
dʒ	voiced palatal affricate	John, wedges, sage
f	voiceless labiodental fricative	fat, sniffle, sniff
v	voiced labiodental fricative	vat, swivel, believe
θ	voiceless interdental fricative	thick, ether, teeth
ð	voiced interdental fricative	then, either, bathe
s	voiceless alveolar fricative	sing, kissing, hiss
z	voiced alveolar fricative	zip, buzzer, buzz
ʃ	voiceless palatal fricative	ship, bushes, bush
ʒ	voiced palatal fricative	genre, treasure, rouge
h	voiceless glottal fricative	hat, ahoy, ___
m	voiced bilabial nasal	milk, simmer, dim
n	voiced alveolar nasal	nun, sinner, fin
ŋ	voiced velar nasal	____, singer, sing
l	voiced alveolar liquid	lap, spilling, spill
r	voiced palatal liquid	right, terror, car
w	voiced bilabial glide	wide, slower, slow
y	voiced palatal glide	yes, layer, stay

FIG. 4.5   Consonants and their properties.

ENGLISH VOWELS

English vowels form the nucleus or musical center to the syllable. The principal vowels of English are distinguished from each other by the shape of the vocal tract when they are produced. The main articulator is the tongue, which is capable of very precise, rapid, and small movements. These movements take only a tiny fraction of a second, but they are enough for us to tell the difference between vowel sounds based on tongue height and tongue position. Pronounce the word in parenthesis to understand the value of each symbol in the Fig. 4.6.

The high front vowels are produced with the tongue relatively high and forward in the mouth, as opposed to the low back vowels in which the tongue is relatively low and back. Thus, the vowels are not distinguished in absolute terms but in relative terms. They are defined with respect to their relative position when compared with each other. We use the terms *tense* and *lax* to get at a very subtle difference in vowels, but it is not useful to spend much time trying to understand these two terms or their definitions. One difference between the tense and lax vowels is a very slight repositioning of the jaw as you make the tense sound and then the lax. In addition, the front tense vowels in English are made longer in duration through the addition of a palatal glide, making them effectively diphthongs. So, /i/ is really pronounced [iy] and /e/ is really [ey]. (Remember, the slashes are placed around mental images of sounds and square brackets are placed around actual pronunciations.) If you have ever tried to learn to pronounce Spanish vowels, you know the difficulty English speakers have in removing the glides to pronounce the shorter and purer Spanish vowels. In fact, a major part of the English "accent" in speaking Spanish and other languages comes from transferring these diphthongized vowels to the other language.

The term *rounding* refers to the position of the lips when the vowel sound is produced. If the lips are somewhat pursed, the vowel is round. Make the sound of /o/; notice the position of the lips. /o/ is a round vowel, as opposed to /a/, which is not. All the back vowels in English are round. When English

			Front	Central		Back	
High	Tense	(beat)	i		u	(boot)
	Lax	(bit)	ɪ	ə (telephone)	ʊ	(soot)
Mid	Tense	(bait)	e		o	(boat)
	Lax	(bet)	ɛ	ʌ (putt)		
Low	Tense				ɔ	(bought)
	Lax	(bat)	æ	ɑ (sod)		

FIG. 4.6   The Vowel Inventory of Standard American English.

speakers try to pronounce French, we may have difficulty with front round vowels in French, because we associate roundness with backness. The tense back round vowels in English /u/ and /o/ are pronounced with a "round" bilabial glide [uw] and [ow]. The round glide, like the palatal glide, causes trouble for the English speaker who is trying to learn any language, like Spanish, that has pure tense, simple vowels. In my classes, I usually contrast the way an English speaker pronounces the word "taco," and the way that a native Spanish speaker says it.

When a vowel is produced right before a nasal consonant, say in the word **band**, the vowel is actually nasalized in pronunciation, although we don't notice it very much in English. In addition, there is very little difference between /ʌ/ and /ə/. The former occurs in positions where there is stress on the vowel, as in words of one syllable like **putt**; the latter occurs in positions where there is little or no stress on the vowel, as the second vowel sound in the word **telephone**. In fact, as we'll see in a later chapter, many vowels that are nonstressed in English are "reduced" to /ə/, so it is a common sound in English.

There is a lot of dialect variation in the vowel system in English as it is spoken across the globe and even within one country. For instance, many American English speakers don't make a distinction between the vowels in **pin** and **pen**. Many don't have the sound /ɔ/ as in the words **bought** or **coffee**. Instead, speakers of this dialect have /ɑ/. (Another factor in dialect variation is the pronunciation of the /r/.) It is helpful for ESL teachers to train students to hear the distinctions in the primary local dialect, but they also need to be able to understand other speakers of English. Students can be instructed that the word **bought** can be pronounced /bɔt/ or /bɑt/, and similarly for other variations. One problem I've had as an ESL and EFL teacher is that my students learn to understand me, but they don't understand the English on the radio or in the streets. Tapes, videos, guest speakers, and team teachers can alleviate that problem. EFL programs should employ native and nonnative teachers, as well as supplemental resources from a variety of origins, so that students have the chance to acquire the flexible recognition strategies based on the invariant properties of sounds.

PHONES, PHONEMES, AND ALLOPHONES

We have been using the word "sound" somewhat loosely to keep our discussion simple, but the word is inadequate for a more accurate and detailed understanding of the unconscious knowledge stored in our memory database. First, we need to be more precise than we have been about the relation between language, the abstract mental system of linguistic knowledge, and the concrete representations which are expressions of it in its different modalities: reading, writing, speaking, and listening.

Language is a complex, abstract, rule-governed, knowledge system which humans have in their minds. It consists of unconscious and informal knowledge of the words, syntax, and meanings, among other things. Language is mental, but it has several "real world" representations: a phonetic system for oral production and listening comprehension, and a writing system for writing and reading. Our concern right now is to describe the relation between these two systems of representation in a way that is helpful for reading teachers. As we saw in chapter 2, logographic writing represents the meanings of language and syllabic writing represents the syllables of a language. Alphabetic writing represents units of language, too, but what exactly are these units of sound?

Any discussion of the phonetic system of a language requires an understanding of three important concepts, which are among the most complex within the field of linguistics: *phone, phoneme,* and *allophone.* A phone is a sound as is it pronounced in speech. In pronouncing the word **fat**, for example, we pronounce three phones. Phones are the real articulations, or vocal noises, that we represent with phonetic symbols inside square brackets, [fæt]. We write phones in square brackets to show that we are talking about sounds as they are actually pronounced, to distinguish them from both mental images of sounds (phonemes) and written letters. In contrast, a phoneme is an abstract symbol, something which is not actually pronounced, but which has a mental reality only. A phoneme is a meaningful symbol in a language, but it is meaningful in a special sense. It is not that the phoneme itself has a meaning like a word does, but rather that the phoneme makes a meaningful difference in comparing two words. Phonemes are the symbols written inside of slanted lines or slashes, /fæt/.

Thus, each phone as it comes out of a mouth is an instance of a mental abstraction, the phoneme. Each [t] that I say is unique, different from any other [t] that I might say on other occasions. However, each [t] is an instance of the same mental abstraction, /t/. It is clear that the number of phones is infinite, but the number of phonemes in a language must be finite. The number of phonemes in English is actually quite small.

Phonemes are mental abstractions; they are never pronounced because when we try to produce them, we are forced to produce phones! Sometimes when we pronounce the phones in the context of a word, the surrounding sounds form a context which can produce a change in a phone. Sometimes phones vary freely from instance to instance (they are in *free variation*), but they are still associated with one phoneme. Sometimes phones are not in free variation; instead a certain phone must occur in one context and another phone must occur in another context. They are in *complementary distribution*. Phones which are related to each other by being different context-dependent or free varieties of the same phoneme are called allophones of a phoneme. One such phone is called an allophone of a phoneme. An example will make these concepts more concrete.

One English phoneme is /t/. We know that it is a phoneme of English because we can find a lot of minimal pairs which show it to be a meaningful contrasting sound. A minimal pair is a set of two different words which are identical except for two phones. If such minimal pairs exist, then it is good evidence that the contrasting phones belong to different phonemes. The contrasting phonemes /t/, /d/, and /k/ are illustrated in Fig. 4.7 with the minimal pairs: **lit** and **lid, ten** and **den, lit** and **lick,** and **till** and **kill.**

When we look closely at the phoneme /t/, we find that the situation is more complicated. For one thing, compare the [t] as pronounced in the word **tick** and the [t] as pronounced in the word **stick.** In the first case, [t] is *aspirated,* or pronounced with a puff of air, so a more accurate phonetic symbol would be [tʰ], where the ʰ represents the aspiration of the puff of air. In the second case, the puff of air is missing. This is an example of complementary distribution.

We also see that in the word **write,** the [t] may or may not be aspirated, but it doesn't seem to make any difference in meaning to the listener because these sounds are in free variation. The word still means the same thing; the words are not minimal pairs, so the sounds do not contrast with each other. In the word **writer,** the [t] seems to sound more like a flap [D] for most Americans, but not for most British English speakers. In fact, we can find no minimal pairs in English which contrast the aspirated version, the unaspirated version, or the flapped version of /t/. Therefore, we know that we are dealing with allophonic variation and not different phonemes. The different ways that /t/ is pronounced in different contexts (of the words **stick, tick,** and **writer**) are allophones of the phoneme /t/, which can be written phonetically as shown in Fig. 4.8.

Contrast			Contrast		
/t/ ◀──▶ /d/			/t/ ◀──▶ /k/		phonemes
[lɪt]	[lɪd]	minimal pair	[lɪt]	[lɪk]	minimal pair
[tɛn]	[dɛn]	minimal pair	[tɛn]	[ken]	minimal pair

FIG. 4.7 Minimal pairs as proof of the status of phonemes.

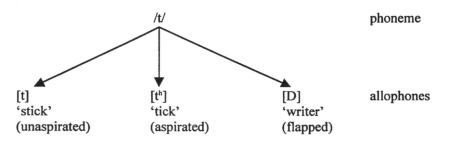

FIG. 4.8 Some allophones of the phoneme /t/.

You already have seen the connection between allophones and "accent." American English has these allophones for /t/, but other dialects of English and other languages have different allophones. Few other languages have the aspirated stop or the flap [D] for /t/, for instance. Because we transfer our knowledge of our native allophones to other languages when we are speaking them, we have an accent.

It is crucial for the reading teacher to understand that individual phones or allophones are not represented by the English writing system; instead, the unit of language that is represented by our spelling is the phoneme. That is why English spelling is called *phonemic* and not phonetic. Some linguistically unsophisticated educators argue that a phonetic system would be better, but that is untrue. First, a phonetic system would require at least three different symbols to represent the allophones of /t/, so the number of symbols needed to write English would increase substantially. Second, English speakers know the allophonic variation in their dialect and it is mostly predictable, so it is redundant to represent it in writing. For example, earlier we discussed how vowels can be pronounced with nasalization if they occur in proximity to a nasal consonant. We don't need to represent that nasalization in writing because that allophonic variation doesn't carry any meaning to us. It is an accident, as it were, of the way that our vocal tract works. We sometimes open the uvula early or close it late in making a nasal consonant sound, so the nasalization leaks onto nearby vowels. This accidental "leaking" is called *coarticulation*.

Third, we don't want to represent allophonic variation in writing because it differs greatly from English dialect to English dialect. English consonant phonemes are quite constant, but allophones may be different in different dialects. All dialects have the phoneme /t/, but not all dialects have all of the same allophones. Around Hartford, CT, for example (and elsewhere), some speakers have the phone [ʔ] as an additional allophone of /t/. When some speakers say the word Britain, they say [brɪʔən]. A writing system that tried to represent phones would be hopelessly confusing and complex; it is more efficient to represent our mental system of abstract phonemes, which is more consistent.

It is true, however, that allophonic variation may cause children and non-native speakers some difficulty in learning to read and write, because they might have incorrect expectations. For instance, there is an aspirated [tʰ] in the word **truck**, which sounds a great deal like another phoneme, /tʃ/. It sounds to many children that the word **truck** is really something like **chruck**. So they would expect it to be written with a **ch** and not a **t**. Someone who advocated a strict phonetic spelling would agree with the child. For teachers, however, it is helpful to understand that spelling errors (or "creative spelling") often follow the phonetic and allophonic values of the sounds, so when a student writes **chruck** they are using sound-to-letter correspondences, but they are not following our conventionalized spelling system. Similarly, the ESL and EFL student may use creative spelling that reflects the allophones they hear instead of the phonemes of English.

SUPRASEGMENTAL FEATURES OF ENGLISH

Besides the inventories of consonants and vowels, each language has different ways to encode other information in the flow of speech. Some languages use systems of tone to differentiate words that otherwise have the same consonants and vowels. A sequence of [ma] is a different word if it is pronounced with a "falling tone" or if it is pronounced with a rising tone:

ma ma

For tonal languages, the tones are suprasegmental phonemes of the language. Suprasegmental means that they "float" above the phonetic segments, the consonants and the vowels.

English does not have phonemic tones, but it does have two suprasegmentals: stress and intonation. Stress is a combination of loudness, duration, and effort in pronunciation. The more highly stressed a syllable or word is, the louder and longer it is and the more effort it takes to pronounce it. Stress differences are relative; they are defined with respect to each other and not in some absolute way. There are two types of stress, word-level stress and phrasal stress. The syllables of words have different amounts of stress. Usually there is one syllable which has primary stress and another may have a secondary amount of stress. In **photograph, pho-** has primary stress, **-to-** is unstressed, and **graph** has secondary stress.

Phrasal stress also occurs in spoken English in addition to word stress. Each main word in a phrase receives more stress than the less important words in the phrase. That means that the stressed word is longer in duration, louder in intensity, and pronounced with more effort than the other words in the phrase. In the following sentence, the phrasal stress is marked with boldface printing:

In the **morn**ing, I have a **cup** of **cof**fee and **read** the **pap**er.

Phrasal stress is involved in the timing of phrases. Each phrase takes more or less the same amount of time to pronounce, but the stressed word takes up more of the time than the unstressed words. This means that the unstressed words are shorter and mushed together. This contrasts sharply with a language like Spanish, which is syllable-timed. In Spanish, each syllable receives approximately the same amount of time. It is for this reason that Spanish sounds more staccato than English does. It is possible that English speakers cue into the phrasal stress to help them determine the phrasal structure of the sentences that they hear because word order and structure are important for understanding English.

Sentences in English also have intonation, which is a cue to meaning. Typically, declarative sentences and Wh-questions have a falling intonation and yes and no questions have a rising intonation. Phrasal stress, timing, and intonation can be used for emphasis and contrast in English, also. Prosody (phrasal stress and intonation) is available to listeners but not to readers. In reading, intonation patterns are represented imperfectly by punctuation: periods reflect falling intonation, commas reflect pauses, and question marks may mark rising intonation in the absence of other syntactic cues, as in the last example sentence. Other languages, of course, have other characteristic intonation patterns.

PHONEMES AND PROCESSING STRATEGIES IN READING

Processing strategies in listening comprehension draw on the knowledge of English phonemes and processing strategies that match incoming phones to the phonemes and understand speech, as illustrated in Fig. 4.9. This occurs automatically, effortlessly, and unconsciously most of the time for native speakers, but we can grasp how it works because sometimes we need to process difficult speech more consciously. If you are listening to someone with a heavy unfamiliar accent, you may need to decide what word you have heard if you are not sure. I have a friend from Atlanta, GA, and at first her words "blind" and "blond" sounded the same. On several occasions, I had to decide if she was talking about someone who couldn't see or someone who had blond hair. I used the sound cue, but I also had to use other areas of my knowledge base, like context and world knowledge. It made for some interesting misunderstandings.

ESL and EFL learners need to acquire the knowledge base of English phonemes so that their aural discrimination of sounds can proceed effortlessly, quickly, and unconsciously. Note that they need to distinguish the phones in hearing based on the mental image of the sound (phoneme), but they don't need to produce phones with complete accuracy. The idea that pronunciation is important in reading stems from a common misunderstanding of the concept of the phoneme, that it is a real sound and not the mental representation of a sound.

Still, more research is needed in this area. Bernhardt (1991) is correct in pointing out that "... the extent to which readers' own accents interfere with, facilitate, or have no impact on their reading process remains uninvestigated" (p. 77). The suggestion made here is that readers' own accents will not affect their silent reading, but it will be affected by their aural discrimination of sounds. Only their oral reading will be affected by their ability to pronounce what they read. Findings by Baddeley et al. (1998) support the idea that phonological accuracy in pronunciation is not crucial for learning new words.

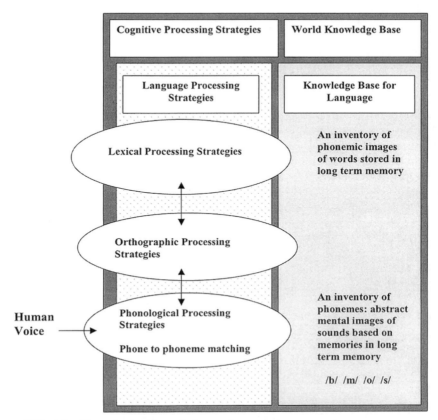

FIG. 4.9   Phonological knowledge and processing strategies.

For quick and efficient silent reading, the ESL and EFL learner should acquire an accurate mental image of the phonemes of English. As previously noted, the image should be based on experiences with different speakers and different situations, but other discrimination activities can also help. Many of these activities are based on minimal pairs like **ship** and **chip,** or **chip** and **cheap**. The knowledge that words are made up of discrete sounds, along with the strategies that allow discrimination and segmentation of the sounds, is called *phonemic awareness,* which has become a "buzzword" in English reading research and classroom practice for native readers. Phonemic awareness is an important precursor for alphabetic reading, but paradoxically people often acquire it as a result of learning to read an alphabet.

One part of phonemic awareness is the segmentation of a spoken word into component sounds. In chapter 1, it was noted that the ability to segment words into component sounds is not very intuitive and that its initial discovery was crucial to the invention of the alphabet. English L1 children often learn segmentation through preschool word play, rhyming games, nursery rhymes, and books like those of Dr. Seuss. These prereading activities prepare them to learn the alphabetic principle. For ESL and EFL learners, there is evidence that Hebrew speakers have difficulty segmenting the beginning consonant of an English word from the rest of the word because of their consonantal writing system (Ben-Dror, Frost, & Bentin, 1995). Arabic readers may have similar difficulties, as well as Chinese readers, who also may not have good segmentation skills because of their sinographic script. ESL and EFL learners can also learn to segment words into component sounds by playing oral rhyming games and learning rhymes and songs. They can pick out words that sound similar to each other.

In addition, English L2 learners can practice manipulating the sounds of words by taking off sounds at the beginnings, in the middle, or at the ends of words. This is an oral task, even a kind of a game; not a reading task. For instance, students can learn to answer "ick" to the following question: "What happens if I take the /t/ off of the beginning of the word 'tick'?" They can answer, "his" to the question, "What happens if I take the /l/ out of the middle of the word 'hills'?" And they can answer "sing" to the question, "What is left if I take the /s/ off of the end of 'sings'?" All of these activities can improve segmentation skills and phonemic awareness. (See, however, Wallace, 1992, pp. 54–57, for an opposing point of view on the value of segmentation activities for Arabic readers.)

Which of our students benefit from instruction in phonemic awareness activities? MariCarmen and Despina are already sophisticated readers of an alphabetic writing system, so we can presume that they have acquired phonemic awareness. If they have accurate mental images of English phonemes, their phonemic awareness will probably transfer to their new language. They may need some instruction and practice to acquire accurate mental images of English vowels. Mohammed, the Arabic reader, may need phonemic awareness activities like segmentation to expand his knowledge of English vowel and consonant segments. Ho, coming as he does from a writing system based on sinograms, may benefit from phonemic awareness and segmentation activities in English to improve his bottom-up reading skills. In addition, Chinese is a tonal language, so Ho may benefit from instruction in phrasal stress, timing, and intonation.

The discussion in this chapter leads to the conclusion that strategies for accurate listening comprehension are more relevant to reading than accurate pronunciation. Pronunciation, in fact, only comes into play in oral reading. Here are more specific ideas for teaching auditory perception and discrimination.

Spotlight on Teaching

Teachers often use auditory perception and discrimination exercises in listening comprehension. Auditory perception exercises are those which practice the perception of the sound; is the sound there? Auditory discrimination exercises are those which practice differentiating the sound from a similar sound. Auditory discrimination exercises are often based on minimal pairs.

Auditory Perception:

1. The teacher asks students to put up one finger if the word has **tʃ**. Then she gives a list of words such as the following: at, chat, apple, chapel, chin, and in. (This can be short.) The teacher can also draw students' attention to the fact that these word pairs rhyme.

2. To test for auditory perception, a teacher might ask students to raise their hands whenever they hear the sound **tʃ**. The teacher then reads the following sentence and similar ones slowly: "Chucky likes to share his chocolate candy bars with Charlotte and Charles." (If some students are waiting to see what other people do before putting their hands up, the teacher should give the students two cards, one with an x and one that is blank. They must put up the card with an x on it whenever they hear the sound.) This can be fun because even if the sentence is read slowly, students will need to listen carefully and respond quickly. It can also be a competitive activity with two or more teams. The team that responds most quickly or accurately wins. Then the teacher does a similar activity for ʃ. (Note that in some ways it is hard to differentiate a perception activity like this from a discrimination activity like those discussed later.

Auditory Discrimination:

3. The teacher makes up a list of minimal pairs with tʃ and ʃ. Have students indicate in some way which they hear: chip or ship, cheap or sheep, watch or wash, or wish or witch. Students who cannot read or write might do this by pointing at the appropriate picture. When the contrasting sound is at the beginning of the minimal pair, the words rhyme, which can also be pointed out to students.

4. In an "odd-man-out" task, students hear four words in a series and they are asked to determine which one of the four words doesn't rhyme with the others, or which one begins with a different sound or ends with a different sound. (The last task is the hardest.)

Now you select an English consonant or vowel contrast that causes difficulty for a certain population of English language learners: (tʃ and ʃ, θ and ð, or s and ʃ; i and ɪ, ɪ and ɛ). Make up creative and interesting auditory perception and discrimination exercise like these examples to teach the sound. Practice your exercise with another student in your group. Remember that this practice is for discrimination; successful pronunciation of the sounds is not necessary. As always, try to make your practice as creative and fun as possible.

Alternatively, make up a rhyming game, song, or story (e.g., Dr. Seuss, for your age level) that can be used to teach phonemic awareness. Follow it up with segmentation activities such as those described in the chapter.

DISCUSSION QUESTIONS

1. Listen to someone with a foreign accent with great attention. How easy or hard is it to understand them? What kind of mental processing do you do when you are trying to understand them? Do you "get used to" someone's accent so that you are aware of it less and less? Describe what must be happening if you get used to someone's accent.

2. Some people find it easy to pick up regional or foreign accents. It is also a skill that some actors have perfected. Discuss what it means to be able to do that in terms of the acquisition of phonological knowledge and motor commands.

3. Say these sentences with different phrasal stress and timing, and different intonation. How does the structure or meaning of each change?
   a. Time flies like arrows.
   b. The man turned on his friend (two meanings; one is bawdy).
   c. This is your handbag, isn't it?

Chapter 5

Processing Letters

Prereading questions—Before you read, think, and discuss the following:

1. Do you remember learning your letters? How did you learn them? What difficulties did you have? Did any particular letters cause you problems?
2. Look at several letters (e.g., a, b, c, f) in a variety of fonts on your computer. What properties do the letters consistently have? What differences are there?
3. How do you read illegible handwriting, if it is important information?

Study Guide questions—Answer these while you read the chapter:

1. Explain the idea that readers just sample the text as they are reading. Where did this idea come from? Why is it harmful for ESL and EFL students?
2. What are graphemes? What are graphs?
3. Consult Appendix A to answer the following questions:
   a. What are the major phoneme correspondences for the following: ch, c, k, g, j, and s?
   b. Why are vowel grapheme-to-phoneme correspondences less predictable?
   c. Which tense and lax vowel phonemes correspond to the graphemes i, e, and a?
   d. What are markers? Give two examples of markers.
   e. What is the main rule describing the alternation between i and y; u and w?
4. What are saccades? What are eye fixations? What are regressions?
5. What knowledge does the orthographic process draw on to recognize graphs?
6. What strategies does it use?
7. What is the most salient information we use to recognize graphs?
8. What accounts for the differences in reading speed between beginning and expert readers?
9. What is pattern recognition?
10. What is the Word Superiority Effect? What causes it?
11. Why is it easier to read a pseudoword like *blash* than a nonword like *hsalb*?
12. What implications are there for ESL reading instruction?
13. Can a typical ESL or EFL reader just sample the text?

We need to understand how expert English readers cope with reading an alphabetic system to know how to help beginning EFL and ESL readers master the same system. What knowledge do English readers acquire or learn to decode the text? What processing strategies do they use? One idea that has been important in recent years is that good readers just pass their eyes quickly across the text, focusing on a few letters or words here and there and forming predictions based on background knowledge. Reading is thought to be a process of "sampling the text" to confirm or disconfirm these top-down predictions. In this chapter I attempt to show that this idea is largely untrue for many typical ESL readers.

Carrell's 1993 characterization of the history of reading theory in the field of English as a Second Language traces the roots of the sampling metaphor to Goodman's early discussions of the "psycholinguistic guessing game." According to Carrell, citing Goodman (1973):

> In this model, the reader need not (and the efficient reader does not) use all of the textual cues. The better the reader is able to make correct predictions, the less confirming via the text is necessary. According to this point of view, the reader reconstructs meaning from written language by using graphophonic, syntactic, and semantic systems of the language, but he or she merely uses cues from these three levels of language to predict meaning, and most important, confirms those predictions by relating them to his or her past experiences and knowledge of the language. (p. 2)

Goodman and other early researchers were characterizing good native English-speaking readers, and they did not minimize bottom-up processing, but by the late 1970s and early 1980s, according to Carroll, second language reading specialists

> began to view second language reading as an active process in which the second language reader is an active information processor who predicts while sampling only parts of the actual text.... The introduction of [this] top-down processing perspective into second language reading has had a profound impact on the field. In fact, it has had such a profound impact that there has been a tendency to view the introduction of a strong top-down processing perspective as a *substitute* for the bottom-up, decoding view of reading, rather than its complement. (pp. 3–4)

The expression "sampling the text" caught on quickly, and it, like the term "psycholinguistic guessing game," created an impression which still prevails among many ESL and EFL reading practitioners today. Some teachers seem to believe that if students have enough cultural background knowledge and prereading strategies, they will be able to make predictions, confirm them, and therefore read, almost without looking at the text at all. For example, in a widely reprinted and excellent article, Clarke and Silberstein (1979) said the following:

The reader, therefore, does not use all the information on the page but rather must select the most productive language cues in determining the message of the writer. From this it follows that reading is necessarily a rapid process that could not proceed word by word.... [R]esearch has shown that reading is only *incidentally visual* (Kolers 1969). More information is contributed by the reader than by the print on the page.... The reader forms a preliminary expectation about the material, then selects the fewest, most productive cues necessary to confirm or reject that expectation. This is a sampling process in which the reader takes advantage of his knowledge of vocabulary, syntax, discourse, and the "real world." (pp. 48–49)

In fact, the word "sampling" is misunderstood just like the word "guessing." Both are extremely complex and cognitively demanding processes which are minimized by the metaphors chosen to talk about them. The idea that readers just sample the text is not very helpful, in a number of ways. First, as Carroll (1993) pointed out, it places too much emphasis at the top of the reading process, skimping the bottom. Although it may be true that expert native English-speaking readers can make top-down predictions and confirm them while reading, they do not just sample the text, as one might sample a variety of the offerings at a banquet table, picking and choosing at random what catches our eye. Reading is not a bit of this and a bit of that thrown onto a plate. As we shall see, expert readers are diligent about looking at the text although they may not fixate their eyes on each and every word. Much of this diligence is unconscious. Good readers' bottom-up processing has gone underground, beneath their awareness, but that does not mean that it isn't happening.

Second, the term sampling does not describe the reading process for beginning or intermediate readers, or ESL and EFL readers, who must process more of the cues in the text to grasp the meaning. Readers must acquire automaticity through ample experience with reading diverse texts before they can make the predictions to be confirmed in the reading process. Third, if teachers believe that readers just sample the text, their instructional methodologies will lack a solid foundation in linguistic knowledge and low-level processing strategies. If they believe that readers are just "guessing" and just "sampling," attention to the nitty-gritty details of English letters and sounds may seem to be a topic to be dispensed with as quickly as possible. Fourth, students are sometimes told explicitly to "sample" the text and to rely on strategies like predicting or skimming. These may work for easy reading for pleasure, but when students must comprehend difficult textbooks or journal articles, these strategies by themselves will not do. In this chapter, we look at the knowledge that beginning English language readers must learn and the low-level processing strategies that they must acquire to read English. At the end of the chapter we again return to the evaluation of this idea.

KNOWLEDGE OF GRAPHEMES AND GRAPHS

For this discussion, we need to discard the word *letter* in favor of the more technical words *grapheme* and *graph*, which parallel our usage of phoneme and phone in the last chapter. A grapheme is an abstract mental symbol of writing which corresponds to a phoneme in our spoken language, and thus, it represents all of the allophones of that phoneme. It is not accurate to say that a grapheme represents a sound, because it really represents more than one sound, usually. A grapheme is an abstraction which we use to recognize graphs. A graph is a real-life written mark on a piece of paper, a page, a billboard, or any other surface which can be written on. A graph is a concrete instance of a grapheme in the same way that a phone is a concrete instance of a phoneme.

In Fig. 5.1 and Fig. 5.2, we can see that neither graphemes nor graphs are the same as alphabet letters: there are 26 alphabet letters but more than 65 graphemes and a potentially infinite number of graphs. In general, we use the term grapheme more often, reserving the term graph to refer specifically to written marks. Single graphemes are: **t, d, f, s, a, o**, and so on. Double graphemes (also called *digraphs*) are **ch, sh, ph, th**, and a few others. Single and double graphemes are called *simple* graphemes. *Compound* graphemes are simple graphemes doubled (or geminated), as in **gg, tt**, or **ck**.

(There is more extensive information about the correspondence between graphemes and phonemes in Appendix A, which is an updated and abridged version of Venezky's 1970 monograph titled, *The Structure of English Orthography*, long out of print.)

As a first step, prereaders must learn to identify and write the letters of the alphabet. It is often helpful for students to make the shapes in a number of different visual, tactile, or physical ways and also to identify them in different fonts. We use the alphabet letters to write English, but students need to acquire the system of graphemes as well. That is why early reading and writing books must contain information about the simple and compound graphemes that make up the English system of writing. This is true for the native English and ESL and EFL prereaders alike.

Graphemes, like phonemes, have invariant properties, and the knowledge base for language must include an inventory of graphemes and their invariant properties. The grapheme **b**, for example, is a lowercase grapheme, a visual symbol made up of a vertical line on the left and a shorter curved line on the right. Our mental image of a **b** must be abstract enough to allow us to read many different real-life **b**s, no matter who writes them, just as our mental image of a phoneme /b/ must be abstract enough to allow us to understand many different voiced bilabial stops, no matter who pronounces them and what position they hold in a word. We must be able to read **b, b, ᑲ, b, b, ᑳ, ᑲ, ᑳ,** or b because of the invariant properties of the shape

English Consonant Graphemes

simple						compound
b	g	kh	q	t	wh	ck
c	gh	l	r	th	y	dg
ch	h	m	s	u	z	tch
d	j	n	sh	v		x
f	k	p	sch	w		all geminated consonants (pp, tt)

Notes: **u** is a consonant unit when it corresponds to /w/, as in **q**uack or lang**u**age.

wh is mainly used as a simple consonant corresponding to the voiced /w/ or the voiceless /ʍ/. In some dialects, **wh** seems to have a compound usage /hw/ as in the "voiceless" pronunciations of the beginning consonants of **wh**at, **wh**ich and **wh**en.

sch is a simple consonant grapheme when it is used as in **sch**ist or **sch**wa.

gn is a simple consonant grapheme when it is used as in **gn**ome, co**gn**ac or poi**gn**ant

Geminated consonants are compound consonants which are simple consonants doubled: **bb, dd, ff, gg, ll, mm, nn, pp, rr, tt, zz**, as in e**bb**, e**dd**y, ga**ff**er, e**gg**, fe**ll**, di**mm**er, di**nn**er, a**pp**le, pu**rr**, be**tt**er, bu**zz**.

In fact, **ck, dg,** and **tch** actually stand for geminate consonants as well: **ck** = **cc** and **kk, dg** = **jj**, and **tch** = **chch**. For some reason, our writing system has resisted writing true geminates for these and has preferred to use **ck, dg,** and **tch**, as in ba**ck**, e**dg**e, and wa**tch**.

FIG. 5.1   Main English consonant graphemes from Venezky, 1970. Used by permission of Mouton de Gruyter.

English Vowel Graphemes

primary		secondary	
a	ai/ay	ie	ue
e	au/aw	oa	ui
i	ea	oe	ae
o	ee	oi/oy	eau
u	ei/ey	oo	eo
y	eu/ew	ou/ow	uy

FIG. 5.2   Main English vowel graphemes from Venezky, 1970. Used by permission of Mouton de Gruyter.

that remain constant throughout its appearance in different fonts. ESL instruction in graphic shapes must extend to at least the variety of fonts available on most computers.

PROCESSING GRAPHS IN ENGLISH L1 READERS

We have seen that the knowledge base needs stored information about English graphemes and their properties to identify graphs in what is called orthographic processing. What processing strategies do English L1 readers develop to process graphs? One source of information comes from the study of the eye movements that take place during reading. When we are reading, the eyes do not move smoothly across a line of words; instead they move across print in very quick jerks which are called *saccades*. During saccades no real sight is possible because the eyes are moving, but between the saccades there are also times, called *eye fixations*, when the eyes are stopped on the print. During eye fixations, light energy bouncing off of the page is received in the eye and transmitted to the brain where the visual stimuli is processed. The adult expert reader has about four eye fixations per second and identifies around one word per fixation, although it is theoretically possible for the eye to read four or five words in a single fixation. This means that the average reader takes in around 240 to 300 words per min although, theoretically again, it would be possible to read at a rate of 900 to 1,200 words per min (Crowder & Wagner, 1992). Presumably, readers prefer a slower speed because it allows for better comprehension of the material that is being read. There is always a trade-off between speed and comprehension and good readers can adjust fixation speed to accommodate to comprehension needs.

In perceiving the graphs on a page, our eyes do not just move from left to right. Our eyes also perform *regressions*, or backward movements, possibly to check information or to reanalyze something we have perceived (Crowder & Wagner, 1992). In addition, we do not use all of the information from the text equally (Weaver, 1994). For instance, it seems like consonant graphs provide a better cue to the identity of a word than do vowel graphs, at least for English. In English, consonants are more frequent than vowels in most words and the consonant spellings are more consistent and predictable than vowel spellings, so it may not be accidental that expert readers use consonant cues better than vowel cues. Consonant graphs carry more "meaning" for readers; the vowel graphs only have meaning when they occur within a framework of consonants. For example, note that sentence a is much easier to decipher than sentence b:

a. Th- qu-ck br-wn f-x j-ump-d -v-r th- l-z- d-gs.
b. —e —i— —o— -o- -u—e- o-e- —e -a-y -o—.

At first, early readers probably look carefully at both vowels and consonants, but soon they develop a strategy of fixating more on the more informative consonants than on the vowels, tolerating incomplete information and projecting vowel information from the peripheral cues they get and from their ample experience with English spelling patterns. Projecting roughly means that the processor makes a best guess about what the graph is based on partial information. Another example of the use of partial information is that readers get more information from the tops of graphs than the bottoms (Weaver, 1994). Again, note the difference between reading sentence c and sentence d:

    c.   The quick brown fox jumped over the lazy dogs

    d.   The quick brown fox jumped over the lazy dogs.

Furthermore, readers fixate more carefully on some words than on others. Stanovich (1991) reported research that indicates that content words receive a direct fixation and that although short function words and highly predictable words are often passed over, there is quite a bit of fixation on them as well.

During an eye fixation, there is a "window" of 10 graph positions on the right of the fixation point where perception takes place (Crowder & Wagner, 1992). (The window is to the left for scripts that go in that direction, like Hebrew, which may require some retraining for the eye for English learners from those languages.) The reader can see word length information a word or two beyond where his or her eyes will be next. The fixation provides a "snapshot" of the text before the eyes move on. The fixated and projected information from the sequence of snapshots must be merged together by the mind at some higher level of processing, maybe at the lexical and syntactic levels. The 10 or so graphs are perceived and recognized, and then held in short-term memory until the next snapshot of 10 or so graphs is processed and recognized. The lexical and syntactic levels of the reading processor supplement any other incomplete information from the snapshots by projecting possible additional data from the previous linguistic knowledge and experience the reader has acquired. The more they have, the better they can do this. This accounts for many of the differences between the beginning and the expert reader.

I recently had an experience while reading that shows some of this in action. While reading a description of bat navigation, I picked up peripheral cues from a later word while fixating on an earlier word. The later word was actually something different, but the peripheral cues from the graphs activated the word **chocolate** in my head. I felt an instantaneous sense of surprise that the substance (chocolate) would occur in a discussion of bat navigation, but in the same instant I fixated on the word **echolocate**. I remained fixated on the word for a long time while I processed the graph **ch** correctly and identified the more unusual verb. After about a millisecond, I succeeded in analyzing the word two ways. First, I saw that it was a compound of **echo** and **locate**, and second I saw that it was a back formation from echolocation, the noun form with which I am more familiar. I noticed myself regressing to that point frequently until I moved onto the next page.

This view of the complexity of "sampling," as summarized in Fig. 5.3, is confirmed when we look at differences in reading speed between beginning and advanced English readers. Crowder and Wagner (1992) told us that there are many differences between the fixations of beginning readers and expert readers. In a study that compared eye movements from native language readers of all grades from 1 to college, beginning readers had about three fixations per second, whereas college students had four. Fixations took about .33 sec for the beginning readers but they took .25 sec for the college students. Thus, beginning readers had fewer snapshots per second, and each one took longer. It is reasonable to think that these beginning

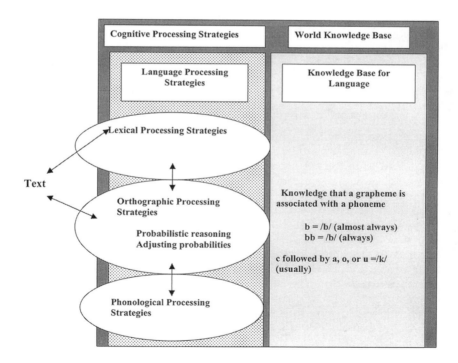

FIG. 5.3   The knowledge base and processing strategies for "sampling" the text.

readers are looking at the visual cues on the page more carefully or that they aren't as fast at information gathering, processing, and projecting.

In a text, beginning readers had more fixations and also more regressions, showing that they process information slowly but carefully, correcting mistakes that they might have made. Readers in Grade 1 had 183 total fixations with 42 regressions for a 100 word passage, but college students had only 75 fixations with 15 regressions for 100 words. The number of words seen in one fixation also changes as readers gain expertise. Beginning readers seem to be reading .55 words in each fixation, whereas the college students were reading 1.3 words in each fixation, with the adults reading 300 words per min. Thus, beginning readers have more and longer eye fixations than do advanced readers, but they are actually reading a smaller amount in each fixation. The efficient and expert readers have fewer, shorter eye fixations in which they can read more than one word; they have truly mastered the process! The so-called sampling of the text, instead of being haphazard and cursory, is actually "dense," with rather complete processing of graphs during each fixation. Efficient readers, it seems, depend on the information from each graph and word that was visible in the fixation.

There is little research on eye movements in the reading of ESL and EFL learners. One study (Tullius, 1971, cited in Hatch, 1979) with university level ESL students found that they did not have more eye fixations per line and they did not have more regressions than monolingual students, but their eye fixations were 3 times longer. This indicates that more processing was involved for them to identify the word or that their processing was not as automatic and effortless. It is probably the case that beginning and intermediate ESL students will require more fixations and regressions in their beginning reading, but that the number and frequency will decrease if they succeed in passing into the later developmental stages. World knowledge and activated schemata will only do so much to help their processing if they cannot learn to read quickly with efficient and short eye fixations, accurate projections, and few regressions. These lowest-level processing strategies are as crucial to reading success as the higher level cognitive strategies.

Along with low-level processing strategies like fixation, projection, and regression, readers also acquire other processing strategies which operate below conscious awareness. One such strategy is called *pattern recognition* (Crowder & Wagner, 1992; Underwood & Batt, 1996). The human brain seems well-suited to recognizing patterns and similarities in the environment. Pattern recognition in reading means matching the shape of a graph with the mental concept of a grapheme stored as linguistic knowledge. There seem to be two possibilities. One is that the graphs are perceived holistically and identified by matching the perception with a "template" or visual image of the whole grapheme stored in memory. The other type of theory suggests that the features of the graph, the shapes of the lines and so on, are detected separately and compared with a visual image of a grapheme stored in memory. The comparison is not done serially, or one by one, but in parallel, a number of features at a time. In either case, pattern recognition, like the phonemic recognition we discussed in the last chapter, seems to rest on associating the token (graph or phone) with the invariant properties of the type (grapheme or phoneme). Each instance of a graph is recognized because its properties are similar to the abstract properties of the grapheme, whether it is done holistically or not. Graphic recognition is really a decision-making process in which a lot of different information and strategies come into play.

In fact, there are further connections between graphemes and phonemes. The orthographic processing which takes the printed text as direct input is connected to the phonological processing which was discussed in the last chapter. In orthographic processing, the graphs in the printed text are perceived and recognized, a grapheme is activated, and because graphemes are associated with phonemes, the activation of the grapheme spreads to the associated phoneme. The phonemic activation is how we know the sound or pronunciation of the grapheme even if we do not actually pronounce it out loud. The visual and sound cues are both used to decide the identity of the word that is being read. Once we have recognized some of the graphs in a written word or a partial word, a phonological representation is also associated with the part of the word. Soon, there is enough graphemic and phonemic information for the reading processor to begin forming a hypothesis about what the full word is. This is the essence of how alphabetic writing works.

There are a number of theories about how words are recognized. For example, it is possible that recognition of graphs causes activation of a graphemic image in our linguistic knowledge, then the activation spreads to those words which have those graphemes in them and causes them to be recognized (Underwood & Batt, 1996). It seems that at this level of word recognition in the reading process, both bottom-up and top-down processing show their greatest overlap. This is because word recognition, like graphic recognition, is a complicated interactive and integrated decision-making process to which the reading processor tries to contribute as much information as possible. The graphemic and phonemic cues are necessary for reading, but the interactive reading processor can also draw on world, semantic, and syntactic knowledge for cues to what the words are that are printed on the page. Many processing strategies also come into play. For instance, the reader can use information from the context of the paragraph to decide what a word is or which of several meanings is the most suitable. The fact that all of this knowledge and these strategies overlap doesn't minimize the bottom-up recognition that must take place. Readers must start with the print and stay close to the print in reading; anything else is not reading, it is imagination.

When we recognize graphs and words, we don't work on each in isolation. It has been found that we cannot process individual graphs as well in isolation as we can when they appear in the context of the word. We process in chunks because information that is organized into a unit is easier to process than the individual bits of information that compose the unit. That graphs are perceived more easily in the context of a word is called the Word Superiority Effect (Crowder & Wagner, 1992).

The Word Superiority Effect can be explained if we assume that readers remember how words typically look. This assumes the storage in long-term memory of a visual image for each word that is frequently read. There is a lot of support for the idea of a visual or graphemic image of words stored in memory. For example, people can read letter sequences that have meaning better than those that don't: **YMCA** is read more easily than **YSSU**. However, that reading advantage disappears if the sequences are presented with mixed typography: **ymCA** is read the same way as **ysSU**. The explanation is that **ymCA** doesn't quite match the pattern of our graphemic image of **YMCA**, so the graphs must be read individually, as in **YSSU** or **ysSU** (Henderson, 1974, cited in Crowder & Wagner, 1992). It seems that the development of a graphemic image based on prior experiences with a word gives an advantage to the reader. (And the writer, too, because one spelling strategy for words we are uncertain of is to write out alternatives and pick the one that "looks right.")

It is interesting that Word Superiority Effects can also be found for nonwords that could be possible English words, or, as they are called, *pseudowords*. It is easier to read **blash** than it is to read **hsalb**. To explain this, we need to suppose, as Crowder and Wagner (1992) did, that the activation that spreads from the graphemic images to the word level activates words that are visually and phonologically similar—**lash, slash**, and **splash**. When these other images are activated, they facilitate the reading of the pseudoword. Facilitation also comes from the fact that pseudowords are pronounceable—a hypothetical phonemic image can be assigned to them. We pick up on this detail again later; this process turns out to be quite important for the English as a Second or Foreign Language learner.

Research also suggests that readers find the beginnings of words more useful than the middles or the ends in identifying words (Weaver, 1994). There may be a number of reasons for this. First, we read from left to right, so the beginning of the word is what we encounter first. The ends of words often contain grammatical morphemes which are largely predictable from context for the native reader at least. It may not be necessary, for example, for the expert English L1 reader to process each verb ending once the context has established that the reading is in the past tense. The morphological information can be projected. Another possible reason has to do with the way that word identification may take place. It may be that the visual images of words are accessed from the beginning to the end and once a word is accessed and identified and the meaning confirmed to fit the context, the rest of the information from the word is not as necessary for identification purposes.

If we think of the reading processor as an expert decision-making system, this use of multi source and extensive, but also incomplete and projected, information makes sense. We have world and linguistic knowledge and different processing strategies that allow us to make a best guess about the graphs and words we are reading. Our best guesses are confirmed by adding in further information from a later fixation. If there is some problem, we can always fall back on the regression strategy to check for a misread graph or a misidentified word.

What can we conclude, then, about the idea of "sampling" the text? It is true that readers do not read every graph or every word, and that their projections and expectations supplement incomplete information. It doesn't take a complete perception to activate stored knowledge, but fairly complete perception may be necessary to store new knowledge. However, it is also true that being able to comprehend the message in the text is a complex decision-making process involving many types of knowledge and processing strategies which interact at different linguistic levels. If we understand the word "sampling" in this more complex and respectful sense, we might say that only the best English readers read by "sampling" the text, especially if they are reading something unchallenging, with little new information to be processed.

Can the ESL and EFL reader read by sampling the text? Yes, if he or she has the knowledge, experience, and low-level reading strategies of the best native English speaking readers. If the ESL and EFL reader is lacking knowledge, experience, or strategies, and if these do not interface automatically and effortlessly, his or her reading cannot be described this way. In the research discussed in previous chapters, we found that there is evidence to conclude that readers develop strategies for the L1, but that these strategies might not be the same for L2, might interfere with reading L2, or that they might not have developed the most efficient strategies for L2. It is hard to imagine that anyone but the most proficient English L2 reader can sample the text and get much from it.

To read English, readers must match a graph on the page to a grapheme stored in their heads, which is matched to a phoneme to form a graphemic–phonemic image of the word, which is then matched to an image stored in our word memory to access the word. For ESL and EFL readers, things can go wrong at any point in this process. The strategies of fixation and regression may transfer if the learner's L1 writing system is similar to English, or they may require some retooling if, for example, the symbols are written right-to-left or top-to-bottom in columns. Some students may need to learn to fixate on both consonants and vowels, but mainly on consonants. They need to fixate more on the tops of graphemes than on the bottoms. They need to fixate more on content words than on function words. Efficient fixation and regression (for example, to detect an error that requires regression) requires extensive L2 knowledge, and the ability to project, say, vowel information from incomplete, uncertain, or missing information, does also.

ESL and EFL students may have trouble with graphic pattern recognition. Teachers often assume that students have already learned how to identify graphs when they come into our beginning reading classes, but they should not take this skill for granted. Learners may not know the alphabet letters or how alphabetic writing works and may be using other cognitive or linguistic strategies that compensate for not being able to recognize the graphs on the page. Illiterate people are not stupid. They become specialists at hiding their illiteracy by memorizing information that is given to them verbally or by memorizing words as holistic units. This is true for English-speaking nonreaders, and so it may also be true for some English learners. People who "read" in these ways do not advance into the later stages of reading proficiency. Students may have learned the alphabet letters, but don't understand how they are used to form graphemes in English. For example, they may not know that **ph** is often /f/, or that **dd** indicates the quality of the previous vowel. They don't have the knowledge of English graphemes stored as units and cannot process them in reading.

Another problem is that some ESL learners have learned the graphemes of English, but they have not acquired them. By that I mean that they know what the graphemes are consciously and formally and can identify them, but they cannot use them to identify graphs quickly and effortlessly as they are reading. The associations between their perception of the graph on the page and the grapheme stored in their memory do not work fast enough, and the associations between grapheme and phoneme may also be missing, faulty, or too inefficient for automatic reading. An ample store of graphemic and phonemic images for frequent words may be nonexistent, which is the topic of a later chapter.

Thus, for many ESL and EFL learners, being able to read by sampling the text must be the ultimate goal to which they aspire, to read quickly and effortlessly. They need low-level L2 knowledge and processing strategies and ample practice to achieve this goal.

Spotlight on Teaching

Texts for English-speaking children use different orders when presenting the consonant grapheme-to-phoneme correspondences. Some of the factors which guide the order of presentation are, according to Gunning (1988), single before digraphs before compound, frequency of occurrence in general, ease of auditory discrimination (stops are least discriminable), frequency of occurrence in the children's reading materials, and not teaching graphemes easily confused together (b, p, and d). Are these factors equally important for ESL and EFL learners? In which order would you teach the consonant graphemes?

According to Gunning (1988), there have been at least three distinct methods of teaching the grapheme-to-phoneme correspondences to English-speaking children over the years. For each one, discuss what might be the advantages and disadvantages for the ESL and EFL learner in terms of what you have learned so far in this text about phonemic awareness, segmentation, and so on. Take notes on your discussion. After discussing each one, put your notes aside until you have read the next two chapters. Then come back and check them to see if you would change your ideas or add more advantages or disadvantages for the ESL and EFL learner.

The three methods follow:

1.   The *analytical* approach is one in which the graphemes and phonemes are never isolated from the context of a word. The teacher might say, "The letter M stands for the sound at the beginning of 'man' and 'monkey.'" The teacher never isolates the sound /m/ for the students.

2.   The *synthetic* approach is one in which the consonant and vowel sounds are isolated and taught separately. The teacher might say, "The letter M stands for /m/." Once the sounds are mastered, then they are blended together (em-aaa-t) to pronounce the whole word: mat.

3.   The *linguistic* approach is one in which a series of words are placed on the board in a vertical column: cat, fat, mat. Each word is read out loud and contrasted with the one above it. Children learn each spelling pattern and "induce" (learn on their own from the examples) the grapheme-to-phoneme correspondences in the patterns.

An analytical lesson plan for presenting a consonant grapheme-to-phoneme correspondence might include the following steps—auditory perception, auditory discrimination, grapheme-to-phoneme linkage within a word, visual discrimination of the grapheme, controlled writing practice, and guided application:

1.   Auditory perception means that the ESL learner can perceive the sound, as in chapter 4.

2.   Auditory discrimination means that the ESL learner can discriminate the sound from similar sounds, as in chapter 4.

3.   Grapheme-to-phoneme linkage within words means that the grapheme is presented visually as the first letter in a word written on the blackboard and pronounced. The grapheme-to-phoneme pattern is reinforced several times with different words, including words in which the grapheme is not word–initial.

4.   Practice visual discrimination of the grapheme, picking it out from other similar graphemes, picking it out in various fonts, underlining examples of it in sentences, and so forth.

5.   Practice printing and writing uppercase and lowercase graphemes, make the grapheme shapes in sand, from beans, and so forth; label objects with names that begin with the grapheme, and so forth.

6.   Read stories with words that have the grapheme in them; draw pictures of things that start with that grapheme and write the word, other writing practice, and so forth.

Now you, individually or in groups, discuss a lesson plan for a common consonant grapheme-to-phoneme correspondence that you pick from Appendix A. Create the materials you would use. Make sure you make them as interesting, meaningful, and "real" as possible. Use cooperative learning in your activities.

DISCUSSION QUESTIONS

1. In this chapter I described an unusual experience while reading the word *echolocate*. Do you recall any similar experiences while reading? Pay attention to the reading that you do in the next few days. What do you become aware of? What problems do you resolve?
2. Are you a fast reader or a slow reader? If the latter, what do you think slows you down?

Chapter 6

The English Spelling System

Prereading questions—Before you read, think, and discuss the following:

1. What complaints have you heard people make about our writing system? Make a list.
2. Some people advocate spelling reform. What are the pros and cons of that? Do you think it will ever happen?
3. How would you pronounce the following pseudo words: habb, spack, hobe, and loce. How did you know how to do this?
4. Compare your pronunciations to that of another person. Are there any differences?
5. What is phonics instruction? What is your impression of it?

Study Guide questions—Answer these while you are reading the chapter:

1. What is the myth that English spelling is chaotic? Where does it come from?
2. What does it mean to say English writing is phonemic? Why is it not phonetic?
3. How do readers use probabilistic reasoning in reading? What are raw probabilities? What are adjusted probabilities?
4. What knowledge do readers need to have to reason probabilistically?
5. Which English consonants have the most unpredictable pronunciations? What increases their predictability?
6. How is reading different from spelling? How is it similar?
7. Give the probabilistic reasoning that might be involved in reading the **c** or **ch** in the words clad, city, pack, chorus, chlorine, and channel.

In an earlier chapter, we saw that the English writing system is called opaque because the correspondence between graphemes and phonemes is not one-to-one. Because of borrowings, historical changes in English, scribal preferences, and so on, our writing system has complexity. If you examine the information from Appendix A carefully, you will see that the consonant graphemes correspond more regularly with phonemes than do the vowel graphemes. Although the consonant system in spoken English has remained fairly stable for the past centuries, spoken English has had a very unstable vowel system. One change was the Great Vowel Shift, which influenced the pronunciation of many vowels, like /i/, /e/, and /a/. Although the change took place in speech, our writing system had been standardized by that time and the changes in pronunciation were not reflected in our writing system. This is why, in other languages, **i** = /i/, **e** = /e/, and **a** = /ɑ/, but in English, **i** tends to be /ay/, **e** = /iy/, and **a** = /ey/.

For these and other reasons, it is a common idea that the English writing system is hopelessly chaotic and random. People point to the old remark attributed to George Bernard Shaw that in English the word **fish** could be written **ghoti**: the **gh** from lau*gh*, the **o** from w*o*men, and the **ti** from ac*ti*on. In the second language field, many reading practitioners believe that there is no system that can be taught to EFL and EFL students to make English reading and writing easier. In fact, English writing is largely systematic; but there are a few anomalies that attract attention and give people the impression of chaos. If people expect to perceive chaos in the English writing system, they will. If they want to perceive the order, they must learn that it is there.

The English writing system is phonemic but the relation between graphemes and phonemes is not one-to-one. The consonant grapheme-to-phoneme relation is quite consistent, however. In fact, for most of the consonants in the English writing system, the probability that a consonant grapheme will be read in a certain way is quite high. The English reader takes advantage of that consistency and uses knowledge of those probabilities in a certain processing strategy to read them, as shown in Fig. 6.1. The processing strategy is called *probabilistic reasoning*, which is a common strategy in judgment and decision tasks (Rachlin, 1989; von Winterfeldt & Edwards 1986).

PROBABILISTIC REASONING

To use the strategy of probabilistic reasoning in reading, readers need to learn the probabilities that certain graphemes will represent certain phonemes. Many English L1 readers learn this information directly from their teachers in their earliest reading instruction in preschool or kindergarten (called *phonics*), or they acquire it unconsciously mainly through exposure to many graphs and words in print. Phonics instruction is instruction in the most common graph–grapheme–phoneme connections in English writing,

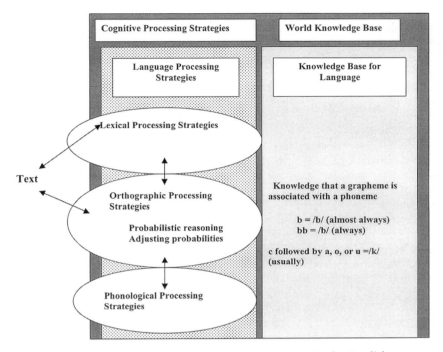

FIG. 6.1   The knowledge base and processing strategies for English consonants.

but not the actual probabilities in the chart in this chapter. Teachers vary as
to how much phonic information they present and practice with
prereaders. At first, in Chall's (1983) first reading stage, reading takes place
out loud (the learning stage), and it probably continues as such until there
has been enough exposure to words for rapid mental processing of
graphemes to take place (the acquisition stage). Once readers have inter-
nalized the main associations between graphemes and phonemes, they begin to read silently.

   To begin our discussion of probabilistic reasoning in expert reading,
and later, in reading instruction, we need to get an idea of what some of the
probabilities are that graphemes will represent certain phonemes. In Table
6.1, you see a chart of English consonant grapheme-to-phoneme correspondences based on, but considerably different from, information in
Dewey (1970). Dewey studied a set or corpus of 100,000 running words, in
which he found 10,119 different words. Function words or frequent content
words were presumably repeated more than once, which accounts for the
difference between the total corpus and the number of different words he
studied for the purposes of the information which I adapt in Table 6.1. Col-

umn 1 has the main simple and compound graphemes of English. Column 2 shows the phoneme to which the grapheme corresponds. The last column gives the percentages of times that the grapheme corresponded to that phoneme in the corpus that was studied by Dewey. The table is to be read the following way: Each time the grapheme **b** occurred in the corpus, 100% of the time its pronunciation was /b/. There were no exceptions. Similarly, each time the compound grapheme **bb** occurred, 100% of the time its pronunciation was also /b/. There were no exceptions. My findings are very similar to those of Berndt, Reggia, and Mitchum, 1987. (See also Carney, 1994, pp. 280–381.)

In Appendix B, my adaptation of some tables in Groff and Seymour (1987) showed that out of another corpus, **b** will occur 97% of the time, and **bb** will occur approximately 3% of the time, overall. That means that overall in our spelling, we spell /b/ more often with **b** than with **bb**. We probably have expectations of that based on the knowledge of English writing that we acquire from our experiences with texts, but that information is really irrelevant to the orthographic processor because it knows that every time it encounters a **b** it will access the phoneme /b/, and every time it encounters a **bb** it will access the same phoneme /b/. It should be obvious that this will not cause any difficulty for the orthographic processor.

Note that the variation between **b** and **bb** can be a problem for someone who is trying to spell, but not for someone who is trying to read. One way to look at it is that the reading "rule" is quite regular, but the spelling rule may be more difficult to apply. In our discussion of the reading processor, our concern has been with a unidirectional correspondence of grapheme to phoneme, because that is what we do in reading. We match incoming printed graphemes to abstract mental units, phonemes, to access words and meanings. These correspondences can be called *reading rules*.

Reading rule: grapheme ⇒ **phoneme**
b or bb ⇒ **/b/**

However, the relation between graphemes and phonemes is really bidirectional. In other words, the relation can be stated the other way as well and when it is, it is called *spelling rule*.

Spelling rule: phoneme ⇒ **grapheme**
/b/ ⇒ **b or bb**

The learner may be able to read **b** and **bb** with ease, without knowing exactly when to write **b** or **bb**, unless he or she has acquired the generalization that the compound grapheme occurs after lax vowels, before certain suffixes, and so on. The English writing system is therefore more complex for the writing decision-making system than it is for the reading decision-making system, which may account for the impression of chaos surrounding the system.

Spelling rules have some similarities with reading rules. For one thing, they draw on the same linguistic knowledge that readers have in their heads about graphemes and phonemes. Reading rules and spelling rules are often taught at the same time. However, reading rules and spelling rules are fundamentally different in their functions and application. The correspondence that goes from grapheme to phoneme is far more predictable, because, for the most part, there are fewer phonemes than potential graphemes associated with them.

People also think that the English writing system is irregular because of their expectations of what an alphabetic writing system should be. Many people have the idea that a perfect writing system would have a certain number of symbols, 26 say, with one symbol for each sound and one sound for each symbol. English writing is not like that. First, we have more phonemes in our language than we have alphabet letters. And second, we have more graphemes than alphabet letters too. A radical solution would be to double the number of alphabet letters, assign one ambiguously to each phoneme, and begin writing in this new way. Indeed, some naïve reformers have advocated this and other similar solutions. However, reforming our spelling has proven to be as resistant to change as the U.S. conversion to the metric system, so such a radical spelling reform is highly unlikely. Although the spelling of some words could benefit from some "pruning," the system itself works well enough.

To see the pattern in English spelling, we must rid ourselves of the expectation that alphabet symbols must have a one-to-one correspondence to phonemes for that alphabetic writing to be regular and consistent. Instead, let's think about a complex system in which, first of all, there are more graphemes than alphabet letters. Both **b** and **bb** are graphemes. Second, most consonant graphemes (except **c**, **g**, and **gh**) are read unambiguously because they do correspond to one phoneme of English. Sometimes the phonemes correspond to more than one grapheme, but that is not the problem for reading as it is for writing. When the aforementioned charts are examined in this new light, regularity and consistency are evident. Regular and consistent patterns of correspondences between graphemes and phonemes, even if they are complex, make it easy for the reading processor to make decisions about assigning a phoneme to a grapheme in reading. Once the orthographic processor is trained (through experience, practice, and direct instruction) to the point of automaticity to recognize these graphemes, it is not hard for it to associate the correct pronunciation with them because they are highly predictable.

We can say that these tables contain raw probabilities that a single grapheme will be pronounced a certain way. However, knowledge and perception of contextual information is important in interpreting consonant graphemes, especially when the probabilities are lower. Contextual information can greatly increase or decrease the raw probabilities that aid the reader in assigning a pronunciation to a particular word encountered in print. Knowledge of these adjusted probabilities also needs to be added by readers to their knowledge base either directly through instruction, or indirectly based on extensive exposure to reading practice.

Here is an example where context increases the probabilities of association between graphemes and phonemes. The grapheme c can stand for either /k/ (72% of the time) or /s/ (28% of the time). Yet, the pronunciation of the grapheme is correlated with the following vowel; the following vowel gives us a context for interpreting the phonemic value of the preceding consonant. If c is followed by a, o, or u, it is likely to be pronounced as /k/. If the c is followed by i, e, or y, it is more likely to be pronounced as /s/. Although we don't know from the information we can find in Dewey (1970) what the adjusted probabilities are, because he doesn't provide information about the contexts for these pronunciations, it is safe to say that they would be much higher than the raw probabilities. The adjusted probabilities are encoded as if/then statements in the knowledge base:

> If c is followed by a, o, or u, then increase the probability that it is pronounced /k/.
> If c is followed by i, e, or y, then increase the probability that it is pronounced /s/.

An almost identical example can be seen in the reading rule involving the grapheme g. The raw probabilities are 73% that it will be pronounced as /g/ as in got and 26% that it will be pronounced /dʒ/ as in general. However, the context for this grapheme is the same as for c, mentioned earlier. If g is followed by a, o, or u, it is likely to be pronounced as /g/, and if it is followed by i, e, and y, it is likely to be pronounced /dʒ/. There are some notable exceptions, of course, like girl and get, but the rule is really quite regular, so it is safe to assume that the real or adjusted probabilities are much higher.

There are also problems in the raw probabilities for the correspondence between spelling and pronunciation for s, which can be either /s/ or /z/. Again, if we know where in the word the graph occurs, we can adjust the probabilities higher. The pronunciation of /s/ is much more frequent when s is syllable initial; /z/ is much more frequent when s is syllable final. Context allows the reader to adjust raw probabilities to make very accurate predictions about grapheme-to-phoneme correspondences. In this case, morphology also plays a part. Plural or possessive nouns and third person singular verbs in the present tense end in the morpheme s (as in books, John's, and goes). The case is complicated, as we see in a later chapter, but sometimes the morpheme is pronounced /s/ (books) and sometimes /z/ (e.g., John's, goes). The native English reader knows which pronunciation to assign to the morpheme, so morphological information allows the reading processor to adjust the probabilities that the grapheme **s** will represent /s/ or /z/. We have seen that many of the phonemic values of English consonants turn out to be much less irregular than previously thought when you add in contextual or linguistic information. The correspondence between grapheme and phoneme in the English writing system is patterned, but the pattern is complex.

It is crucial to note that human brains are willing and able to store this much information and more in their knowledge base to use as a basis for probabilistic reasoning and decision making. (However, reading problems are more frequent in English readers than in readers of more transparent systems, so this is not true for everyone.) In general, our minds are capable of handling much more complexity; indeed, many of the decisions and judgments we are asked to make instantaneously every day are far more complex than the interpretation of **g** or any other grapheme, which become, for expert readers, nothing more than routine. Just as we can gauge the probabilities of getting caught if we go through a red light, or the probabilities that we will be late if we have that extra cup of coffee in the morning, we can gauge the probabilities that a certain grapheme will correspond to a certain phoneme. The basis for this knowledge is experience and learning, through which we build up expectations that aid us in future situations.

Let's examine an example of probabilistic reasoning involving the graph **ch**. From Appendix A we see this information which we can augment with probabilities from this chapter:

ch		
a.	**ch** in fuchsia or yacht = /0/	less than .5%
b.	**ch** = /k/ before l, n, r, and in words of Latin or Greek origin	8%
c.	**ch** = /ʃ/ in words of French origin	less than 1%
d.	**ch** elsewhere = /tʃ/	90%

When the orthographic processor sees **ch** in a word that it is processing, the main (or default) option is /tʃ/ (as in line d), so it will assign **ch** a pronunciation of /tʃ/ until further notice. (Recall also the relevant example of **echolocate**, from the last chapter, in which I first assigned the **ch** the pronunciation of /tʃ/ and then had to fixate to repair it.) If further information from other graphs and the lexical processor contradicts that first assignment, the lexical processor will override the first assignment to correct it. For example, say the processor perceives an l after the **ch**, as in the word **chlorine**, and it realizes that this is a contingency that it knows about, as in line b. At some point, the orthographic processor or the lexical processor must "fix" the mistake and assign **ch** the pronunciation of /k/. Let's say I've had some unfortunate experiences with the pronunciation of French words, so I am attentive to them in reading. Over time, based on these cases, I develop the expectation contained in line c. When I come across the word **chamois**, I think it is a French word because of the unusual **ois** at the end and so my first attempt at pronunciation /ʃamoy/ is not too far off but still not quite right.

Although probabilistic reasoning works well for consonants, it is less useful for vowels. An examination of Table 6.1 shows that although the correspondence between vowel graphemes and vowel phonemes is less predictable than the correspondence between consonant phonemes and spellings, the orthographic processor does have some expectations with which to work. Let's say the processor comes across a new word: *tun*. How would we pronounce it? By consulting with the Table 6.0, we can see that there are three alternatives: /tʌn/ with a vowel like **pup** (63%), /tʊn/ with a vowel like **put** (10%), or /tun/ with a vowel like **truth** (2%). The processor will choose /tʌn/ because the grapheme-to-phoneme correspondence has the highest probability of occurrence.

However, context also plays a part in adjusting these probabilities. The vowel graph **o** has the probability of 40% of having the phonemic value of /ɑ/ according to the first part of Table 6.1. That is its most consistent correspondence. The main phonemic value for **o**, when placed in the context of **o–e**, is 60% for /o/, which is its most consistent pronunciation. This tallies with our expectations that overall, our graph **o** is most commonly pronounced as in **pot**, unless it is followed by a consonant and a "silent" **e**, as in **tone**. This is the major reading rule for vowels as reported by Venezky (1970) and reprinted in Appendix A. The orthographic processor can use this raw and adjusted probabilistic information about vowel graphs to assign pronunciations to the flow of incoming graphs while reading, as it does with the more predictable consonants. Nevertheless, another type of reasoning is thought to be more valuable for vowels, reasoning by analogy to known spelling patterns. We discuss that topic in the next chapter.

PROBABILISTIC REASONING FOR ESL READERS

Seidenberg (1990) said that orthographies in different languages differ as to how much phonological information they encode. He cited a number of languages with alphabetic writing systems which are more regular than English in their grapheme–phoneme correspondences. We have called these writing systems, like Spanish, German, or Greek, transparent. According to Seidenberg (1990), readers "adjust their processing strategies in response to the properties of writing systems ... [and that] there are very basic difference in the types of knowledge and processes relevant to reading different orthographies" (pp. 49–50). What potential differences are there in the knowledge and processes of L1 and English as an L2?

TABLE 6.0

English Consonant Grapheme to Phoneme Correspondences

Grapheme	Phoneme	Approximate Percentage of Times that the Grapheme Spells that Phoneme:	
bat	b	100	
ebb	b	100	
debt	0	100	
cat	k	72	
city	s	28	
back	k	100	
church	tʃ	90	
choir	k	8	
dot	d	98	
add	d	100	
fat	f	60*	*Note: this result is skewed by three very frequent words in the corpus in which f =>/v/. One is **of**. Except for those frequent words, the correspondence between f and /f/ is probably very high.
of	v	40*	
cuff	f	100	
got	g	73	
general	dʒ	26	
egg	g	99	
edge	dʒ	100	
laughter	f	100*	*Note: in syllable final position. There were no occurrences of words like bough or daughter in the corpus.
ghost	g	100*	*Note: at the beginning of a syllable.
gnome	n	100	
hat	h	100	
jet	dʒ	100	

keep	k	100	
know	n	100	
leap	l	100	
hill	l	100	
met	m	100	
lamb	m	100	
hammer	m	100	
never	n	100	
sing	ŋ	100	
dinner	n	100	
pat	p	100	
phone	f	100	
pneumonia	n	100	
happy	p	100	
quick	k	100	
run	r	100	
purr	r	100	
sat	s	54*	*Note: /s/ is frequent when s is syllable
as	z	45	initial; /z/ is much more frequent when s is syllable final. The frequency of the word **as** may have affected the results.
sword	s	100	Note: This result is questionable.
less	s	93	
pressure	ʃ	5	
shirt	ʃ	100	
tap	t	99	
putt	t	100	

TABLE 6.0   *(continued)*

action	ʃ	96	
thimble	θ	20*	*Note: 113 items with **th** => ð account for
then	ð	80*	80% of the pronunciations of **th**. These will be high frequency function words like **the** and **that** which distort the figures.
vat	v	100	
water	w	100	
who	h	100	
what	w	No figures	
write	r	100	
tax	ks	No figures	
yes	y	100	
zebra	z	96	
buzz	z	100	

We have already seen that L1 logographic reading doesn't transfer at all or negatively to alphabetic writing, so those readers must start from square one. Readers of consonantal systems must learn to look at vowels and know something of their pronunciations. Readers of different alphabets must learn the Roman alphabet. Everyone must learn to discriminate English phonemes.

However, there are more differences based on our discussion in this chapter. Some ESL and EFL readers may be accustomed to the Roman alphabetic writing system, but it is likely that they are not accustomed to all of the strange English graphemes listed in the last chapter and this one: for example, gg, ck, gh, and x. Readers from an L1 transparent writing system have the task of assigning a phoneme to a grapheme, but it is a fairly straightforward process of matching one-to-one. The knowledge base for their L1 will not contain information about the probabilities that a certain grapheme will be pronounced a certain way because that information is moot if all the probabilities are 100%. The knowledge base will not contain information about the contextual information which plays a role in assigning pronunciations in English.

TABLE 6.1

English Vowel Grapheme to Phoneme Correspondences

Grapheme	Phoneme	Approximate Percentage of Times that the Grapheme Spells that Phoneme
a	æ	52
	ə	22
	e	8
	ɔ	5
	ɑ	4
	ɛ	1
e	ɛ	50
	ə	23
	i	15
	ɪ	12
i	ɪ	89
	ɑy	9
	ə	1
o	ɑ	40
	u	15
	o	15
	ə	12
	ɔ	11
	ʌ	3
	ʊ	2
u	ʌ	63
	ʊ	10
	yu	8
	w	6
	ə	6
	u	2
	ɪ	1

TABLE 6.1 (*continued*)

y	ɪ	78
	ɑy	22
ai	ey	71
	ɛ	23
	ɪ	6
au	ɔ	49
	ɑ	42
	o	4
	æ	4
aw	ɔ	100
ay	ɑy	95
	ɛ	4
ea	i	63
	ɛ	18
	ey	11
	ə	6
	ɑ	1
ee	i	76
	ɪ	24
ei	e	77
	i	17
	ɪ	5
eo	i	97
	ə	2
ie	ɪ	53
	ɑy	24
	i	17

	ɛ	6
oa	o	94
	ɔ	5
oe	ʌ	56
	o	37
	u	10
oi	oy	99
oo	u	50
	ʊ	45
	o	3
	ʌ	2
ou	aw	38
	u	30
	ʊ	15
	ʌ	14
	o	3
ue	yu	33
	u	27
	ʊ	25
	ɛ	13
ui	ɪ	69
	yu	17
	u	12

Similarly, ESL and EFL readers may not have needed to use a strategy of probabilistic reasoning to read their L1, if the matching between grapheme and phoneme is completely regular, or they may have relied on probabilistic reasoning only exceptionally. If this is true, they will most certainly not have acquired the ability to apply the strategy continuously, assigning phonemes to graphemes by weighing probabilities and examining the context, adjusting probabilities higher so that a decision can be made, and all of this with little if any conscious effort.

All of the students we have been considering (MariCarmen, Despina, Mohammed, and Ho) may require extensive experience with reading in English to achieve the knowledge base of probabilities and contextual information, processing strategies, and the automaticity that depends on them. Braten, Lie, and Andreassen (1998) reported a study that showed automatic orthographic word recognition was directly dependent on the amount of leisure reading children did while away from school. This suggests that unless ESL readers are reading an abundance of English inside and outside of the classroom, they may not develop efficient grapheme-to-phoneme knowledge and processing strategies. Naturally, students like MariCarmen, Despina, Mohammed, and Ho should be encouraged to read as much as possible, but it may also be helpful to provide direct phonics instruction in the classroom as an entry point to enable them to do extensive reading without frustration. Such phonics instruction should obviously emphasize the visual recoding of the graph into a phoneme, but it should involve accurate listening discrimination activities and only secondarily pronunciation, although students will probably read out loud.

As a primary background for phonics instruction, teachers should be more optimistic about the learnability of the English writing system. At least for the purposes of reading, it is a patterned and consistent system, although the system is complex. It should be presented to students as such, and not as a confusing mass of contradictions no one can learn. The next chapter explores the system for reading English vowels, another complex but fairly consistent system.

Spotlight on Teaching

A lesson plan for a linguistic generalization may have these components: presentation, practice with presented data, application to new data, common exceptions, controlled and free practice, and assessment of learning.

The presentation of a linguistic form may be inductive or deductive. In a deductive lesson plan, a generalization is presented first, then it is applied to examples to show how the rule works. In an inductive lesson plan, the examples are presented first and then the rule is presented by the teacher or "induced" by the learners on their own. In groups or as individuals, invent either deductive or inductive presentations for the following examples. Think of an original activity to present or practice with the generalization and examples to increase contextual knowledge that "adjusts" probabilities:

1.	gain	gym
	go	giant
	gun	gentleman
2.	cap	city
	copper	cement
	cup	cycle
	came	cinder
3.	lace	picnic
	peace	Lac
	nice	tarmac
	fleece	comic
4.	cage	bag
	huge	hug
	change	log
	village	Ag

After you have finished the deductive or inductive presentation or practice, think of several other examples which follow the same generalization. Add these new examples to model reasoning by probabilities. An example is provided for you: If "cap" is pronounced with a /k/ at the beginning, how do you think "car" is pronounced? Then think of some counterexamples to the generalization and find a way to practice with these exceptions.

Your next activity should be designed to have the students practice writing the words that follow the generalization and those that don't follow the generalization. The activity might be a dictation, a structured Language Experience Approach (in which students write a communal composition using specific words and then practice reading), a spelling bee game, or something similar.

You can then assess if the generalization has been learned through an activity in which students restate the generalization that they have learned in their own way. Assess if the generalization has been acquired (albeit consciously) through an activity that requires them to apply the generalization. Build in other activities throughout the school term to apply the generalization to make it more unconscious.

DISCUSSION QUESTIONS

This chapter touches on the relation between spelling and reading. Some researchers believe that learning to spell should take place within the context of reading and writing because spelling and reading are based on the same data: the visual images of words we have stored in the mental lexicon. The following words seem particularly difficult to spell. Discuss various reasons why these words may be difficult to spell. Do you have difficulty with any of them?

beautiful	relevant		
lieutenant	grammar	foreign	conscious
unnecessary	accommodate	receipt	misspell
conscientious	noticeable	muscle	vacuum

What words would you add to this list? What makes them difficult for you?

Chapter 7

Approaches to Phonics

Prereading questions—Before you read, think, and discuss the following:

1. How old were you when you learned to read?
2. What activities do you remember? Make a list of activities and evaluate their purpose and effectiveness. If you have ESL and EFL learners in class, compare how they learned to read in English.
3. What reading materials did you read in preschool, kindergarten, or first grade?

Study Guide questions—Answer these questions as you read the chapter:

1. What is phonics?
2. What are phonic generalizations? Why did many teachers stop using them? What is blending? Why did teachers stop using it as a strategy to sound out new words?
3. What is reasoning-by-analogy? What knowledge is necessary for the strategy? Why it is better for reading vowels?
4. What are Ehri's stages of development of reading strategies?
5. What is the structure of the syllable for English?
6. How do the strategies ESL and EFL learners develop for their L1 reading relate to Ehri's stages of English L1 acquisition?
7. How can reading instruction for vowels be taught most efficiently?

In previous chapters, I introduced the idea of teaching phonics to expose beginning readers to the predictable consonant grapheme-to-phoneme correspondences and contextual information in English writing. In this chapter we see that context is important for another type of reasoning that is useful for reading vowels in English with maximum efficiency. Before going on to that, let's look at the issue of phonics instruction. I often call phonics the "f-word" in reading instruction because it has such a bad connotation for many reading practitioners. This bad connotation stems, I think, from the way some phonics instruction was done in the past or people's somewhat muddled ideas about the way that phonics instruction takes place at present. The prevailing idea for many seems to be that phonics instruction is useless (because English writing is so chaotic), pointless (because readers are just guessing anyway), a waste of time (because readers will automatically learn grapheme-to-phoneme correspondences), and boring (because it involves memorizing rules that don't work or reading sentences that don't make any sense). Other chapters have shed a different light on some of these ideas; this chapter is about the last. Phonics is not about memorizing rules that don't work. It is not about reading sentences that are meaningless.

There have always been a number of phonics methodologies (Adams 1990; Hatch, 1979; Tierney & Readence, 2000). In one, grapheme-to-phoneme correspondences were taught directly and explicitly through the use of rules which were called *phonic generalizations*. Here are two examples of phonic generalizations from Clymer, 1963, with their percentage of utility (or percentage of times that the rule actually works) from a certain corpus of words. (The complete list can be found in Adams, 1990, and Weaver, 1994.) "When there are two vowels side by side, the long sound of the first one is heard and the second one is usually silent." (45%) "When there are two vowels, one of which is final e, the first vowel is long and the e is silent." (63%)

Phonic generalizations were taught as part of an explicit synthetic and deductive phonics program for children learning to read. Often the rule was explained in terms the beginning reader could understand. The first generalization was a common one taught as "When two vowels go walking, the first one does the talking." Then the rules were applied in worksheets and workbooks which had many examples of words that illustrated the generalization. Once the phonic generalizations had been learned, they were applied as part of a synthetic strategy of sounding out words. Each individual graph was assigned a pronunciation and then the individual pronunciations were blended together (synthesized) by saying them quickly in sequence. For example, to sound out the word **cat,** the learner was taught to say something like " kuh æ tuh." This synthetic method of teaching phonics is often called "blending."

When we consider phonic generalizations, we note that their utilities range from high to low. The utility of the 45 phonic generalizations studied by Clymer (1963) ranged from 0% to 100%, but the high range was mainly for consonants and lower ranges were found for vowels, as we might expect.

There is much we can say about phonic generalizations, but the long and the short of it is that the low or unpredictable utility of many of them made teachers feel that they were not useful to teach and practice. Sometimes although the generalizations were often true (when a word begins with **kn,** the **k** is silent), it seemed a waste of class time to explain it and then do a worksheet on that one pattern. Many teachers were eager to turn away from this type of phonics instruction and embrace whole language methods that often assumed that beginning readers would just learn phonic generalizations on their own through exposure to print (Weaver, 1994). It is true that readers do unconsciously acquire knowledge of these phonic generalizations through exposure to print, but they are not in the form of overt rules. Rather, they form the unconscious probabilistic and context-dependent knowledge and processing strategies we saw in the last chapter.

From our current perspective in ESL and EFL, we can see that phonic generalizations and the deductive synthetic phonics instruction that accompanied them fall into the category of learning about the language rather than acquiring the use of the language. We think it commonplace now that learning a grammar rule doesn't necessary imply that the learner will be able to apply the rule in speaking or writing. Likewise, learning the phonic generalizations such as those previously mentioned doesn't lead to automaticity; so those teachers who found these phonic generalizations tedious and unhelpful were probably right. When the teaching of phonic generalizations was largely discarded, however, an important thread of reading instruction was also lost for some teachers. In their eagerness not to teach phonic generalizations, some teachers stopped explicit phonics instruction altogether.

A similar thing has happened with the blending strategy which used to be quite commonly taught in English L1 reading instruction. Teachers saw that trying to figure out the pronunciation of a graph in isolation led to many errors and problems. Some children would say the letter name instead of the sound; siy ey tiy for **cat** will never "blend" into its proper pronunciation. Some children, although they could assign a sound and not a letter name, chose the wrong sound to assign and they also encountered problems when trying to blend the sounds together to figure out the word. For many teachers, blending also went out the window as they began to prefer whole language methods.

Although some phonics instruction in the past was rule-based and synthetic, another phonics instructional method, called the Linguistic Method, was based on learning key spelling patterns like -at, bat, cat, sat, fat, etc. (Tierney & Readence, 2000) Although this has turned out to be a good method of teaching reading in English, at the time the method was in vogue the materials were based largely around meaningless nonwords or silly stories with sentences like "Dan can fan Nan." Teachers quite rightly criticized this phonics method because it did not provide early readers with much motivation to read. It was dull and unrealistic. The purpose of these stories was to illustrate and practice spelling patterns, but that is not an authentic purpose for literature or any other types of written material. The purpose for this phonics-based reading was to acquire low-level reading skills, but the purpose for real reading is getting the meaning, enjoying a story, learning about a subject matter, and so on. The whole language methodology, with its focus on real children's literature, was much more attractive.

The good news is that researchers have now given us a justification and a methodology for teaching the grapheme-to-phoneme correspondences and sounding out strategies in a way that leads to acquisition rather than learning. We do not need to choose either phonics or whole language because we can do both. In modern phonics instruction, the consonant grapheme-to-phoneme correspondences are taught because we know that readers apply a probabilistic reasoning strategy acquired through direct instruction and through extensive reading for pleasure. It involves reading graphs in word and sentence contexts and not in isolation.

Modern phonics instruction also involves a different kind of knowledge of basic English spelling patterns and reasoning by analogy to similar patterns to decode words. Phonics can be taught in an efficient way if we understand how readers read, and it can be embedded as one element within a whole language reading program.

REASONING BY ANALOGY

When the correspondence between a grapheme and a phoneme is not very predictable, as is the case with vowel spellings in English, probabilistic reasoning can take place as we saw in the last chapter, but expert readers also use another strategy: reasoning by analogy using contextual information in the form of frames (Goswami, 1998, and others). The frames are the typical rimes, morphemes, or syllables that show consistent spelling patterns over a number of English words. Frames provide a context that allows for easier graphic recognition. Frames are also very useful because they provide a context to disambiguate the pronunciation of vowel graphemes. This information is illustrated in Fig. 7.1.

An example will make this clear. Take the grapheme **a**. When we see it in isolation, we cannot assign it a pronunciation with accuracy. It could be pronounced [ɑ], as in **father**, [æ], as in **hat**, [ey], as in **rate**, and in fact, some other pronunciations are also possible. However, as soon as we provide the bare grapheme **a** with a context: _at, we instantly seem to know how to pronounce it. We have stored the chunk _at in our linguistic memory as a graphic image with a strong connection to its pronunciation: /_ æt/, so that as soon as we see it, we know how to pronounce it.

Ehri (1998) hypothesized that there are four stages in the acquisition of expert English L1 reading shown in Fig. 7.2. At first, readers "read" by remembering certain features of the way words look; this "reading" is nonalphabetic (as in, say, Chall's [1983] Stage 0). As readers learn the al-

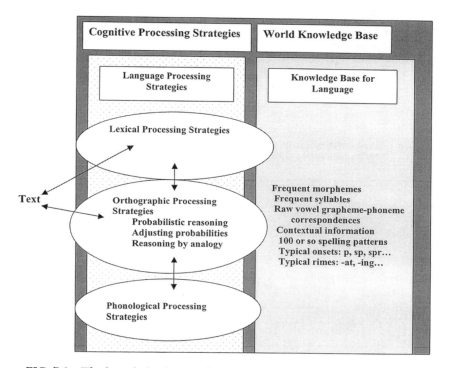

FIG. 7.1 The knowledge base and processing strategies for reading English vowels.

phabet, they begin to use their knowledge to connect the graphs on the page to the phonemes in their heads. Early on (e.g., in Chall's [1983] Stage 1), the connections between graphs, graphemes, and phonemes are partial, but later the connections are complete and sophisticated. At Ehri's third stage (which might still be in Chall's [1983] Stage 1), we might hypothesize that readers have a good knowledge of probabilities and contingencies that allow them to read accurately and automatically. In Ehri's fourth stage of reading (which may occur in Chall's [1983] Stage 2), as we acquire extensive knowledge of graphemic and phonemic patterns that hold true over a number of words, frames that can be used for reasoning by analogy emerge in our knowledge base.

It is in the full alphabetic phase that rapid growth in our knowledge of printed words becomes possible. As we become more and more knowledgeable about words and spellings through more and more exposure to print, grapheme-to-phoneme patterns that occur again and again begin to merge and "consolidate." Information in our knowledge base is restructured into

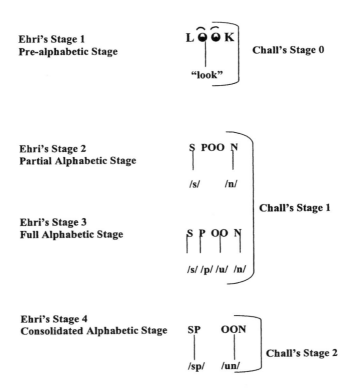

FIG. 7.2   Probabilistic reasoning restructured as Reasoning by Analogy. Figure adapted from Ehri, 1998, p. 18.

chunks of information called frames. Frames may be morphemes (e.g., -tion, -ness, pre-), syllables (e.g., at, in, ten), or smaller parts of syllables called **onsets** and **rimes**. The onset is the first consonant or consonant sequence in a one-syllable word if there is one; the rime is the vowel and final consonant or consonants. Words that share the same rime with different onsets are called *word families* or *phonograms*.

Rime: _at   Examples: at, bat, cat, chat, fat, hat ...
Rime: _in   Examples: in, bin, din, chin, fin, spin ...

Probabilistic reasoning can take English readers only so far, but it is not the most efficient way to deal with English vowel graphemes, so English readers develop different knowledge and a different strategy. We might say that cognitive restructuring takes place because of the demands of reading an opaque script. That is, up to a certain point, readers get by on their knowledge of how individual graphemes are to be read, along with some contextual information. After a while, readers realize unconsciously that there is an even more efficient way to read vowels if the common spelling patterns of English are stored in memory too. Thus, along with the probabilities discussed in the last chapter, readers begin amassing a store of chunked information in the form of frames with which to assign vowel pronunciations by analogy. The strategy of storing frames and relying on analogy allows the reader to resolve important decision-making problems quickly and accurately in the incoming textual data.

Ehri (1998) believed that the larger grapheme-to-phoneme units reduce memory load and increase our ability to understand words with several morphemes such as happy + ness or pre + own + ed. Because we have seen that graphs are easier to identify in contexts, she argued that remembering larger units like rimes will make identifying the graphs even easier. Ehri believed that it is in second grade that English speaking readers begin the consolidated alphabetic phase. So we might say that most beginning readers begin by learning the shapes and pronunciations of graphs formally. They go through a period of fairly painstaking application of their learning to reading texts and as they acquire automaticity with the graph-grapheme-phoneme connection, they begin to build up speed and read for more enjoyment. As readers acquire more and more stored knowledge about the way that spelling patterns work in English, it becomes more and more efficient to store larger chunks of words too. Common rhyming games and stories probably facilitate passage into this phase. The awareness of rhyme has been correlated with reading success for English early readers. That is, readers who can segment words into onsets and rimes and pick out or produce words that have the same rime are generally better readers than those who cannot. This is the value of Dr. Seuss books and similar rhyming material for prereaders and early readers.

Seymour (1997) cited a model of the internal structure of the syllable from Treiman (1992) and others, which I adapt for our purposes in Fig. 7.3. The discussion so far leads us to posit that both the bottom level of phonemes and the higher level of onset and rime (and other frames, too) are important in English reading. The bottom of Fig. 7.3 is the basis for probabilistic reasoning based on grapheme-to-phoneme correspondences and develops first, most likely in Stages 1 and 2 of Chall's (1983) stages of reading development. At some point, as a result of restructuring, the higher level of onset and rime are added, because of the demands of dealing with English vowel grapheme-to-phoneme unpredictability. It is a way of building in context, which is so necessary for reading vowels. At this point, analogy to known rime patterns can become a useful strategy for reading. English-speaking children acquire knowledge of frames and analogical reasoning as they gain automaticity with graphs. But what about our ESL readers?

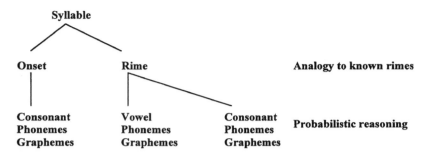

FIG. 7.3 The structure of the syllable for English-speaking readers. Adapted from Seymour, 1997, p. 323.

Recall that there is evidence that readers of sinograms and Kanji are using a meaning-based strategy in which the written symbol is associated with a meaning and only secondarily with a set of phonemes. The meaning-based strategy is quite similar to Ehri's (1998) Stage 1 prealphabetic reading stage, in which the early readers use visual cues in the word to associate with a meaning and thus to figure out the sound of the word. We saw evidence that some ESL and EFL readers use the meaning-based strategy for reading English words; they may need assistance to develop more appropriate alphabetic strategies.

Likewise, some evidence indicates that Arabic or Hebrew readers might use a strategy very similar to Ehri's (1998) partial alphabetic Stage 2 reading strategy, in which readers use their knowledge of consonant grapheme-to-phoneme correspondences to guess the English words. Consonants are more informative to readers than vowels are and English readers fixate more on them than vowels, but ultimately the information from vowels must come into play as well. We can see this in those readers from L2 transparent alphabetic scripts who may be using a strategy like Ehri's fully alphabetic strategy. Readers using the fully alphabetic strategy process all of the letters and this strategy would work for transparent scripts. There would be no need to develop the consolidated alphabetic strategy, based on frames as English readers do.

For example, Goswami (1998) found that the correlation between rime awareness and reading ability has not been consistently found for early readers of other alphabetic languages. Goswami theorized that the importance of rime units in reading different languages could be studied by looking at whether familiarity with rimes aided reading for early readers. English, French, and Greek were studied. Greek has a nearly one-to-one correspondence between graphemes and phonemes and French has a closer connection between them than English. Goswami found that rime familiarity aided English readers quite a bit, French readers somewhat, and Greek readers not at all. It seemed that the Greek children were not using rimes in reading their orthography.

If we look back at Ehri's (1998) phases, it is possible that, because Greek writing has great consistency in grapheme-to-phoneme correspondences, Greek readers can read efficiently at the Fully Alphabetic Phase. There is no need for them to develop further strategies, like English readers do. In fact, Goswami (1998) argued that it is dealing with English writing that causes strategies based on using rimes to emerge. Cognitive restructuring only happens if it is necessary. Readers like MariCarmen and Despina may have greater problems with orthographic processing than we had previously thought. Not only do they lack knowledge of English grapheme-to-phoneme correspondences and probabilistic reasoning as a strategy, they may also not be able to read most efficiently by using consolidated chunks of words because the orthographies of their languages may not have required development of that strategy. Rather, there is some evidence that students from transparent alphabetic writing systems acquire a syllabic processing strategy, dividing words into predictable syllables based on the vowels, for the purposes of reading (Aidinis & Nunes, 1998).

(For example, a colleague [Andrea Voitus, personal communication, March 20, 2000] whose first language was Hungarian, which has a transparent orthographic script, reported that when she was acquiring English reading skills as a young immigrant child, she mentally "translated" all the letters of English words into Hungarian sounds and syllables and then "translated" this into the English pronunciation to identify the word she was reading. Although Andrea eventually became very adept at reading English fluently [and indeed is now a native speaker of English], it is to be wondered how and when she dropped this reading strategy in favor of more efficient ones. She reports that she still uses this strategy to help her spell sight words such as **Wednesday**.)

We may presume that those of our students who become good readers of English will learn the grapheme–phoneme correspondences in their earliest reading classes, that they may, like English-speaking children, go through a painstaking phase of matching the graphs to graphemes and phonemes, and that this laborious process will become more automatic as the connections between the units become fully defined as probabilistic knowledge and reasoning. Unless learned material becomes acquired material, some of our ESL readers may be blocked at any of these stages. However, under no stretch of the imagination can we think that our ESL students like Mohammed or Ho, or even MariCarmen and Despina, will come to us fully prepared to use analogy to frames to read English most efficiently. Can we expect them to acquire the strategy on their own, as Andrea did? Or can we expect at least some of them to keep on reading English orthography in a fully alphabetic way? That is, can we expect restructuring to occur naturally or should we help them?

Goswami (1998) reported that a few studies have been conducted with English-speaking children which show the potential for instruction in analogy-to-frames. In one study, children who had long-term training with a strategy of analogy based on rimes and word families were better at reading new words than an equivalent control group, although the ability to make use of rimes also depended on phonological segmentation abilities. Rime analogy benefitted phonological segmentation, as we might expect. In another study, children in the analogy classroom were trained for 1 year and in a posttest, were shown to be better in decoding and in reading comprehension than their equivalent control group which had not received the training.

Instruction and practice in using an analogy to frames strategy may benefit ESL and EFL students because it increases their ability to sound out words that they are reading accurately. Earlier we saw that English readers can read pseudo words that were possible more easily than impossible nonwords because of their graphemic and phonemic similarity to real words. The same could work for ESL and EFL students if they store common frames and use an analogical strategy. Sounding out new words is an important skill for ESL and EFL students, but it is one they often do poorly. If they can sound out the words accurately, they can tell if they know the word in their oral or aural language. If they don't know the word, they can still begin to form a lexical entry with the visual and auditory image of the word, which can't help but improve their reading skill over time. In addition, they may be able to read faster and with better comprehension because more efficient bottom-up reading leaves more attention for higher level processing.

ESL READING INSTRUCTION BASED ON ANALOGY TO FRAMES

The best way to teach the analogy strategy is to introduce the idea of phonological segmentation of spoken words into phonemes and into onsets and rimes. Reading instruction begins with the graphs and their letter names and common sounds associated with them. Learners should read simple words that they know orally. Teachers should provide instruction about rimes in the written language and their connection to pronunciation through the use of word families. In addition, Goswami (1998) suggested that teachers should model the use of analogy to frames by asking questions:

"How can we use our clue to read this word? What is our clue word? Yes, it's *cap*. What are the letters in **cap**? Yes, **c, a, p**. What are the letters in this new word? Yes, **t, a, p**. So which bit of the new word can our clue help us with? Which part of the words are the same? That's right, the **a, p** part. What sound do the letters **a, p** make in **cap**? Yes, *-ap*. So what sound do they make here? Yes it must be *-ap*. So now we just need the sound for the beginning letter, which is—yes, **t**. What is the sound for **t**? Yes, **t** as in **teddy**. So our new word is? Yes, **t-ap**, **tap**. We can use **cap** to figure out **tap** because they rhyme." (p. 58)

There are many places where teachers can find lists of common vowel spelling patterns. One is from the Benchmark School in Pennsylvania (Downer, 1991; Gaskins, 1997), which has used the decoding by analogy strategy to help children who have had difficulties learning to read, as shown in Fig. 7.4.

Teachers can model the use of analogy to sound out new words in the course of their whole language reading and writing class. Rather than spending time learning the words on the Benchmark (Downer, 1991; Gaskins, 1997) list, for example, the teacher can select five frames that naturally occur in the reading text that the students are using for that day or week. Take a few minutes to look at the pattern and pronounce it. Talk about other words that have the same pattern or words that have a different pattern.

For example, these are five patterns from the Benchmark list:

fl ag   r ed   kn ife   br oke   j ump

Let's say your reading text contains the following: rag, bed, wife, spoke, and lump. Isolate these words from your text and discuss the meaning if necessary. Then look at the spelling and the sound. Have the students repeat the words while looking at them. Play games with them, make up rhymes with them, use them in oral sentences, or use them in a spelling test or dictation. The more familiar the students become with these patterns the more available they will be for the orthographic processor. The Benchmark Method (Downer, 1991; Gaskins, 1997) rests on teaching students the use of overt analogy to sound out the words that they don't know. Although that method is mainly for native-speaking students, it can be applied profitably to the ESL situation. The pattern words are written on cards and displayed on a wall in the classroom. When the student comes across an unknown word, he or she learns to break it up into syllables and break each syllable up into onsets and rimes. He or she then finds the rime that is like the rime in the unknown word and the student pronounces the new syllable by analogy. He or she then reassembles the unknown word, pronouncing each syllable. Again, that seems complex when you describe what the mind is doing, but in actual practice it is simple.

Let's say the student sees the word **ornery**. Its three syllables are **or**, **ner**, and **y**. The rimes in the spelling patterns are **for**, **her**, and **baby**. The analogical process the student goes through follows:

if **for** is /for/, then **or** is /or /
if **her** is /h ə r/ , then **ner** is /n ə r/
if **by** in baby is / biy/, then **y** is /iy/
The written word **ornery** is pronounced /ornəriy/.

-a		-e		-i		-o		-u		-y	
gr	ab	h	e	h	i	g	o	cl	ub	m	y
pl	ace	sp	eak	m	ice	b	oat	tr	uck	bab	y
bl	ack	scr	eam	k	ick	j	ob	gl	ue	g	ym
h	ad	y	ear	d	id	cl	ock	b	ug		
m	ade	tr	eat	sl	ide	fr	og	dr	um		
fl	ag	r	ed	kn	ife	br	oke	j	ump		
m	ail	s	ee	p	ig		old	f	un		
r	ain	bl	eed	s	ight	fr	om	sk	unk		
m	ake	qu	een	l	ike		on		up		
t	alk	sl	eep	sm	ile	ph	one		us		
	all	sw	eet	w	ill	l	ong		use		
	am	t	ell	sw	im	z	oo	b	ut		
n	ame	th	em	t	ime	g	ood				
ch	amp	t	en		in	f	ood				
c	an		end	f	ind	l	ook				
	and	t	ent	w	ine	sch	ool				
m	ap	h	er	k	ing	st	op				
c	ar	y	es	th	ink	f	or				
sh	ark	n	est	sh	ip	m	ore				
sm	art	l	et	squ	irt	c	orn				
sm	ash	fl	ew	th	is	n	ose				
h	as			w	ish	n	ot				
	ask				it	c	ould				
c	at			wr	ite	r	ound				
sk	ate			f	ive	y	our				
br	ave			g	ives	c	out				
s	aw					c	ow				
d	ay					gl	ow				
						d	own				
						b	oy				

FIG. 7.4 The spelling patterns from the Benchmark Program (Downer, 1991, p. 11). Used by permission.

(If you're from a dialect region that prefers /ɑnriy/, then this is probably best taught as a sight word, a word that must just be learned as is because analogy is not practical.)

In summary, pronouncing the word and looking at its graphemic shape help the student form a new entry in the mental lexicon for the new word. Obviously, meaning clues from context will help the student begin to elaborate an associated meaning in semantic memory. The analogical strategy not only helps the student build up his or her mental lexicon and semantic memory, but it also helps the student recognize words that he or she already knows orally but may not know in written form. As the student gains practice with conscious analogy, he or she also gains practice with using his or her knowledge base of frames unconsciously to read faster and more accurately.

The Benchmark Method (Downer & Gaskill, 1991) also provides a method for learning sight words because they happen to be common and frequent function words like **would**, **too**, and **they**. Teachers write those words on different colored cards and place them on the wall. This procedure will help ESL students learn to automatically identify the written forms of common function words.

Once the students have learned the grapheme-to-phoneme correspondences with the contexts they occur in, frames, probabilistic reasoning, and the strategy of using analogy to common spelling patterns for vowels, they need to practice with reading texts, but not texts that are too difficult for them. Instead, the texts should be very easy but age-appropriate. They can be encouraged to read aloud to the teacher and to supportive reading groups, because reading aloud forces the student to associate graphemes with phonemes, but it is imperative that reading aloud not be competitive or graded. Anxiety will lead to mispronunciations and other mistakes because students are too concerned with pronouncing accurately. Comprehension questions and testing on content must wait until students have had a chance to read and study the text silently by themselves. Reading aloud often requires so much concentration on the part of the student that he doesn't have much attention left for comprehension.

Another good activity is to read along silently while a tape of the story is playing because that not only improves the association between grapheme and phoneme, but it also improves pronunciation, as an added by-product. Students can follow along in their books as other students read aloud, provided the readers are accomplished and interesting. There is nothing less motivating than listening to a poor reader stumble through a text, no matter how short, so poorer readers should read aloud to the teacher, their parents at home, and to a supportive and small reading group or reading partner. Another activity is called *shadowing*. In this activity, the beginning reader is matched with a more advanced reader. The advanced reader begins reading the text aloud and the beginning reader follows along reading aloud a few seconds behind the advanced reader, so that they are both reading aloud, but one is slightly ahead of the other.

Spotlight on Teaching

Review—A lesson plan for a set of common spelling patterns may have these components: presentation, practice with presented data, application to new data, common exceptions to the spelling pattern, controlled and free practice of the spelling pattern, and assessment of learning. The presentation of a spelling pattern is best done inductively: the examples are presented first, and then the pattern is presented by the teacher or "induced" by the learners on their own.

Using an inductive presentation, how would you treat the following as onsets and rimes so that your students can use analogy to decode similar words or syllables?

bake	back
lake	lack
rake	rack
make	Mack

Now you write an inductive presentation and lesson plan for the spelling pattern bead = /biyd/. (Its most common alternative pattern is bread.)

DISCUSSION QUESTIONS

1. We have discussed a couple of strategies for spelling words correctly. What strategies do you use for spelling words? How do you use a dictionary to look up a word if you don't know how to spell it? What kind of knowledge does this strategy use?

2. Do this quiz again. What have you learned so far? What remains to be learned?

- Logogram.
- Transparent orthography.
- Phoneme.
- Phone.
- Grapheme.
- Morphology.
- Derivation.
- Inflection.
- Onset.
- Rime.
- Tense vowel.
- Morphophonemic writing.

English Morphophonemic Writing

Prereading questions—Before you read, think, and discuss the following:

1. The words **naked** and **baked** look much the same but their pronunciations are very different. What can explain the difference in pronunciation?
2. Why do we spell the word **sign** with a **g** in it? If you look at Appendix A you will see that we specify that word final gn = /n/. Could there be another generalization that would make this spelling more explicable? What might that be?

Study Guide questions—Answer these questions while you are reading:

1. Define these terms and give examples of each of the following: morpheme, free morpheme, bound morpheme, derivational morpheme, infix, inflectional morpheme, and bound root.
2. What is the morphological structure of the words Massachusetts, cannibal, congregational, carpet, disapproval, disproved, proven, Polish, and liked?
3. How might the reading processor store morphological information in the knowledge base?
4. Give an example from the book of pronunciation changes due to derivational morphology: a vowel, consonant, or stem change, and a stress change with vowel reduction. Then give an original example of each.
5. What does it mean to say that English writing is morphophonemic?
6. Give another example of each of the three principles involved in spelling morphemes consistently although pronunciation changes due to derivational morphology: tensest vowel, stops>affricates/fricatives, and most complete spelling.
7. Would you, at any point in your spelling career, have benefitted from an explanation that English writing is morphophonemic? Would it help you spell better to know the principles?
8. What are the four morphological types of languages?
9. Could a language's predominate morphology type affect the structure of the mental lexicon? How?
10. Could morphological processing in English be problematic for the ESL and EFL learner?

We have been looking at the bottom levels of the reading processor which deal with the connection between graphemes of written language and phonemes of spoken language. But English, like other languages, is made up of other units of organization which are important in understanding the system of English writing: *morphemes*. We have described the English writing system as phonemic, but, in fact, we shall see in this chapter that it is actually better described as *morphophonemic*. For teachers, a key to understanding that the English writing system is indeed a system, and being able to present it as learnable to students, is knowing how English morphology affects pronunciation and spelling.

Readers process morphology while reading based on the level of morphological awareness they have achieved. Levin et al. (1999), and Bryant, Nunes, and Bindman (1999), proposed that morphological awareness plays a causal role in the learning of morphological spelling patterns. The causal link is not uni-directional, but rather they bootstrap each other. As children become morphologically aware, they develop knowledge of written spelling patterns. As their knowledge of morphological spelling patterns matures, their morphological awareness is also maturing (Nunes, 1999).

Because morphology differs from language to language, it is reasonable to think that readers develop different strategies to process it in their L1 writing system. For instance, Levin et al. (1999) suggested that children learning to read Hebrew as a first language showed a lag in writing vowels compared to consonants. It is possible that this lag in writing may reflect a different reading strategy based on the relative prominence of consonants in their writing system or their heavier meaning load. As we have seen, low-level processing strategies can transfer positively or negatively, and there is some evidence that this is also true for morphological processing. After an examination of English morphology, pronunciation, and spelling, this chapter looks briefly at morphology in other languages, the possibility that different languages require different morphological processing strategies, and some suggestions for ESL and EFL instruction.

WORDS AND MORPHEMES: BASIC UNITS IN LANGUAGE

The word is in many ways the most basic unit of language, but in spite of that (or maybe because of it), there is really no adequate definition of what a word is. Part of the problem is that words are very different from language to language. Some languages have very short and simple one or two syllable words which mean only one concept, but some languages have words which are formed of many syllables all strung together forming a complex concept. Some languages, like English, show a variety of word structures. Some are simple (e.g., sun, moon, chair, man, and girl) and some are complex (bookkeeper, antediluvian, developing fluid). People used to think that there might be a millisecond pause between words in the flow of speech and that we could define words that way. However, technology has shown this not to be true; there is no pause between words as we speak unless we consciously make a pause. The pauses in speech tend to mark off phrases or clauses, not individual words. Because the word is difficult to define precisely, linguists talk instead about morphemes.

The definition of the word morpheme has three parts. First, there must be a form, a unit of language which usually consists of a sequence of sounds. Second, this unit of language must be associated with a meaning, either a grammatical meaning or a meaning with real content. Third, the form must be minimal in that it cannot be broken down into any smaller meaningful units. Some morphemes are called *free morphemes*, which are words in and of themselves. The word **sun** is a free morpheme. It has a form consisting of three sounds: / s / / ʌ / / n /. It has a meaning which could be found in any dictionary. And finally, the form cannot be broken down into smaller meaningful units. The /s/ by itself is not meaningful; it is the same with the / ʌ / or the /n/. Other free morphemes are **moon**, **Fresno**, **school**, or **Oklahoma**. In the case of the latter word, it may have more than one morpheme in the original Native American language from which it came, but in English, it has only one morpheme.

Some morphemes are bound morphemes, which are words that can stand alone, but must occur attached to another either free or bound morpheme. The prefix **un-** is such a bound morpheme: it has a minimal form associated with a meaning, but it cannot occur meaningfully by itself. It must be attached to another morpheme to be meaningful, as in the words **undo** or **untie**. Other examples of bound morphemes are **de**code, **re**take, **pre**fix, judg**ment**, comic**al**, and sanit**y**.

All of the bound morphemes exemplified in the preceding paragraph are derivational morphemes, and they are either prefixes or suffixes in English. Other languages also use infixes, morphemes that are placed within the context of a word, not before it or after it.

Derivational morphemes are used to derive or create a new word from an old word:

- Derivational morphemes often (but not always) result in a *change in the part of speech* when the derived word is compared to the *base* to which they are added.
- Derivational morphemes can be either *prefixes, infixes*, or *suffixes*. In English they are prefixes or suffixes.
- Derivational morphemes vary in *productivity*. In other words, some derivational morphemes can be added to many words, and some can be added to few words.
- Derivational morphemes make a *substantial and sometimes unpredictable change in the meaning* of the word.
- In fact, derivational morphemes are *creative*; they result in what we would think of as a *new and different word*.

Derivation is a common word formation process in English. From then noun **care**, we form the adjective **careless**, which, through the addition of the suffix, has a different part of speech and a different meaning. Most would agree that **careless** is not at all the same word as **care**, but an entirely different but related word. We can continue to form new words almost indefinitely. For instance, to **careless**, we can add another suffix to form an abstract noun: **carelessness**.

There is another kind of bound morpheme, however, which we must not overlook, the inflectional morpheme:

- Inflectional morphemes *do not usually change the part of speech* when the inflected word is compared to the base to which they are added.
- In English, inflectional morphemes are always *suffixes* and never prefixes.
- Inflectional morphemes are *very productive*; they can be added to almost any word of a certain part of speech.
- The *change in meaning* inflectional morphemes cause is a quite predictable grammatical detail.
- Inflectional morphemes are *mechanical*; they do not result in a new and different word, just *a different form of the same word*.

An example of an inflectional morpheme is the **-ed** past tense ending or the **-s** which is added to form plural nouns.

When the past tense ending **-ed** is added to the verb **play**, the result is the word **played**, which we would all agree is not a newly created innovation, but merely a different form of the original base word. This process, when grammatical suffixes are added to bases to cause a change in grammatical form, is called *inflection*. Inflectional processes are rule-governed; that is, past tense verbs, plural nouns, and so on are formed by means of grammatical and morphological rules which add a certain morpheme to the base word to encode grammatical information. Inflection is an important process in many languages of the world, but in English there are only eight inflectional morphemes.

English Inflectional Morphemes

Nouns: **-s** marks the regular plural: He needed two book**s**.
-s marks the possessive form (especially of animate things): The dog**'s** dish is empty.

Verbs: **-s** marks the third person singular present tense: He want**s** the newspaper.
-ed marks the past tense for regular verbs: He want**ed** the newspaper.
-ed marks the past participle for regular verbs: He has stud**ied** in Canada for years.
An *allomorph*, **-en**, marks the past participle for many irregular verbs: He has spok**en** French since then. (Can you guess what the word 'allomorph' means?)

-ing marks the present participle for all verbs: He is lear**ning** Japanese.

Adjectives and Adverbs: **-er** marks the comparative form: He has bought a new**er** car.

-est marks the superlative form: He can't afford the new**est** car.

There is one other kind of bound morpheme in English, usually called a *bound root*, which is a root to which a prefix or suffix must be added to form a word, but the root itself never occurs alone. Many of the bound roots we have in English came from words of Greek and Latin origin which were borrowed as "learned vocabulary" or through French. Examples of bound roots are pre**cept**, pro**vide**, super**vise**, and im**port**.

You will already have noticed that English words can have quite complex morphological structures made up of many different kinds of morphemes: free, derivational, inflectional, or bound roots. In any word, however, if there is an inflectional morpheme, it will be the last one because it is the last part of speech that determines the type of inflectional morpheme that can be added. Examples follow: progressives = pro + gress + ive + s, untied = un + tie + ed, and preceptors = pre + cept + or + s.

Adding derivational morphemes to bases and roots can affect the derived words in several ways. Sometimes, the pronunciation of the derived word changes when compared to the original base or root: **sane** + **ity** = **sanity**; **pro** + **gress** + **ion** = **progression**. Sometimes both the pronunciation and the spelling changes, as in **re** + **ceive** + **tion** = **reception**. Although these seem like random events, they can be explained by regular morphological and phonological processes. The apparent spelling anomalies which can result are reduced when you understand the underlying system.

**PRONUNCIATION CHANGES
AND MORPHOPHONEMIC WRITING: THE SYSTEM**

English has many words that are derived from a simple base by adding prefixes and suffixes. Prefixes don't usually cause pronunciation changes except assimilation in place of articulation, as in **im**perfect versus **in**decisive. The final nasal phoneme of the prefix, presumed to be alveolar /n/, becomes bilabial /m/ when it is placed before a bilabial /p/ or /b/. This is why some people misspell **input** as **imput**. However, derivational suffixes often change the pronunciation of graphemes in the word. There are four different types of pronunciation changes: a vowel change, a consonant change, a stem change, and a stress change with vowel reduction.

Vowel Change

Some suffixes, when added to a base word, have the effect of changing the pronunciation of a vowel in the derived word. Examples are **deprave-de-**

pravity, divine-divinity, or extreme-extremity. The base word deprave has
the tense vowel /ey/ in the second syllable, whereas the derived word deprav-
ity has the lax vowel /æ/. Similarly, the base word divine has the diphthong
/ay/, whereas the derived word divinity has the lax vowel /ɪ/ in the second syllable. Extreme has the tense vowel /iy/ in its second syllable but extremity has
a lax /ɛ/ in that position. Because of the alternation between tense and lax
vowels, *vowel laxing* is a more technical name for this type of change. The
tense vowel or diphthong alternates with its most similar lax vowel.

Consonant Change

The addition of some suffixes results in a change in the pronunciation of a
consonant. In *palatalization*, a stop or fricative consonant becomes palatalized; it becomes a palatal fricative or affricate. Examples are suppress-sup-
pression or native-national, and nature. In the first example, the final alveolar /s/ sound of the base word suppress is pronounced like the palatal
fricative /ʃ/ in the derived word pressure. In the second example, the same
root word (a bound root which also occurs in the word innate) is pronounced with an (alveolar stop) /t/ in some words, but with a palatal fricative
/ʃ/ in national. In the word nature, however, the t has become a palatal affricate, /tʃ/.

Velar softening is a term for another type of consonant change. In this
case, a velar stop, either /k/ or /g/, becomes "softened" to /s/ or /dʒ/, respectively. Examples are electric-electricity and analog-analogy. In the first
example, the velar stop /k/ in electric is softened to /s/ in the derived word,
electricity. In the second case, the final /g/ of analog is pronounced as /dʒ/
in the derived word analogy.

Stress Change and Vowel Reduction

Stress means a louder or more forceful pronunciation of one syllable of a
word than of other syllables in a word. The word confessor, for example, is
stressed on the second syllable fess. The addition of suffixes can change
the stress on a word, meaning that in the base word one syllable is stressed,
but in the derived word, another syllable is stressed. Change of stress is
complex, but it is not really a problem by itself. What happens is that, because of a phonological rule of English, a change in stress can result in a
change in pronunciation. The phonological rule in question is that of
vowel reduction. Vowel reduction refers to the fact that when vowels have little or no stress on them, their pronunciation is reduced to /ə/. In fact,
sometimes a vowel is reduced so much that it disappears from the pronunciation altogether.

Examples are grammar-grammatical or labor-laboratory. In the first
case, the word grammar is stressed on the first syllable, so its vowel has its

full value of /æ/. The second syllable is unstressed, so the vowel is pronounced as /ə/. However, in the word **grammatical**, stress has shifted from the first syllable to the second syllable. The pronunciation of the second vowel is now its true value of /æ/, and the first vowel is reduced to /ə/. Thinking of the derived word **grammatical** is a good way to remember that the commonly misspelled word **grammar** is spelled with two **a**s. The example of **labor-laboratory** is more complex. In American English, **labor** is stressed on the first syllable and the second syllable receives a secondary stress. In **laboratory**, primary stress remains on the first syllable although vowel laxing takes place /ey/ /⇒/ æ/, but the second syllable's stress is reduced to nothing because of the addition of **-atory**. The reduction in stress on the second syllable is so severe as to cause it to disappear. In British English, the primary stress shifts to the second syllable, so it doesn't disappear, but the vowel in the first syllable is reduced to /ə/.

Stem Change

Sometimes the pronunciation changes from a base word to a derived word, but it isn't explained by a phonological process. Instead, the cause is a change in the stem of the word itself. In other words, some words historically have two stems, one which serves as the basic word, and another one which serves as the base for derivation. Examples are **receive-reception**, **permit-permissive**, or **divide-divisive**.

To sum up, we can say that English relies heavily on derivational morphemes to create new words, but because of certain phonological processes such as vowel laxing, stress change with vowel reduction, consonant changes like velar softening and palatalization, the derived words aren't always pronounced like the bases from which they come. Sometimes a different stem is used to form the base of a derived word. These processes have the effect of changing the pronunciation of English derived words quite a lot, sometimes to the consternation of English speakers and ESL and EFL learners alike. These processes involve only a segment of the English vocabulary, the Latinate vocabulary, or words and morphemes which have come from Latin and Greek origins. Native Germanic vocabulary, or words and morphemes which have come down through the history of English from its earliest days as a Germanic language, do not undergo the same word formation processes, phonological processes, and pronunciation changes. Still, Latinate vocabulary now comprises roughly half of the words and morphemes commonly used in English, so the pronunciation changes have caused a problem with the writing system, which does not reflect this variation.

The problem resides in the fact that our writing system represents both phonemes and morphemes; it is morphophonemic. In other words, our writing system is phonemic in that it represents the sounds of our language, but it is also morphemic in that it also attempts to represent morphemes consistently. For example, study the following set of words: **physics**, **physi-cist**, and **physician**. This set of words shows evidence of velar softening and palatalization, leaving three pronunciations at the end of the base word: /k/, /s/, and /ʃ/. Would it be best to change the spelling to reflect the pronunciation (as in, say, **fiziks**, **fizisist**, and **fizishen**) or to maintain the spelling to show clearly that the words have a morphemic relation? For our spelling system, the latter is more important. The different pronunciations are not represented in writing so as to show that the same basic morpheme is involved in this set of words.

However, this presents a dilemma. There are various pronunciations of a morpheme because of derivational changes, but the English writing system prefers to write morphemes consistently. In the word set discussed earlier, we have one morpheme with three alternative pronunciations for the final grapheme in the base word: **physics** with a /k/, **physicist** with an /s/, or **physician** with a /ʃ/. Which pronunciation is to be preferred for spelling the word consistently?

The operation of English morphophonemic writing can be described in three rules of thumb.

Tense Vowel or Diphthong. To write a morpheme consistently in spite of variations in vowel pronunciation, the spelling that represents a tense vowel or diphthong is basic, as in **produce-production**. Similarly, always represent the original vowel although it may be reduced to [ə] with a change of stress, as in **define-definition**. Vowel laxing and vowel reduction are disregarded for the most part.

Stop ⇒ Fricative ⇒ Affricate. Where there are stops and fricatives, prefer a spelling that indicates the stop pronunciation, as in **physics-physicist** and **physician**, where the **c** indicates the stop /k/. Where there are stops and affricates, as in **innate** and **nature**, prefer the stop spelling. In **press-pressure**, the **ss** indicates the alveolar fricative /s/ and not the palatal fricative, indicating that alveolar is written in preference to palatal even if both sounds are fricatives.

Most Inclusive Spelling. And finally, if there are graphemes that are pronounced in some cases and not pronounced in other cases, choose a spelling that shows the grapheme in question and keep the spelling consistent, as in **sign-signature**, and **bomb-bombard**.

ENGLISH MORPHOLOGY AND READING STRATEGIES

The last section describes some problems resulting from English derivational processes, namely, that the addition of suffixes (and prefixes to a lesser extent) brings about changes in the pronunciation of the base word. The English writing system, on the other hand, prefers to maintain the spelling of the original morpheme, before vowel laxing, reduction, palatalization, or velar softening occurs. This is one of the main reasons for the opacity of the English writing system, the fact that graphemes and phonemes do not correspond in a one-to-one fashion. Looking back to the charts in chaps. 5 and 6 and Appendix A, one can see that many of the apparent problems in English grapheme-to-phoneme correspondences are explained. For example, a common spelling for /ʃ/ is **ti**. It is clear that this is caused by one extremely productive derivational suffix in which palatalization has occurred: **-tion**. The most efficient way to deal with this is to store that morpheme as a graphemic and phonemic image in the mental lexicon, which is what expert readers mostly likely do. In this way, the reader can read **ti** as /ʃ/ unambiguously, easily and effortlessly, if it occurs in the context: __**on**. Other examples where morphology and phonology explain unexpected spellings listed on the charts follow: a common spelling for /tʃ/ is **tu**, which is another example of palatalization, as in **culture** or **picture**; the specifications that **gn** or **mb** are pronounced as /n/ or /m/, respectively; and the tense vowel and lax vowel correspondences.

If expert English readers store common morphemes with their phonological representations and can read them efficiently, then there are two issues of concern. First, as we have seen elsewhere, problems with the English writing system are mainly problems in writing or spelling, not in reading. The expert reader can read **grammar**, **definite**, or **misspell** with no difficulty. These words do not present problems for expert readers because the graphemic and phonemic image is matched in its usual way with the visual stimuli. In spelling, the graphemic and phonemic image may not be as usable or productive except as a check after the fact.

The English writing system, as we see once again, is mainly problematic only for two groups of people learning to read English: native English-speaking children and ESL and EFL students, because they must build up a vast knowledge of graphemic and phonemic images encoding, for instance, that **c** is usually pronounced /k/, unless it occurs in the context **i_ity** or **i_ist**, as in **electricity**, **toxicity**, or **classicist**. This knowledge is stored in the mental lexicon, our extensive storage of English graphemic and phonemic images, each with a number of associations to semantic memory, or our memory for word meaning. Accessing the words and morphemes in the mental lexicon is called word recognition.

Knowledge of derivational morphemes must be contained in the mental lexicon because people can use them to make up new words if they need to. For instance, sometimes people forget or don't know a word. One strategy is to use morphemes to make up a word: for example, **sensitiveness** instead of **sensitivity**, and so on. Also, sometimes people make a slip of the tongue in saying words, adding the wrong suffix. However, it is probably the case the case that derived words are also included in our lexicon. That means that our mental lexicon lists **sane, sanity,** and **ity**. It lists **progress, progression,** and **ion**. It lists **receive, reception,** and **tion**. The English mental lexicon is probably redundant, to allow flexibility in the processing of the inconsistent derivation in English. In decision-making systems, there is a trade-off between redundancy in knowledge or information storage and efficiency in processing. Sometimes it is more efficient in processing time to store information inefficiently and redundantly, rather than storing in the most efficient way, which can increase the complexity of the processing and therefore the processing time.

However, readers differ in what they know about morphology. Knowledge of derivationally suffixed English words facilitates accurate reading in the school years and even in high school for English readers (Fowler & Liberman, 1995; Tyler & Nagy, 1990). The ability to see the derivational morphemes in an English word is dependent on the knowledge that a reader has about the language, which is acquired mainly through schooling (Derwing, Smith, & Weibe, 1995). The greater the reader's knowledge about prefixes, roots, and suffixes, the greater his or her ability to see structure when looking at words.

In any case, in word recognition, the reader has unconsciously formed a graphemic–phonemic image of the word in question and matched it with a representation of a word contained in the mental lexicon. The word is recognized and the meaning in semantic memory can then be accessed. If the reader reads a new word, it won't be recognized because there is no match for the new word stored in their mental lexicon. However, the new word then can be added to the reader's mental lexicon and any meaning which can be gleaned from the text (or the dictionary) will be associated with it. If the new word is morphologically complex, containing a prefix, a free morpheme, and a suffix, the reader can use his or her knowledge of derivation and decision-making strategies to try to guess the meaning of the new word. This is not always easy because, as we have already seen, when prefixes and suffixes are added, the meaning changes can be unpredictable. Still, the meaning of the derivational morphemes stored in the mental lexicon are clues to the meaning of new words.

This discussion has been fairly abstract, so let us make it more concrete with an example or two. The reader's eyes take in the graphs **s u n n y** and associate them with the phonological representation /sʌniy/. The resulting image is matched with the word **sunny**, which is part of the lexicon of English; recognition of the word is achieved and the meaning is accessed. Suppose the reader's eyes take in the graphs **b e e r y** and associates them with a phonological representation /biriy/. Suppose this reader has never encountered this word before (as in, "**The police officers thought the interior of the car smelled beery after the crash.**"). The reader can use a number of strategies to deal with it. The reader can recognize that this is a possible word in English, separate the two morphemes, and access them—**beer** and y, and combine them to infer what the meaning of the whole word must be—**like beer**. **Beery** can also be understood using a straightforward analogical strategy to words like **sunny**. This is shown in Fig. 8.1.

It is easy to see that there are some implications for teaching ESL and EFL reading. The knowledge of derivational morphemes and the phonological changes that go with them may be helpful to the ESL and EFL reader. Although many of the patterns are somewhat inconsistent and do not allow automatic processing, they are very productive and useful as patterns. Recall that there is evidence that some ESL and EFL students do not use a phonological strategy when they come across unknown and "unpronounceable" words in their reading. Instead, they use a meaning-based strategy of trying to associate a visual image with some kind of meaning association, whatever that might be. For English, a phonological strategy is more empowering. Knowing how derivation works can aid students in this because morphemes can be segmented and pronounced. Knowledge of the pronunciation changes that occur in derivation can result in more accurate pronunciations.

Further, derived words are not all listed in dictionaries, especially the abridged dictionaries that nonnative speaking students carry around. To look up derived words, it is often necessary to look up the root word and

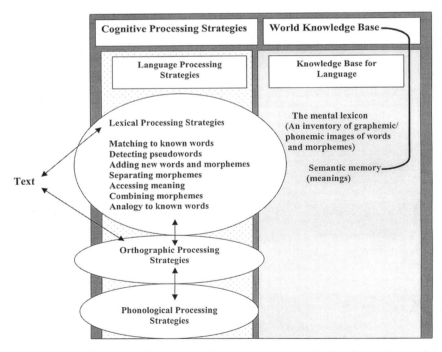

FIG. 8.1   The knowledge base and processing strategies for derivation and word identification.

then apply knowledge of the prefixes and suffixes. For nonnative speaking students whose linguistic competence develops slowly and whose reading vocabulary is often meager, direct instruction in the derivational morphemes of English, although time-consuming, may be extremely helpful, especially to those who wish to pursue higher education in an English-speaking environment.

Do ESL and EFL readers use knowledge of English morphology and processing strategies to read unknown words? The main strategies that ESL and EFL learners can use in word recognition are cognate recognition (Carroll, 1992), context (Bensoussan & Laufer, 1984), graphemic similarity (Walker, 1983), and morphological processing. The cognate strategy is only available to ESL and EFL readers of languages that are Germanic or Latin-derived. The use of context is only available if there is sufficient surrounding information and it can be utilized by the reader. Graphemic similarity is of limited use in English. Osburne and Mulling (1998), in their survey of this literature, found that students prefer these strategies and rarely rely on a morphological strategy to help them identify unknown words. In a new study Osburne and Mulling (2001) found that many Spanish speaking ESL students could use a morphological strategy if necessary, but they preferred not to, presumably because of the cognitive load that morphological processing entails. Cognitive load refers to the amount of mental work involved in a task—the more work there is, the more reluctant the reader is to do it.

There are a number of reasons that might account for the large cognitive load involved in processing English morphology. First, processing derivational morphology involves disassembling the word into component morphemes (which could be ambiguous), matching them with sound representations (which are opaque, as discussed earlier), accessing them in the mental lexicon and semantic memory (where they might not occur), and reassembling the pieces into the whole word. ESL and EFL students may not have the knowledge base or processing strategies to do that, or their processing strategies might not work with automaticity. A further contributing factor might be that the students' own knowledge of their L1 morphology and the processing strategies they have already developed may interfere with processing English morphology.

MORPHOLOGY IN OTHER LANGUAGES

Comrie (1981) offered a useful way to discuss morphology in the world's languages by introducing the concept of two morphological dimensions. One dimension concerns the number of morphemes per word and the other dimension concerns the extent to which the morphemes within a word can be segmented or separated from each other. Languages can be placed on the axes of two continua, as shown in Fig. 8.2.

Languages at point A are called *isolating*; normally, each word is made up of one morpheme. For example, although Chinese has some com-

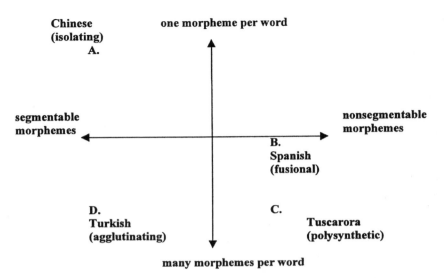

FIG. 8.2   A continuum of morphological variation in the world's languages. Adapted from Comrie, 1981, pp. 39–49, and used by permission of the University of Chicago Press.

pound words made up of two morphemes, the typical word has one segmentable morpheme. Languages at point B are called *fusional*; normally words will have more than one morpheme per word and the morphemes often cannot be easily broken down into components. Languages at point C are called *polysynthetic*; words can be made up of many morphemes, but the individual morphemes may be hard to separate out. Languages at point D are called *agglutinating*; there are many morphemes and it is easy to segment the morphemes within a word. In general, languages can be characterized by how they fall within the quadrants formed by the lines on the chart. Keep in mind that any time a linguist sets up a neat dichotomy such as this one, he or she finds that it is sometimes difficult to wrestle the world's languages into the perfect position. Languages, the ultimate human creations, resist neat and tidy classifications.

Vietnamese, for instance, is an isolating language, in which each word usually has one morpheme. Comrie (1981) gave this example of a Vietnamese sentence (in which I have omitted some phonetic markings):

Khi toi den nha ban toi, chung toi bat dau lam bai

when I come house friend I PLURAL I begin do lessons

"When I came to my friend's house, we began to do lessons." (p. 40)

Note that there is no past tense marking on the Vietnamese verb and that plural and first person (which would be "we") are also separate morphemes. Chinese languages, like Mandarin, are isolating.

An example of a fusional language is Spanish, in which the verb endings encode grammatical information which cannot be split into components of meaning:

To speak	hablar
I speak	hablo
you speak	hablas
he/she/it speaks	habla
we speak	hablamos
you plural speak	hablais
they speak	hablan

The ending on the Spanish verb encodes person, number, and tense grammatical meanings all rolled up into one morpheme. For example, **-o** in **hablo** captures these grammatical meanings (which could be separable morphemes but aren't): first person singular present tense. Which part of the **-o** means first person singular? Which part means present tense? They are fused together into one form and cannot be pulled apart. Many European languages have fusional verb endings which indicate person, number, and tense. Some also have extensive fusional noun endings which indicate number, gender, and grammatical relations like subject, object, possessive, and so on.

This example, from Napoli (1996), is a polysynthetic language, Tuscarora, a Native American language. The first word includes a number of different nonsegmentable (bound) morphemes:

Ae-hra-taskw-ahk-hwa?   ha? tsi:r
PREFIX-3rd Person Masculine-domestic animal-pickup-
                                    ASPECT MARKER   PARTICLE dog
"He regularly picks up dogs." [He is a dog-catcher.]

Many American Indian languages are polysynthetic; so are some Bantu languages and some Australian languages.

An agglutinating language is Turkish. In this partial example of a noun declension (adam means "man"), the morpheme boundaries are clear, so it is easy to segment the words into component morphemes:

	Singular	Plural
Nominative	adam	adam-lar
Accusative	adam-ı	adam-lar-ı
Genitive	adam--ı n	adam-lar-ı n

A casual look will indicate that "lar" means plural, **ı** means accusative (direct object), and **ın** means genitive (possessive). Another agglutinating language is Hungarian. In agglutinating languages, the words can be quite long, but they can be processed automatically because the morphology is transparent and consistent.

English has words that fall into all of the quadrants. Examples of isolating words (words made up of one free morpheme) are **sun, moon,** and **carpet.** Fusional words, where the morphemes are fused together and inseparable, are words like **were** (be + past tense + plural, although English verbs tend not to be fusional, as in **play + ed**, in which the -ed only indicates past tense) or **people** (human + plural). Examples of agglutinating words are compounds like **bookkeepers,** where each morpheme is easily pulled apart and the meaning of the whole is made from adding each part together. Polysynthetic words, made up of many inseparable morphemes, might be long derived words with Latin roots, like **antediluvian, antebellum,** or long chemical and medical terms. This variety in word types in English might cause increased cognitive load for ESL and EFL students whose languages contain predominately one type of word and who therefore might not be used to the other types. The problems might reside in their knowledge base (mental lexicon and semantic memory) or their processing strategies.

L1/L2 TRANSFER PROBLEMS IN MORPHOLOGY

To understand possible problems for the ESL and EFL reader in processing morphology, we need to consider two areas: the knowledge base and processing strategies. In each case, research is scanty but suggestive. First, the knowledge base, or mental lexicon, might be organized differently for different languages. (At present, it is unclear whether there is separate storage for L1 and L2, or whether there is one mental lexicon that serves more than one language, or whether there might be two interconnected lexicons for L1 and L2. See discussion in Singleton, 1997, and elsewhere.)

However, Schreuder and Baayen (1995) proposed that different language-specific characteristics of morphology may affect the way that the mental lexicon develops. Evidence from Caramazza, Laudanna, and Romani (1988) and Jarvella, Job, Sandstrom, and Schreuder (1987), which was reported in Schreuder et al. (1990), indicated that differences in the reading processes for Italians reading Italian (verbs with fusional endings) and Dutch can be attributed to the fact that Italian has a more complex (and fusional) verb system than does Dutch (which is more like English), and therefore knowledge of the verbs and verbal endings are stored in memory in different ways that are efficient for each language. Although still hypothetical, it is not unreasonable to think that isolating languages have separate words stored one-by-one as whole unchanging entities (and syntax operates to put them into the right order in that sentence.) Agglutinating language like Turkish might have all the morphemes listed and word formation processes (not syntax) operate to construct the predictable series of morphemes that make up the long words (and syntax operates to place these long words into their correct order).

Furthermore, words and morphemes in the mental lexicon might be stored in different relations to each other. For example, Serbian has an extensive and complex fusional case-marking system for noun phrases. There is a base noun form, which adds inflections based on how the noun is used in the sentence: subject, direct object, and so on. Lukatela, Gligorijevic, Kostic, and Turvey (1980) proposed an organization of the mental lexicon in which the nominative case (for subjects) is the central one; the others "revolve" around it as satellites. This is a rather ornate organization for nouns is probably unnecessary for English, because nouns do not change their form according to their use, except as singular or plural.

Bentin and Frost (1995) also argued for the influence of different morphology on word storage and identification. For example, they suggested that Lukatela et al.'s (1980) model of word identification based on the frequency of the nominative singular and not the frequency of other inflected versions of the noun is heavily dependent on the richly-inflected Serbo–Croatian language and has little plausibility for English, which has few nominal inflections. They argued the following:

> ... the lexical presentation and parsing of morphologically complex words which are possible in language with an agglutinative word structure such as Turkish must be different than those in a language with a nonconcatenative morphology such as Hebrew, in which different inflections and derivatives are formed by infixing word-patterns within the consonantal string that forms the root morpheme. (pp. 272–273)

They suggested that fusional languages like Serbian, agglutinating languages like Turkish, and infixing languages like Hebrew, have different word storage in the mental lexicon, and these, presumably, are also different from English. If ESL and EFL learners have a mental lexicon organized in a certain way for their L1s, do they use the same organizational principles and structure in acquiring an English mental lexicon or do the demands of learning English words necessarily create a mental lexicon appropriate for English? Alas, we do not know the answer to that.

Is there any evidence that readers of different L1s develop different low-level morphological processing strategies because of differences in the morphological structure of their words or mental lexicon? The answer here too is sketchy, but interesting. We saw earlier that patterns of derivational morphology do not seem to be very accessible to English speakers unless they have been schooled in them, but they can use morphology to read unknown words if they have the knowledge. We have also seen that words in English can be of any of the four morphological types. This leads to the hypothesis that native English readers do not rely much on consistent morphological processing strategies, but rather have a number of strategies that they can employ if necessary, depending on how transparent or segmentable the word is: matching the perceived word or morpheme to a word or morpheme stored in the mental lexicon or detecting pseudo words (that is, words that could be English but aren't in the mental lexicon). If a word is identified as unknown, the reader can separate potential morphemes if necessary, accessing the meaning of the words and morphemes, and recombining the pieces. The reader can also use analogy to similar known words to get a hypothesis about what the word is and its meaning.

Schreuder and Baayen (1995), who proposed that different language-specific characteristics of morphology may affect the way that the mental lexicon develops, also assumed different "language-specific models of morphological processing" (p. 132). We might imagine that languages that have words made up consistently from one type of morphological pattern might encourage readers to use one strategy uniformly. For example, the matching strategy is useful for isolating languages. If the word is found to be an unknown pseudo word, the L1 strategy might be to add the new word without any further analysis because morphological analysis is not an option. Matching one-to-one may be less useful for agglutinating languages. Readers might have to do morphological analysis or analogy to process words in reading, thus, separating, accessing meaning, and recombining might be frequently used strategies. If students are used to applying one strategy to the exclusion of others, they may show signs of only partial positive transfer or negative transfer to English reading, which seems to require both.

For example, Chinese writing doesn't contain information about morphology because it is an isolating language not given to morphologically complex words, although compound words are common. In addition, the sinograms themselves do not lend themselves to indicating any changes in the words that they encode, because they are printed "as is," unlike alphabetic writing which can print the words in present tense or past tense, singular or plural, through changes in spelling. Taft and Zhu (1995) discussed a number of questions concerning morphological processing in Chinese writing; they made some suggestions for morphological processing that are quite different from any ever proposed for English. It is quite possible that Chinese learners of English reading do not process the grammatical information from derivational and inflectional morphemes in English, or they do not process it efficiently and automatically.

Garnham, Oakhill, Ehrlich, and Carreiras (1995) showed that gender marking in languages like French and Spanish is used to determine reference between a pronoun and a noun phrase. In French and Spanish, all nouns are either "masculine" or "feminine" and adjectives, determiners, and pronouns must match them. It seems like readers of Spanish and French have developed a strategy to process gender marking of nouns, but English does not have the same type of gender markings. In English, most nouns are neutral with respect to gender and are referred to with "it," unless there is some reason to assign them a gender (as in referring to boats as she). French and Spanish speakers will not be able to rely on their L1 strategy to process nouns and they may lack the strategies that English speakers develop.

Koda (1993) studied second language learners of Japanese (21 Americans, 12 Chinese, and 13 Koreans). A sentence completion task measured knowledge of case-marking particles. The data confirmed that sentence comprehension differs among second language readers of Japanese with varying L1 backgrounds and suggested that reading skills transferred from native language interact with L2 linguistic features in shaping processing strategies. Besides the potential difference in reading strategies, ESL and EFL learners are affected by lack of knowledge of English inflectional and derivational morphology. The Japanese learners studied in Schmitt and Meara (1997) showed "a rather weak awareness of derivative suffixes and their use [and they] lack convincing mastery of even inflectional suffixes" (p. 26).

IMPLICATIONS FOR ESL READING INSTRUCTION

As ESL and EFL students are learning words in English, they should be building up such a storage of morphemes, rimes, and syllables through direct instruction and through extensive reading practice. This morpheme store will help with reading and with effective use of English dictionaries. Students, whose first languages are isolating, like Ho, may have difficulty with the complex morphological structure of some English words. Their mental lexicons may need restructuring to include knowledge of derivational morphemes and they must learn the inflectional morphemes of English. If the L1 writing system doesn't encode morphological changes in words, readers may not have efficient processing strategies like separation and recombination for morphological changes in English words, such as tense, possessive, or plural. They may be relying on a simple matching strategy, which is not effective unless they have a perfect match for each word in their mental lexicon.

Students who speak Hebrew may have L1 processing strategies that focus more on infixed morphological changes rather than on the prefixed and suffixed morphology of English. This would be similar, say, to detecting the difference between **sit** and **sat**, for example, which is not a very useful strategy to generalize for English. English has a small set of verbs that form their past tenses by "infixed" (in a way) vowel changes; although these words may be frequent, their number is small. Students like Ho may benefit from direct instruction in reading derivationally complex words and inflectional endings so that their lexical processor works optimally using matching, separating and recombining, and analogy to morphologically similar words.

Students like MariCarmen and Despina come from languages that are largely fusional with complex verbal systems of many inflectional endings and complex noun, adjective, and pronoun agreement systems that use gender and case markings to show relations and reference. This rich and informative inflectional morphology is probably processed with more attention than the meager inflectional morphology of English, which provides few cues to verb tense and noun agreement. Japanese uses a system of particles (not inflections) to indicate the functions that nouns have in sentences (e.g., subject, object, indirect object, etc.). Readers who come from these languages need to learn that English uses strict word order more heavily to encode meaning relations. They, like Mohammed and Ho, benefit from direct instruction in derivational and inflectional morphology, and strategies like separating and recombining. Students from Latin- or Greek-based languages have the benefit of shared derivational morphology with English (pre-, post-, -ment, -tion, etc.); they may focus more exclusively on Germanic morphology (-ness, -dom, -ly).

For some ESL and EFL advanced readers, it may be useful to comment on the fairly consistent phonological rules of English which affect the pronunciation of derived words (press-pressure) and therefore complicate our spelling. This may enable students to sound out words more effectively to determine if they know the word by sound and to discard a meaning-based reading strategy for words that are hard to pronounce. It may even be useful to tell students that English writing is not just phonemic but also morphemic in that the accurate representation of sound is sacrificed to maintain the semantic connection between words that can be perceived if the root morphemes are spelled consistently. Our system tries to strike a balance between representing phonemes (sound) and morphemes (small meaning units) and sometimes the need to represent morphemes overrides the need to represent sound accurately. This may help students form a lexical entry for a word and see meaning relations between words, or at least connect words in the mental lexicon. The point of morphological instruction and practice with processing strategies must be to reduce the cognitive load associated with the task, so students must understand the system, practice the strategy overtly, and generalize the strategy to all of their reading. It is only then that they will make use of English morphological cues in reading.

Spotlight on Teaching

Gunning (1988) provided a list of prefixes, suffixes, and Greek and Latin bound roots. He listed these common prefixes and suffixes with their level of difficulty for English speakers. Do you agree with this order of difficulty for the nonnative speaker of English? Is this order of difficulty related to the productivity of the morpheme? Which ones cause phonological changes in the base words to which they are attached?

	Prefixes	Suffixes
Primary:	dis-, pre-, re-, un-	-able, -er, -ible, -ful, -less, -ness, -y
Intermediate:	anti-, co-, de-, en-, fore-, il-, im-, in-, ir-, inter-, non-, over-, post-, semi-, sub-, super-	-age, -al, -an-, -ant, -ent, -ese, -est, ic, -ive, -like, -ment, -or, -some, -th, -ward
Advanced:	ad-, circum-, contra-, counter-, -ex-, extra-, out-, sur-	-ance, -hood, -ism, -ity, -ize,-osis, -ship

The following inductive sequence can be used for teaching morphemes like **un-**.

Step 1: Show examples like **happy** and **unhappy**. Discuss the difference in meaning between the two words. Contrast other words that students also know, such as **kind** and **unkind**, and so forth.

Step 2: Have students articulate what **un-** adds to the meaning of the base word; but if they can't, articulate it yourself for them. Have them write it down in a vocabulary notebook.

Step 3: If you are introducing a suffix, discuss how it changes the part of speech of the original word: **care/careful**, **help/helpful**, and **use/useful**. Show these words in different grammatical contexts. "I care for my pets. I am careful to give them water." Have students articulate the difference if they can.

Step 4: Have controlled practice with typical activities on a group or individual worksheet:

a. Rewrite "He was not happy ⇒ He was unhappy."

b. Complete the sentence with the correct word or fill in the blank.

c. Match the correct word with its definition.

d. Provide the morpheme and a list of words to which it can be added. Have students make up words, define them, and write sentences with them.

e. Contrast the morpheme with others that are like it, if any: -less,/ -ful, pre-/post-.
Step 5: Have guided practice, such as the following:
a. Have a structured language experience, using words with the morpheme.
b. Bring in examples of the morpheme from other books or readings. They should write these in their vocabulary notebook.
c. Allow students to identify the morpheme in the reading when they see it. You probably selected this morpheme for a minilesson because it appears in something that your class is reading.

Now you choose one of the morphemes from Step 5 and write a lesson plan for teaching it.

DISCUSSION QUESTIONS

1. Have you figured out the **naked** and **baked** example? If not, look them up in the dictionary and try a little morphological analysis.
2. What is strange about the pronunciation of the word "beloved" with three syllables (be-lov-ed)? Where did this pronunciation come from?
3. In which "order" were the suffix and prefix added to the word **hurry** to make **unhurried**? That is, was the **-ed** added first and then the prefix **un-** or vice versa? What is your reasoning for your answer? Is this the same reasoning for **daunt** ⇒ **undaunted** or **unbridled** from **bridle**?
4. Besides derivation, one common word formation process in English is *compounding*. Noun compounds may be made up of noun-noun combinations (tomato juice), Adjective-noun combinations (blackbird), and even verb-particle combinations (pick up). Say these sentences. What do you notice about the way that the compound is pronounced in "i," when compared to the other sentence in each pair? What is the difference in meaning?
   a. i. Please bring me some orange juice.
      ii. This is the red juice and that is the orange juice.
   b. i. The president lives in the White House.
      ii. The white house on the corner is new.
   c. i. She drives a pick-up truck.
      ii. Please pick up some eggs on your way home.
5. Is there any rule about when to write compound words as one word, with a hyphen, or as two (or more) words?
6. If you know another language, think about its morphology: for example, it may be isolating, polysynthetic, agglutinating, fusional, or a combination of these. What evidence do you have for your answer?

Chapter 9

Vocabulary Acquisition

Prereading questions—Before you read, think, and discuss the following:

1. What is the structure of the word **unruly**? Why do we not say **ruly**? What might be the origin or derivation of the word **unruly**?
2. Are the words **park** (as in park the car) and **park** (city park) one word with two meanings or two words with separate meanings? What does the dictionary say?
3. How do you understand words that you've never seen before in print?

Study Guide questions—Answer these while you read the chapter:

1. What is the idea of skipping words you don't know in reading?
2. What is the phonological loop?
3. What properties of words make them easier to learn?
4. How can you define the word "word"? Look it up in the dictionary.
5. Can you think of some other examples of the word formation processes mentioned (borrowing, blending, acronym, abbreviation, back formation, clipping, coinage, and generalization)?
6. How are compounds interpreted?
7. What special problems are caused by conversion?
8. How are metaphors interpreted? Give an original example of a metaphor.
9. Explain the following terms: polysemy, homophones, homographs, and homonyms.
10. What information is needed to have native-speaker mastery of a word?
11. What is the difference between connotation and denotation?
12. What applications are there for vocabulary recognition or acquisition?

Many reading textbooks for the ESL and EFL learner suggest higher level cognitive reading strategies or learning strategies that can benefit the student who is trying to learn to read. For instance, a prereading examination of the text for organization, headings, summaries, and so on, will help the reader make predictions about the content and locate sources of help within the text. Learning to pick out the topic sentence in each paragraph will allow the student to get most of the essential information in the text, taking full advantage of the predictable and formulaic nature of English written organization. Acquiring a repertory of reading skills like reading in depth, skimming for the gist, and scanning for specific information, permits ESL and EFL readers to adjust their reading to the task that they need to perform.

However, lack of vocabulary remains one of the major obstacles for the ESL and EFL reader. As a result, many ESL and EFL textbooks offer valuable learning strategies for vocabulary. Students learn to distinguish and look up the words that seem most essential to the meaning of the text, such as those that are repeated four or five times. They are shown how to look at morphological cues within the word that might indicate something about its meaning or part of speech, although students seem to avoid this strategy because of the cognitive load involved in it (Osburne & Mulling, 2001). Students may be encouraged to keep a vocabulary journal while reading so that they can use their new words actively in speaking or writing. Students become adept at finding cues in the context of the sentence or paragraph to guess what the word means. Students can also apply a cognate strategy, that is, they look for similarities between the English word and a word in their native language. Because cognates may be understood and acquired with support from the L1 lexical knowledge store, L2 readers seem to apply this strategy automatically. In the case where the student's L1 has many cognates with English, a valuable vocabulary strategy might be to "be wary of false friends," which are those words that are cognate but have very different meanings in L1 and L2.

Many teachers teach students to use these word identification strategies in reading, but they do not consistently advocate vocabulary building during reading for comprehension. Instead, some teachers commonly advocate one reading comprehension strategy at the expense of vocabulary building, that is, to "skip the words you don't know and get the gist of the meaning." Although no reading textbook promotes this strategy outright, many teachers adopt it in the classroom, as I, myself, did at one time in my life. The idea seems to stem from conclusions drawn from a number of sources in the reading literature in the past 30 years, some of which have been discussed elsewhere in this book: for example, "readers are just guessing anyway," or "readers just sample the text and don't fixate on every word." In addition, some common assumptions inadvertently have led some teachers to accept the idea of skipping over unknown words in hot pursuit of comprehension.

ASSUMPTION 1: L2 READERS CAN COMPENSATE FOR LACK OF SPECIFIC LANGUAGE KNOWLEDGE WITH BACKGROUND KNOWLEDGE

Coady, 1979, said the following:

> Since the various process strategies interact among themselves, the ESL student should take advantage of his strengths in order to overcome his weaknesses. For example, greater background knowledge of a particular subject could compensate somewhat for a lack of syntactic control over the language.... The proficient reader learns to utilize whatever cue systems render useful information and to put them together in a *creative* manner, always achieving *at least some comprehension*. This weakness in one area can be overcome by a strength in another. (p. 11; emphasis added)

ASSUMPTION 2: READERS DO NOT NEED TO UNDERSTAND EVERYTHING IN THE TEXT FOR ADEQUATE COMPREHENSION

Clarke and Silberstein, 1979, said the following:

> Students must be made aware of the number of language clues available to them when they are stopped by an unfamiliar word. They should realize that they can usually continue reading and obtain a general understanding of the item.... Most importantly, they must be taught to recognize situations in which the meaning of the word or phrase is *not essential for adequate comprehension* of the passage. (p. 51)

Been, 1979, said the following:

> The readers should be given cues which lead him to ignore linearity, help him to exploit redundancies, and demonstrate *that meaning can be apprehended even though he does not understand every word*. (p. 98)

Day and Bamford, 1998, said the following:

> Part of fluent and effective reading involves the reader *ignoring unknown words and phrases or, if understanding them is essential, guessing their approximate meaning*. (p. 93)

ASSUMPTION 3: VOCABULARY INSTRUCTION TAKES UP TOO MUCH TIME IN THE READING CLASS

Gaskill, 1979, said the following:

> Many instructors ask their students to learn vocabulary items which are found in their reading selections. This can be helpful if the number of words is held

to a reasonable ten to twenty words per selection and if the list of words is accompanied with contextualized examples and practice. Preparing lists of vocabulary items and contextualized practice requires *additional preparation* on the part of the instructor.... Discussion of and practice with such lists takes *a lot of class time.* (p. 148)

Clearly, it is impossible to argue against these commonsense assumptions for the reading comprehension classroom. They have validity, but the conclusion that some teachers have drawn seems to be that, given that the goal of the reading class is improvement in the comprehension of a message, and not word learning, and that background knowledge can make up for lack of vocabulary anyway, and that readers don't need to understand every word, and that vocabulary learning is not an efficient use of reading class time, a good strategy is for ESL and EFL readers to skip over words they don't know.

Again, there is some merit in the suggestion. Lack of vocabulary is a serious problem for ESL and EFL students in reading independently. Many ESL and EFL students, especially those in higher education, are required to read stories, articles, or books that are too difficult for them to read because there are too many words they don't know. It is frustrating to read something incomprehensible, so the natural inclination for the reader is to stop reading and do something else. If readers don't read, they don't improve. It is equally frustrating for most people to consult the dictionary for every unknown word. Dictionaries are fallible, the definition may be unclear or incomplete, and by the time the reader has found the definition he has lost track of what the sentence was about anyway. Teachers don't want students to be frustrated; they want them to read extensively because that is the one sure way to improve reading.

It is a common impression among teachers I have talked to that students will learn words automatically while they are reading, that they will at least acquire some new vocabulary while reading, even if they skip over unknown words. And anyway, teachers are cognizant of the fact that the goal of reading is to get meaning, not to read and remember words. So, it was probably inevitable that reading teachers at one point began to advise students to skip the words that they didn't know to focus on getting the overall meaning of the text.

The strategy was designed to keep reading interesting and fun so that readers would read and, as a short-term task-limited procedure, it probably accomplishes its goal. One problem, however, is that it can become a long-term task-unlimited procedure for students. Some students adopt this strategy for the long run because it is easier than learning new words. They get into the processing habit of disregarding words that they fixate on as soon as they decide that it is not a word in their L2 mental lexicon. Once this habit is formed, it is hard to break. Students also apply this processing strategy to all of the reading that they must do, even the reading in which it is essential to get more than just the gist. Rather than a strategy they can apply to challenging but relatively unimportant reading, it becomes their exclusive reading policy. Rather than applying it to the preliminary reading of a text which they are going to read more carefully again, they use it as the one and only "careful" reading they do. The simple truth is that if readers skip the words they don't know, they don't learn them, and often, they don't understand the texts they need to understand. The conclusion is that the short-term reading comprehension strategy is very detrimental to long-term vocabulary building. Even Day and Bamford (1998) cannot report substantial and consistent vocabulary gains through extensive reading programs.

(To provide a more personal example, an ESL student of mine was once involved in volunteer work that required him to read a short training manual. He took it home overnight and read it, but the next day, when the volunteer coordinator asked him a few questions, he couldn't answer. She was peeved and expressed irritation to me. I was surprised, because he was a serious student. When I asked him about it, he told me that he had just skipped the words he didn't know. He didn't realize that he should have read any differently because this is what his teacher had advised him to do to cope with difficult reading. This is probably an extreme case but I think of it every time I hear employers, teachers, and professors complain that their non-native speaking students can't understand what they read.)

The purpose of this chapter is to suggest additional word learning strategies for ESL and EFL readers to use to read efficiently at the same time that they improve vocabulary. We have seen that reading familiar words depends on low-level processing strategies and specific linguistic knowledge of writing systems, spelling patterns, morphemes, and so on. It turns out that learning unfamiliar words depends on the same sorts of knowledge, as well. It follows that improving low-level processing strategies and linguistic knowledge might help students retain more vocabulary words from their reading and vocabulary exercises.

LEARNER VARIABLES IN VOCABULARY ACQUISITION

First of all, what makes a person a better word learner? Ellis and Beaton (1993) gave us some ideas. There is a lot of evidence that a better word learner can repeat new words easily and repetition ability depends on the short-term memory (processing strategies) and the long-term memory (knowledge store) of the learner (Baddeley et al., 1998; Cheung, 1996; Service & Kohonen, 1995). To repeat a new word (a sequence of graphs) that the learner has read, he or she must access (at least some of the) graphemic images stored in long-term memory and hold them in short-term memory while they are matched to a phonemic image from the inventory of phonemes stored in long-term memory. Then the graphemic and phonemic image is held or rehearsed in short-term memory while the motor commands to the mouth are formulated and executed. If the learner's short-term memory or long-term memory is not adequate to the task, the learner cannot repeat the unknown word and cannot store it as easily. The storage of words in the mental lexicon in long-term memory is an important part of the knowledge base.

The reader's abilities to repeat new words is part of an interactive cycle as noted by Gathercole, Willis, Emslie, and Baddeley (1991, and cited in Ellis & Beaton, 1993). Repetition ability and existing vocabulary knowledge "bootstrap" on each other. Phonological skills influence the learning of new words, but also, the larger the storage of words in the mental lexicon, the easier it seems to be to come up with phonological analyses. From the point of view taken in this book, it is clear that this supports the idea that readers use probabilistic reasoning and analogy to known spelling patterns to read unknown words, and the better able readers are to do this, the better they can retain a new word, as well.

These findings come from the study of what has come to be called the phonological "loop" in vocabulary acquisition (Baddeley et al., 1998). The phonological loop, shown in Fig. 9.1, comes into play in listening compre-hension and in reading to allow the listener or reader to learn unknown words. After the word is heard or read, a phonological image is formed. The loop allows for the retention of the phonological image for short periods of time in short-term memory. The loop consists of a phonological store, which stores the image, and a rehearsal process, which serves to refresh de-caying representations that might disappear from short-term memory. The function of the loop is to store unfamiliar forms in short-term memory while permanent memory structures can be constructed in the mental lexicon, thereby leading to word learning. Repetition ability is taken to be an indica-tor of the loop. People with poor short-term memory have a hard time re-peating words. Likewise, vocabulary knowledge is also related to repetition ability. These findings are consistent for both L1 and L2 word learning.

An ingenious type of experiment shows the effect of the phonological loop in reading (at least the reading of single words). In reading, the graphs on the page are matched to graphemes in our head and these, in turn, are matched with a phonological image of the phonemes associated with the graphemes. This is the phonological "loop." The functioning of the loop can be disrupted in reading by having readers say a nonsense syllable (like "bla bla bla") while they are reading. This method, called *articulatory suppression*, has a "clearly deleterious effect on the acquisition of foreign language vocabulary" (Baddeley et al., 1998, p. 162). The idea is that if the reader does not, for some reason, form and retain a phonological image of an unknown word which is being read, he or she will not form an entry in the mental lexicon, and therefore will not recognize the word when it is read again.

Baddeley et al. (1998) offered a dynamic model of word learners as active processors of new words through phonological storage and rehearsal to add to their knowledge base in the mental lexicon. Why is it that many ESL and

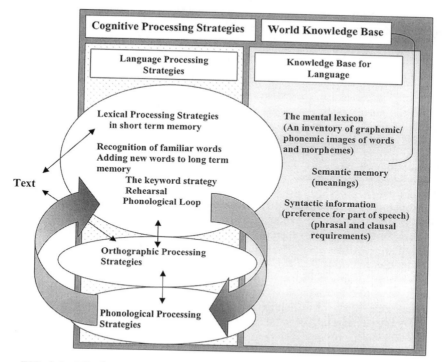

FIG. 9.1   The human word processor.

EFL learners fail to learn much vocabulary while they are reading? One reason might be that they are overwhelmed by the sheer number of new words in some of the texts they are asked to read. Other reasons may be found if we look at the lexical variables in word learning: acoustic similarity, word length, pronounceability or other phonological factors, orthography (script, direction of script, sequential letter probabilities, familiarity with grapheme–phoneme mappings), and word class or part of speech (Ellis & Beaton, 1993).

LEXICAL VARIABLES IN VOCABULARY ACQUISITION

Acoustic Similarity

Papagno and Vallar (1992) found evidence that acoustically similar words confused the phonological loop in the L2 learner even in visual presentation. In the phonological loop, the phonological image in short-term memory may be confused with similar words already learned, and the confusion may impede or prevent storage of the new item in long-term memory.

Word Length

Word length affects storage and retention in the phonological loop. Cheung (1996) found this to be an important factor for Hong Kong seventh graders whose vocabulary size was smaller than the median for all the students studied. The longer the word, the harder it is to store and retain in the loop so that it can become permanently stored in the mental lexicon.

Pronounceability

The more pronounceable a word, the more easily it is learned. Ellis and Beaton (1993) made the point that the more a word conforms to the expected phonological forms of the language, the more pronounceable it is. In matching graphs–graphemes–phonemes, the more knowledge about the typical phonological structures of the language, the better the reader can predict the sound of the word and the easier the storage and retention in the phonological loop. In this book, we have already considered the problem of pronounceability elsewhere. We saw that there is a tendency for Japanese readers of English to use a visual strategy to remember words, that is, they try to match the visual appearance of the word with a meaning concept, as if the English word were a Kanji or logographic symbol. I think this explains some unusual findings by Saito (1995), who was investigating the effects of pronounceability and articulatory suppression on phonological learning in Japanese learners of Japanese nonwords presented in Katakana or syllabic writing. In this study, participants were shown easy and difficult-to-pronounce "nonwords" under a control and an articulatory suppression condition. Then they were asked to recall the words in a free recall task in which they were asked to write down the words they remembered. Then there was a cued recall task in which the participants were given the first syllable of the word and had to complete the word. The prediction would be that pronounceability of nonwords would result in better word learning, and it did. Articulatory suppression, however, was expected to inhibit word learning for the nonwords. In contrast, Saito found that in both the free recall and the cued recall, the unpronounceable nonwords were learned better in articulatory suppression than in the control condition. I think that articulatory suppression inhibits phonological storage in short-term memory and favors visual or graphemic storage, which could be expected to be well-remembered in recall writing tasks. In other words, the Japanese participants reacted to the articulatory suppression condition by treating the unpronounceable Katakana nonwords as Kanji, just as they seem to do with unpronounceable English words. This strategy led to success in the experiment but is less useful in actual reading tasks or in learning new words productively, as we have seen.

Orthography

In Ellis and Beaton's (1993) study of English learners who knew no German, the degree to which the German word conformed to the orthographic patterns of English affected their ability to translate from English to German. It is obvious that these individuals who knew no German had no knowledge of German letter-to-sound patterns and could only learn words based on their similarity to English. This study does, however, reinforce the idea that L1 orthography can help in reading L2 to the extent that there is overlap between the two systems. Where there is little or no overlap, L1 interferes or does not facilitate. Problems with English orthography may be significant contributors to the lack of vocabulary acquisition in reading generally. If ESL and EFL learners cannot match graphs to graphemes to phonemes quickly and automatically, the phonological loop may not be able to function to store and retain the word in long-term memory. If the phonological loop is not able to function, students may fall back on visual strategies for reading, which, we have argued, are not the most efficient way to read English words.

Word Class

Ellis and Beaton (1993) found that nouns are easier to learn than verbs, and this finding is consistent with other psychological literature for first language acquisition. It is unclear why nouns should be easier to learn than verbs, but one reason given is that their meaning tends to be more imageable or easy to visualize. In the case of English and German, probably the nouns and verbs correlate highly with each other because the two languages are closely related in syntax. For other languages, however, part of speech differences may be a cause for confusion in reading, because it is necessary for the reader to understand parts of speech to assign the correct syntactic structure to a sentence. Correct comprehension of syntactic structure is an important precursor to correct comprehension of meaning. The quote from Coady (1979), cited earlier, which said that background knowledge can make up for a lack of syntactic knowledge, must be tempered with a consideration that, as one of my linguistics professors used to say, syntax was made so that we can talk about things that are contrary to our expectations about the world. How else could we understand the sentence, "A man bit a dog," if it weren't for the dominance of syntax over background knowledge.

Part of speech information is opaque in English. A fusional language like Spanish marks part of speech clearly because it marks nouns with (generally) either an **-a** ending or an **-o**, and adjectives and pronouns carry corresponding markings with the nouns they match. The Spanish noun and adjective system of marking is different from the system which marks verbs, a three-way (-ar, -er, and -ir) series of conjugations in different tenses, persons, and numbers. Because of the noun, adjective, and verbal inflections, many words in Spanish, even in isolation, are unambiguous as to grammatical category, There are many languages with even stricter marking of grammatical category information than Spanish; in these languages there is no ambiguity at all between different parts of speech. The nouns are often clearly marked as to their function in the sentence (e.g., subject, direct object, etc.) and verbs are clearly marked with their inflections of person, number, and tense. For students from these languages, the scarcity of overt marking in English causes uncertainty in attributing a part of speech to an English word, and therefore phrasal structure is hard to compute and accurate meanings are difficult to comprehend. Further, any factors which favor noun learning over verb learning will not operate if the student cannot identify a word as a noun.

On the opposite side of the spectrum, some isolating languages have even fewer consistent markings of parts of speech than does English. Although spoken Chinese words have different categories, the written sinograms don't reflect grammatical parts of speech at all; they are invariable. Students whose L1 is like this may also have problems with English parts of speech because they may be unable to take advantage of the morphological information that is present in the English text.

Most native English readers don't have conscious or learned knowledge of the part of speech of each word in each sentence as it is being read, but they have unconscious knowledge which allows them to compute phrasal and sentential structure quickly, then discard it as soon as the meaning is clear. Given the incomplete marking of English grammatical categories and given how common conversion is as a word formation process in English, perhaps it is more accurate to think of parts of speech as weighted probabilities or frequencies from which we form grammatical expectations. For example, from our experience with language, we form the expectation that **floor** will be a noun, say, 95% of the time and a verb 5% of the time, except in certain registers (such as the carpet installer).

Expert English readers use these lexical expectations, the cues from the text like word order and grammatical function words like **the, of**, or **to**, and their knowledge of typical English syntactic structures, to determine the syntactic structure that they are reading. English speakers intuitively know that the subject of an English sentence is most typically a noun phrase, they know that **floor** is most likely going to be a noun, and they know that nouns are often preceded by **the**, so when they see the following sentence, **The floor the man swept was clean**, they will take the subject to be the first noun phrase **the floor**.

In addition, words themselves place requirements on the words that can or must go with them and this is part of the knowledge that readers must have about words. It is often called *collocational knowledge*, the stored information in memory about the lexical, phrasal, or clausal requirements of a word. For example, the verb **put** might occur in the predicate of a sentence. If so, there are certain collocational requirements placed on the verb phrase that forms the predicate. **Put** requires two other types of phrases within the verb phrase, a direct object, and a location phrase, as in the following sentence: **He put the car in the garage**. Taking away either the direct object **the car** or the location phrase **in the garage** would yield an ungrammatical sentence. The verb **remember** can take an infinitive or V + ing (**I remembered to go/going**), a that + sentence (**I remembered that he went**), or an OBJECT PRONOUN V + ing (**I remembered him going**). Each of these structures is associated with a certain semantic interpretation.

OTHER LEXICAL VARIABLES IN READING ENGLISH WORDS

As we saw in the last chapter, languages can be isolating, agglutinating, polysynthetic, or fusional, so even the concept of "word" is different from language to language. Words can be formed through different processes: for example, prefixing, suffixing, infixing, concatenation of morphemes, compounding, and so on. The processes typical in a student's L1 may not prepare him or her for the variety of word formation processes in English: acronym, blending, coining, generalization, back formation, clipping, conversion, and compounding. Students may benefit from direct assistance from teachers to learn processing strategies for these new words.

Another problem for students is that even if they know words, they may not have all of the necessary semantic information to understand the word and its meaning if they read it. They may lack knowledge of meanings other than the most common or the most literal. They may lack knowledge of the social, political, or religious connotation that words have. They need to be able to process and understand metaphor, discard inappropriate meanings for polysemous words, and resolve lexical ambiguity problems. They may lack knowledge of the grammatical requirements that words place on their syntactic contexts. If semantic and syntactic information about words is not automatically available to readers from their knowledge base as they process the text, comprehension of meaning is compromised.

Borrowing is a word formation process because it does result in a new word in the lexicon of a language. English has no problem borrowing words from other languages (e.g., **taco, patio, Wiener schnitzel, glasnost**), which has given English a very extensive, heterogeneous, and unruly vocabulary compared to languages which resist borrowing, whose lexicons are very homogeneous and rule-governed. Because of borrowing in English, there can be more than one word to refer to similar objects (e.g., sausage, bratwurst, chorizo, pepperoni). In most borrowings in English, the written word is copied letter by letter closely, but it is pronounced more or less as an English word with perhaps some concern to authenticity, depending on the speaker. ESL and EFL readers can benefit if the borrowed word happens to be from their own language, but otherwise, recent or uncommon borrowings are probably all going to be new and unknown.

Besides derivation and borrowing, English frequently uses *compounding* to form new words. Compounding is also common in German, which allows long compounds of many free morphemes put together, and in Chinese, which prefers short compounds of two free morphemes. It is not as common in some other languages. For instance, many speakers of Romance languages like Spanish, French, or Italian, prefer possessive structures instead of the more typical compounds in English. For instance, they might say **the leg of the table** or even **the table's leg** instead of the more correct **the table leg**. When they read this compound they might wonder about the relation between the two nouns. They might lack an interpretive strategy for these words because of their structure. The strategy is that the second noun is the object and the first noun is descriptive.

Long compound nouns made up of a number of words can be very confusing because the interpretive strategy must be applied over and over again; the English Department Curriculum Committee Summer Retreat Planning Committee requires quite a bit of mental gymnastics to understand. To understand what this compound means, first the student must realize that this is a compound and not a sentence or clause. The capital letters in this compound indicates that this is not a sentence, but if the compound is not capitalized, students may not understand that such a long group of words is a compound noun and not a sentence. Then the student must apply the interpretive strategy first to the individual two-word compounds and then to the four-word compounds and then to the eight-word compound.

(((English Department) (Curriculum Committee)) ((Summer Retreat) (Planning Committee)))

There are other types of compounds also, among them, compound adjectives (e.g., red-hot, candy apple red, etc.) and compound verbs made up of a verb and a particle (e.g., pick up, pick on, pick out, etc.) Compound verbs require an interpretive strategy that differentiates them from verbs with prepositional phrases. (This is often treated as a grammar issue but not necessarily a reading comprehension issue. However, syntax and reading comprehension are intimately connected.)

Common word formation processes in English besides derivation, borrowing, and compounding are blending, coining, generalization, acronym, back formation, clipping, and conversion. *Blending* is a process where two separate words are reduced and combined. For example, **brunch** is a blend of **breakfast** and **lunch**. In the case of **brunch**, it might be hard for ESL and EFL students to apply a strategy of breaking up the two parts to combine the meaning, because they might not recognize it as a blend. Other blends are more recognizable; reaganomics or chocoholic come to mind. *Coined words*, or words "minted" out of thin air, are harder to detect. Many are trademark names like kleenex or xerox, so they might, in fact, be multinational. Sometimes trademark names or other proper names become common nouns or verbs through a process of *generalization*, as in **kleenex** or a **quisling**.

Another much-used word formation process in English is *acronym*. The words **radar**, **AIDS**, and **NATO** are formed by taking the first initial of each word or main part of a word in the originating phrase and pronouncing them together as one word. This is distinguished from an *abbreviation*, where the initials are pronounced as letters, as in **FBI** or **CIA**. (Another type of abbreviation is a shortened form of the original word which is written with a period at the end. This is not really a word formation process, that is, **Dept.** for **department** is not a different word.) It may be my imagination, but it seems like acronym and initial abbreviations are becoming more common in some other languages, possibly due to U.S. influence. One strategy for dealing with these might work for students from Romance languages: reverse the direction of the letters and translate them. In Spanish, for example, NATO is OTAN and the UN is La ONU. Other students should recognize them as acronyms or abbreviations and look in the text for cues as to what they represent.

Back-formation and clipping are similar processes which yield different results. **Edit** is a back-formation from the word **editor**. In *back-formation*, the original word (editor) is analyzed as having a derivational morpheme at the end **-or**, which means "one who does X." The suffix is removed to form the new verb (**edit**) on analogy with pairs like **act-actor** and **bake-baker**. Thus, usually the word that is formed through back-formation has some kind of grammatical difference from the original word. Often, its part of speech is different, as with **enthuse** from **enthusiastic**. If students know the original word **enthusiastic**, they can use it as a cue to meaning, but they should also notice the change in part of speech. Back-formation explains the neologism echolocate from echolocation that was mentioned earlier.

Prof is a clipped version of **professor**. *Clipping* means shortening a multisyllable word either from the end or from the beginning without much regard for the morphology of the word. Clipping doesn't really derive a new word with a different meaning and part of speech, but rather a different word that is just shorter than the original. **Prof** and **professor** mean the same thing, **math** and **mathematics** mean the same thing, and **golf pro** and **golf professional** mean the same thing. Clipped words differ from abbreviations (of the second type, mentioned earlier) because clipped words can take on a life of their own. They are easier to pronounce and usually slangy or informal. The strategy for reading clipped words is to recognize them as such and relate them to the longer word if it is known. Alternatively, students may be more familiar with the clipped word; if so, they can relate the longer word to it when they see it.

These word formation processes may cause the ESL and EFL student some difficulty in reading, especially authentic materials like academic texts or articles, magazines, and newspapers because acronyms, new blends or coinages, back-formations, clipped forms, and abbreviations may not be in the dictionary and their meanings may not be self-evident.

The use of metaphor to refer to an object, although technically not a word formation process, can also create challenges for readers. A *metaphor* is a figure of speech in which a word which denotes one thing is used in place of another to suggest a likeness or similarity between the two things. Using the word **ice** instead of **diamond** is a metaphor drawing on our awareness that diamonds and ice have similarities in appearance. If a waitress uses the term **ham sandwich** to refer to a customer in the sentence, "The ham sandwich left without paying," she is using a figure of speech drawing on the associated concepts of the individual customer and what he ate. This example of *metonymy*, where a word meaning an attribute or a part (the sandwich) is used in place of another which is the whole (the customer), is a specific type of metaphor.

Understanding a metaphor requires reasoning by analogy. To understand the use of **that old goat** in reference to an elderly character, students must first know that **goat** is being used to refer to the character and not some extraneous animal in the story. They must know what a goat is and what properties could be shared by a goat and an elderly man (e.g., smelly, shaggy, stubborn, reclusive, bossy, stringy, and thin) to successfully understand the analogy. Native-speaking readers can usually understand figures of speech because the meaning associations stored in semantic memory are not self-contained and isolated one from another. Rather, they are widespread networks of interconnected concepts and associations (called schemas) which have been built up through the years as we have learned about words, culture, and the world. Thus, when native-speaking readers come across a figure of speech, the associations evoked allow the readers to understand what the writer is trying to say. ESL and EFL readers may not have the stored cultural concepts and associations to understand common metaphors in English, or they may understand them in an unintended way. In addition, comprehension of metaphor is not universal. It is learned and developmental, and as such, it is reasonable to expect cultural variation in its use and interpretation.

Metaphors can, through repetition, become so conventionalized that they lose their special status as a figure of speech and become merely cases of polysemy. *Polysemy* is not a word formation process, but it can be confusing. It refers to any words which have more than one meaning. In some cases of polysemy, the meanings of the word are clearly related to each other and yet we are quite sure that the meanings are different. An example of this would be the use of the word **mouse**, which began as a metaphor to describe the computer part because of its resemblance to the animal in color, size, and shape, and possession of a tail. Now, many would probably say that the word **mouse** has two clearly different meanings equal in importance: the small animal and the computer part. It is ceasing to be a metaphor and becoming a case of polysemy.

In cases with a longer historical background, the meanings may seem more distant from each other, but we would agree, still, that they are related. An example is the word **point**:

He sharpened the point of the knife (sharp end).
He wasn't sure of the point of the story (purpose).
He made an interesting point (an important detail in his argument).
He walked to a point 10 feet from the outhouse (specific location).
He made a point for his team (a score).
The decimal point is in the wrong place (a mathematical punctuation).

The problem with polysemous words for English L2 learners is that the commonest words tend to have the most meanings and the students only know one or possibly two of the main definitions for a word. Because the word is common, teachers may overlook the difficulty students have with polysemy because they think that students must already know the word.

Polysemous words must be distinguished from homonyms, homophones, and homographs. *Homophones* are different words which happen to have the same pronunciation. There are two types of homophones: those that have different spellings (e.g., through–threw, bear–bare, eight–ate, you–ewe) and those that have the same spellings (e.g., bear–bear, bank–bank, quail–quail). *Homographs* are different words which happen to be spelled the same. Again, there are two different types of homographs: those that are pronounced differently (e.g., bow–bow, lead–lead), and those that are pronounced the same way (e.g., bear–bear, bank–bank, quail–quail).

Homophones		Homographs
I.	II.	III.
through–threw	bear–bear	bow–bow
bear–bare	bank–bank	lead–lead
eight–ate	quail (n)–quail (v)	does–does
sole–soul	left–left	dove–dove
stile–style	file–file	close–close

The words in Column II, which are both homophones and homographs, are called *homonyms*, two different words which have both the same form and the same pronunciation. We can rule out metaphor in these cases because there is no similarity in meaning and we can rule out polysemy in these cases because it seems quite clear that different words are involved, not different meanings of the same word. Homophones, homographs, and especially homonyms, present some of the same decision-making dilemmas as polysemous words. Students may know only one word from a pair, so the meaning they assign is wrong and they won't detect it. If the readers know both words, this can still cause problem-solving nightmares for the reading processor that is developing in the ESL and EFL students because they create lexical ambiguity. If students are aware of two different homonyms, how do they know which one is the intended one for this context? If their comprehension of a text is already shaky, lexical ambiguity could sabotage it completely.

Top-down schema-activating strategies can help with polysemous words and homonyms because they will prime the reader to understand the text the right way from the beginning. Other than that, one strategy is for students to acquire as extensive a semantic memory as possible in L2 and to use syntactic cues to narrow down the part of speech of the word in question.

Any teacher, no matter how novice, will agree that ESL and EFL readers face challenges with vocabulary acquisition, word recognition, word meanings, and grammatical information. This is, of course, supported by research. For example, Schmitt and Meara (1997) found that L2 learners did not have extensive mastery of the word associations even for verbs they reported they "knew." They were only able to produce 50% of the word associations possible as compared to native speaker norms. This indicates that the meaning associations for the verbs they were tested on were only half as elaborated as they were for native speakers. In an earlier paper, Meara (1983) found that L2 learners gave more varied responses to test words than native speakers did and that their associations are often nonrelated words that sound similar instead of words that are related in meaning. This tells us that students' intuitions about words are not conventional. Their associations are simply from phonemic image to the similar phonemic image of other similar words. Their associations between words may not be through meaning at all. Fragmentary knowledge of word meaning has an impact on comprehension. Ying (1996) found that adult English learners' incomplete knowledge of certain types of verbs (e.g., psychological verbs like **think** and perception verbs like **hear**) prevented them from processing sentences like the native speakers did.

ESL and EFL readers also lack syntactic collocational information about the phrases and clauses that the word requires. Lennon (1996) found that advanced learners of English have a broad concept of verb meaning for simple verbs, but their knowledge of contextual and collocational restrictions is not precise. If this is the case, then even advanced ESL readers may have difficulty interpreting syntactic structures and this may influence their ability to comprehend what they are reading. Lennon concluded that even advanced learners may require classroom vocabulary work on simple verbs within their common lexical and syntactic contexts.

PEDAGOGICAL IMPLICATIONS FOR WORD LEARNING AND RECOGNITION

When the participants in Ellis and Beaton's 1993 study repeated the unfamiliar L2 word, their ability to produce the unfamiliar word later was enhanced, presumably because the phonological loop was used and an entry in the mental lexicon was constructed. When they used a keyword strategy, their ability to translate the L2 word to the L1 word was enhanced. Translation of the L2 word to L1 is considered to be a receptive skill, but probably appropriate to reading. A keyword strategy was one where the foreign word is associated with the L1 word by means of a mediating word which is similar to the foreign word in sound. For example, the Spanish word for **bread** is **pan**; English-speaking learners of Spanish might visualize a loaf of bread in a pan. The Spanish equivalent (pan) for one word (bread) is learned by mediation of a similar sounding English word (pan). The keyword in this case is the English word "pan." The keyword strategy in some ways might be similar to a visual or Kanji strategy for word identification, but there are some important differences. First of all, Ellis and Beaton found that acoustic similarity enhanced the association between the target unknown word and the native language keyword. This means that the target word is being processed phonologically and a phonologically similar (but not orthographically similar) word is chosen as keyword. In the Kanji strategy, the target word is not processed phonologically. The keyword strategy is also different in that the mediating image or sentence probably improves memory for meaning over a purely visual strategy in which an English word is associated by rote with a sinogram.

According to sources cited in Ellis and Beaton (1993), the keyword method of learning vocabulary is superior to rote rehearsal or presenting vocabulary in context; however, they pointed out the following:

> However, theories of FL vocabulary learning and the role of phonological memory systems typically fail to make the important distinction concerning direction of translation. The present study's finds suggest that phonological factors are more implicated in productive learning when the student has a greater cognitive burden in terms of sensory and motor learn. Ellis and Beaton (in press) demonstrate from individual differences analyses that *although keyword techniques are efficient means for receptive vocabulary learning; for productive learning they are less effective than repetition* (at least for learners naïve to the pronunciation patterns of the foreign language). (p. 601; emphasis added)

MariCarmen and Despina can supplement their natural tendency to use L1 to L2 cognates to identify new words with these methods. Mohammed and Ho especially need these methods to increase their productive and receptive vocabulary for reading and writing. They will be a lot better off in the long run than if they just skip the words they don't know. Certainly, at the early stages of English L2 reading, all new words should be learned productively through repetition, because the words common in early reading are likely to be common in listening, speaking, and writing, as well. Even in later advanced reading, most words should be learned productively so that they can transfer from reading to writing. However, there might be occasions, in very advanced stages of reading acquisition, that readers might wish to apply the keyword strategy to remember some unfamiliar words which they will not be using in writing. These findings suggest that teachers should teach vocabulary in reading class in certain ways to empower students to become active human word processors:

- To the extent that it is possible, choose readings that contain only a limited number of new words. Readings should be considered comprehensible input, that is, just slightly above the student's true reading level at present.
- Provide ample opportunities for students to read on their own for pleasure outside of class.
- Continue using the top-down reading strategies to prepare students to read effectively.
- Teach vocabulary and reading in the context of English phonology, orthography, morphology, word formation processes, and grammar to make more new words more pronounceable, repeatable, and comprehensible to the students.
- Teach vocabulary items with their part of speech and teach words, especially verbs, in collocations (Lewis, 1993, 1997).
- Teach students different word learning and recognition strategies to apply on their own while they are reading, to be proactive about increasing their overall vocabulary and comprehension and to decrease reliance on ineffective visual strategies.
- Teach students to distinguish between words to be learned productively (most words) and words to be learned receptively (a few words).

Spotlight on Teaching

These two strategies, repetition and keyword, can be modeled and practiced for learning new words, instead of skipping them. For words to be learned productively, the repetition strategy is best:

- Look at an unfamiliar words carefully using an onset-rime strategy and knowledge of English morphophonemic writing (to form a graphemic image); try to pronounce it (to form a phonological image and to activate the phonological loop). Pronounce it several times (to store it in long-term memory). An incorrect pronunciation probably doesn't matter and is better than no pronunciation.
- Look at the syntactic and meaning context and try to determine something of the new word's part of speech and definition.

For words to be learned receptively in reading, model and practice the keyword approach:

- Look at the word carefully (to form a graphemic image). Try to pronounce it once.
- Try to determine something of the word's meaning and part of speech from the context.
- Associate the sound of the L2 word with a similar L1 word and relate them through a visual image or a sentence.

Select a reading passage from an ESL and EFL textbook. Identify five words to be learned productively and two words to be learned receptively. Design classroom activities around these words.

DISCUSSION QUESTIONS

1. Do you have any idea why ESL students made these mistakes in compositions they wrote while consulting small L1 to L2 dictionaries?
    a. The ambulance went down the street with its mermaid on.
    b. Please cast the sugar into the coffee.
    c. That joke shamed me.
    d. We were expecting the bus for 45 min and then we left.
2. In this chapter, we discussed what information there might be within the lexical entries. Write lexical entries for the following verbs: **expect, hope, wait for**. Comment on similar aspects of the meanings of these words. Can this explain some of the ESL learner's difficulty with these words?
3. Lexical entries containing grammatical information are linked by association to meaning concepts (memories) in semantic memory, where we store the encyclopedic knowledge of the words of our language. Words have denotations and connotations. What is the denotation of the following words: chair, art, density, and happy? What is difference in the connotation of the following words: slim versus skinny, mother versus welfare mother, and statesman versus politician?
4. Try to identify the following words as homophones, homographs, or homonyms (use a dictionary if necessary): tied–tide, do (v)–do (musical note), pine–pine, row–row (a kind of fight), tea–tee, seal–seal, toe–tow, tic–tick, polish–Polish, and colon–colon.
5. Go through the steps of what would happen in your reading processor if you came across the following new words in the newspaper: (a) When the congressman spoke to the women, his *Clintonism* was apparent, and (b) It's time to apply some *orlandotherapy*.
6. Is it possible to put all of your thoughts or experiences into words? What thoughts or experiences are resistant to "lexification"? (Can you understand that new word based on its morphology?)

Chapter 10

Getting to the Bottom of English L2 Reading

This book has explored some of the exciting new research in the area of English L1 and L2 reading and offered a new concept of the proficient ESL and EFL reader: that of an expert decision-making and problem-solving mind that uses extensive knowledge of language and the world, effective cognitive comprehension strategies, and quick automatic low-level processing strategies to interact with the text efficiently. The discussion in this book has aimed specifically at getting to the bottom of the reading processor, that is, reinforcing and strengthening our understanding and appreciation for the details of low-level knowledge and processing strategies our students need to read in English.

This focus, however, doesn't mean that higher-level knowledge of the world and top-down processing strategies are less important. In fact, the bottom of the reading processor serves the top because the more efficiently and "quietly" the bottom functions, the more attention there will be for higher-level processing of meaning, implications, outside references, and so on. Language processing skills are one subcomponent of more general cognitive processing; linguistic knowledge is just one area of the complete knowledge about the world, culture, or personal memories of the reader. This is a more balanced and integrated view of reading, worthy of the name "whole language."

The balanced integrated perspective offers a different picture of what "guessing" involves: split-second decisions based on accurate perception, reasoning abilities, and stored knowledge. To make good guesses, an ESL and EFL reader must pass through the various stages of acquisition posited by Chall (1983) and Ehri (1998). Although they can be assisted through early to advanced reading by teachers who get them started and guide them with the right strategies and knowledge, the best way for readers themselves to acquire automaticity with bottom-level processing is by extensive active practice with reading material that is enjoyable and easy. Extensive practice means students reading inside the classroom to learn and apply strategies, and reading outside the classroom to perfect their skills with interesting relevant fiction or nonfiction. If readers are motivated to read on their own (and this is where social factors such as peer pressure or cultural appreciation and ownership of literacy and literature also play a role), they will become expert unconscious decision makers and problem solvers.

They say that a long journey always begins with the first step. A lifelong rewarding journey of English reading also begins with the first tentative attempts of EFL and EFL students like Mohammed, Ho, Despina, and MariCarmen to decode our morphophonemic writing. The earliest step (in fact, a prereading step) in learning to read is, of course, listening comprehension. Study after study has shown the importance of phonological awareness, especially segmentation skills, in early reading for native English readers. Phonological awareness is acquired through aural and oral activities, but total mastery of the sounds of English is not necessary before beginning to read. Often, learning the letter shapes and sounds together can bootstrap phonological awareness. Students need to learn the alphabetic principle anyway, so teachers should teach it explicitly.

For some learners, their L1 orthography matters a lot. For them, the process must begin with slow and laborious acquisition and practice with English orthography. Teachers must not rush ESL and EFL students through this stage, but allow them to continue to read easy texts for as long as necessary. It is important to recall that native-speaking children learning to read English show great variety in how long it takes them to become good readers. Some are reading well at 4 years of age; others take until the age of 7 or 8 to read well. In our anxiety to show progress in English L2 reading, we often rush students into texts that are too difficult, without allowing them the time to acquire automaticity with English graphemes and common spelling patterns. We will rush our students if we overlook or minimize the complex task of switching from their L1 orthography to English.

Just as we have gained insight into the need for a "silent period" in speech production for some students, and have therefore tried to avoid pushing learners into speaking before they are ready, we also need to respect the need for ESL and EFL students to have the time and opportunity to acquire automaticity in reading before moving on to challenging material. To build this time and opportunity into the reading curriculum may mean expanding our notion of the beginning and intermediate student. One or two courses at these levels may not be sufficient for everyone.

During this expanded curriculum, students may benefit from practice sounding out words without worrying about their pronunciation. They also need numerous ways of getting feedback on the connection between graphemes and phonemes: listening to stories while they follow along or reading out loud to someone else in a safe, nonjudgmental environment. They should not resort to the strategies that may have transferred from the L1 orthography, such as the visual strategy or the partial alphabetic strategy. The fully alphabetic strategy may be a good jumping off point for ESL and EFL students, because it helps them implicitly learn the probabilities that a grapheme will be pronounced a certain way, as long as they are getting accurate feedback. However, instead of using each syllable as a reading unit, teachers need to instruct students in the 100 or so common spelling-to-sound patterns that form the basis for reading by analogy in the consolidated alphabetic stage.

Only very advanced ESL and EFL readers can read by "sampling" the text, with few short fixations and few regressions. It often takes a lot of effort, practice, and learning to get to that point. All of the processing strategies summarized in Fig. 10.1 must be working together so accurately and efficiently that they work at an unconscious level. All the knowledge of English graphemes, morphemes, and words must be readily accessible in long-term memory. ESL and EFL readers must be active, soaking up and storing new words, morphemes, and meaning in their knowledge base for receptive and productive use. For them to learn to do this, early reading must be carefully controlled to be at their comfortable but challenging level and they should not be pushed into reading texts that are too challenging too soon. They should be able to take to time to practice word learning strategies like the phonological loop or the keyword strategy.

As our students take their first steps on the reading pilgrimage, let's give them the best provisions and tools we can. Let's make their first steps as confident and effective as possible so they can read faster and easier later. We can do this if we get to the bottom of English L2 reading.

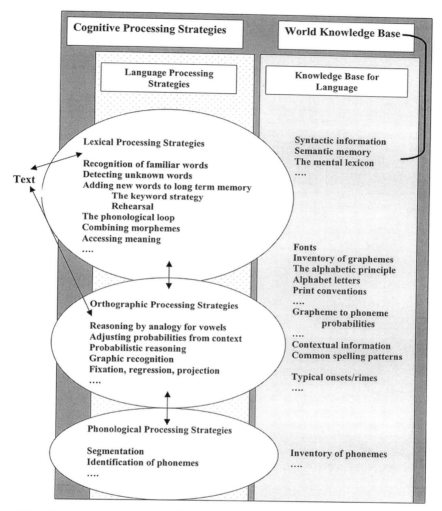

FIG. 10.1   A hypothetical model of the bottom of the reading processor.

Appendix A

ENGLISH GRAPHEMES

Venezky's 1970 book, *The Structure of English*, is still one of the most comprehensive treatments of English spelling conventions, and I summarize and update a significant portion here with permission of the publisher, Mouton de Gruyter.

Most people can understand that consonant and vowel graphemes are used to correspond roughly to consonant and vowel phonemes, and that is our first topic in this appendix. However, there is another use for graphemes. Graphemes are sometimes used merely to give hints to the reader about how to pronounce other graphemes in the word; if they serve this purpose, they are called **markers**. The most common example of that is the so-called silent **e**, which clues the reader in to the pronunciation of the previous vowel, as in **pine** versus **pin**, or **vane** versus **van**. We start our discussion with an exposition of the major and minor graphemes in English, then we explore some of the uses of graphemes as markers. Simple graphemes or digraphs are those that correspond to a single phoneme; compound graphemes act as if they were "doubled."

The Consonant Grapheme to Phoneme Correspondences

Consonant Graphemes

simple						**compound**
b	g	kh	q	t	wh	ck
c	gh	l	r	th	y	dg
ch	h	m	s	u	z	tch
d	j	n	sh	v		x
f	k	p	sch	w		geminated consonants

Notes: a. **u** is a consonant unit when it corresponds to /w/, as in qu**a**ck or lang**u**age.

b. **wh** is mainly used as a simple consonant corresponding to the voiced /w/ or the voiceless /ʍ/. In some dialects, **wh** seems to have a compound usage /hw/ as in the "voiceless" pronunciations of the beginning consonants of **wh**at, **wh**ich, and **wh**en.

c. **sch** is a simple consonant grapheme when it is used as in **sch**ist or **sch**wa.

d. **gn** is a simple consonant grapheme when it is used as in **gn**ome, co**gn**ac, or poi**gn**ant

e. Geminated consonants are compound consonants which are simple consonants doubled: **bb, dd, ff, gg, ll, mm, nn, pp, rr, tt, zz, ck, dg,** and **tch**, as in e**bb**, e**dd**y, ga**ff**er, e**gg**, fe**ll**, di**mm**er, di**nn**er, a**pp**le, pu**rr**, be**tt**er, bu**zz**, ba**ck**, e**dg**e, and wa**tch**.

---

b   **b** in de**b**t, dou**b**t, su**b**tle = /0/.

final **b** in bom**b**, com**b**, tom**b**, crum**b** = /0/.

b and **bb** elsewhere = /b/.

Note: 1. /0/ means that the grapheme is not pronounced.

2. When there are two bilabial consonants in the middle of a word, only the second is pronounced: cu**p**board, su**b**poena, cla**p**board, ras**p**berry.

3. Note these **nonproductive** alternations. Nonproductive means that people do not make up new words following this pattern:

bombard	bomb
crumble	crumb
debit	debt
iambic	iamb
indubitable	doubt
number	numeric
rhombus	rhomb
thimble	thumb

c c in cello and concerto = /tʃ/.

c in victual, czar, and indict =/0/.

c before i, y, e (and in facade) = /s/.

c elsewhere = /k/.

Note: 1. Unproductive alternations: corpuscular–corpuscle, muscular–muscle.

ch ch in fuchsia or yacht = /0/.

ch = /k/ before **l**, **n**, **r**, and in the following examples of words of Latin or Greek origin:

ache	chasm	hypochondria
alchemy	chemi-	lichen
anarchy	chiropodist	machination
anchor	choir	mechanic
archaeology	cholera	monarchy
archaic	choral	orchestra
archangel	chord	orchid
archetype	chorus	parochial
architecture	dichotomy	patriarch
archive	echo	pentateuch
catechism	epoch	psych-
chameleon	eucharistst	omach

chaos eunuch character

hierarchy

ch = /ʃ/ in the following words of French origin:

cache	chassis	chivalry
chagrin	chateau	chute
chaise	chauffeur	cliche
chalet	chauvinism	crochet
chaperon	chef	echelon
chamois	chemise	machine
champagne	chiffon	mustache
chandelier	chevalier	parachute
charlatan	ricochet	
charade	chic	

ch elsewhere = /tʃ/.

d   **d** = /0/ between /n/ and another consonant, as in han**d**kerchief or gran**d**mother.

d elsewhere = /d/.

Note these unproductive alternations: defend–defense, expend–expense, respond–response.

f   **f** in of = /v/.

f elsewhere = /f/.

Note that in the following words, **f** becomes **v** when the word is made plural: calf, elf, half, knife, leaf, life, loaf, self, sheaf, shelf, thief, wife, wolf.

In the following words, **f** becomes **v** when a noun becomes a verb: belief, grief, half, life, proof, relief, shelf.

Similarly, there are some other unproductive alternations: bereft–bereave, cleft–cleave, drift–drive, fifth–five, gift–give, left–leave, serf–serve, twelfth–twelve. The **f/v** alternations stem from a regular phonological process in the history of English. This phonological process is no longer productive.

g   **g** = / ʒ / in the following words of French origin:

bourgeois	mirage
camouflage	prestige
corsage	protege
garage	regime
lingerie	rouge
massage	sabotage

g = /g/ before e, i, y in the following large number of "exceptions."

begin	gift	girth
eager	finger	gear
geese	get	gig
giggle	gild	gill
gird	girdle	girl
give	gynaecology	hunger
lager	linger	malinger
target	tiger	yogi

g = /dʒ / before e, i, and y, generally

g = /g/ elsewhere

Notes   **ng** becomes / ŋ / except in comparative and superlative forms of adjectives, where it remains /ng/ as in strong–stro**ng**er.

gn in word initial position = /n/ as in **gn**ome.

gm and **gn** at the end of words = /m/ and /n/ respectively.

gh   **gh** = /f/ in these: cough, rough, enough, tough, laughter.

gh = /g/ at the beginning of words: ghost, ghetto, and in aghast, spaghetti.

gh elsewhere = /0/.

h   **h** = /0/ in heir, honor, herb, hour, vehicle, and other words of
    French origin.

h = /0/ preceded by a consonant: philharmonic.

h = /h/ elsewhere.

j   **j** = / dʒ/ except in words borrowed from Spanish:
    Juan, marijuana.

k   **k** = /k/.
    Note: in **kn**, **k** = /0/ except in **acknowledge**, possible because of
       the **c**.

    Nonproductive alternations: speak–speech, leak–leach,
       wreak–wretch, wicca–witch.

l   **l** in the word colonel = /r/.

    l in would, could, should, half, calm, chalk = /0/.

    l otherwise = /l/.
    Note: **l** occurs in many consonant clusters: **pl, bl, cl, chl, gl, fl, sl,
       spl** at the beginning of words; **lp, lt, ld, lk, lch, lm, rl, rld,
       lb** at the ending of words.

    le at the end of words is syllabic (is pronounced like a syllable / əl/)
       as in sim**ple**, ket**tle**, and net**tle**.

m   **m** = /m/.
    Note: the initial cluster **mn** = /n/ mnemonic.

n   **n** = /n/.
    Note: **n** before **k** and **g** becomes / ŋ /.

p   **p** = /0/ in corps, coup, and receipt and the first p in sapphire.

    p in clusters **pn, ps**, and **pt** = /0/, as in pneumonia, psychology, and
       ptomaine.

    p elsewhere = /p/.

ph ph = /f/.

q q = /k/ and always appears before **u**.

r r = /r/.

Note: r occurs in many clusters: **br, chr, cr, dr, fr, gr, phr, pr, scr, shr, spr, str, thr, wr** at the beginning of words; and **rb, rp, rd, rt, rg, rf, rth, rsh, rch, rm, rn, rl, rpt, rst, rld** at the end of words. **r** in the sequence **er** becomes a syllabic r as in butter, better, and baker.

rh rh = /r/, as in rhino, cirrhosis.

s s = /s/ at the beginning of words and at the end of words, generally.

s = /s/ in the middle of a word before or after a voiceless consonant.

s = /z/ after a voiced consonant and in as, has, his, is, and was.

s = /z/ elsewhere, as in design, dissolve; the verbs: house, use, and close.

Note: s occurs in many clusters: **ps, sc, sch, schw, scl, scr, sk, sl, sm, sn, sp, sph, spl, spr, squ, st, str, sv, sw** at the beginning of words; and **sp, st, sk, rst** at the end of words.

Note: s = /0/ in aisle, corps, island, isle, bourgeois, chamois, Illinois, debris, and rendezvous. Some of these words have an s inserted in the spelling for no good reason and some are of French origin.

sh sh = /ʃ/.

t t = /0/ in some clusters as in listen, often, soften, and castle.

t = /t/ elsewhere except when palatalized in derivational morphology.

t = /0/ in depot, debut, and mortgage, and in words ending in et with the accent on the final syllable: valet, buffet, and ballet. These words are of French origin.

Note: t occurs in many clusters: **pt, st, str, tr, tw** at the beginning of words; and **ct, ft, ght, lt, mpt, nct, nt, pt, rpt, rst, rt, st, tz, xt** at the ending of words.

th   **th** in thyme and Thomas = /t/.

     th in clothes, isthmus, and asthma = /0/.

     th at the beginning of function words = /ð / as in the, this, that, and then.

     th in the middle of words and in -the, or -ther = / ð /, hither, clothe, and brother.

     th elsewhere = / θ /.
     Note   these nonproductive alternations: bath–bathe, breath–breathe, cloth–clothe, north–northern, south–southern, teeth–teethe, and worth–worthy.

u   **u** = /w/ after **q** and in some cases after **s**: suede, persuade.
    Note   in forms ending in -que, -quet, quette, and in the words liquor, piquant = /0/.

v   **v** = /v/.

w   **w** = /0/ in answer, sword, two, and toward.

     w = /w/ elsewhere.

wh **wh** in who, whore, and whole = /h/.

     elsewhere, **wh** = /w/.
     Note: Some people have /hw/ or / ʍ / in what, where, which and so on, but this is becoming increasingly rare.

x   **x** = /z/ at the beginning of words.

     x = /gz/ in the middle of words, if the preceding vowel is unstressed: exaggerate.

     x = /ks/ elsewhere.

y   **y** = /y/ as in yes, yet.

z   **z** in final **tz** = /s/ as in chintz or glitz.
     z = /z/ otherwise.

tch tch = /tʃ/ as in kitchen, match.

ck ck = /k/ in back or pick.

dg dg = /dʒ/ in edge, midget.

> There has been a general tendency to replace geminate consonants in Latin words with the aforementioned English complex digraphs, but these are exceptions: exaggerate, account.

gn gn = /n/ in champagne and /ny/ in mignon, poignant and vignette.

kh kh = /k/ in khan and khaki.

sch sch = /ʃ/ in shist and schwa.
Note: All of these words are borrowed from other languages.

THE VOWEL GRAPHEME TO PHONEME CORRESPONDENCES

The grapheme to phoneme correspondences for consonants are fairly regular, in spite of what you might think after reading the previous information, but the correspondence between vowel graphemes and vowel phonemes is more unpredictable. Spoken English has had a very unstable vowel system for a number of centuries. Sociolinguists tell us that vowel changes are still occurring.

Vowel Graphemes			
primary	**secondary**		
a	ai/ay	ie	ue
e	au/aw	oa	ui
i	ea	oe	ae
o	ee	oi/oy	eau
u	ei/ey	oo	eo
y	eu/ew	ou/ow	uy

MAJOR PATTERNS FOR VOWELS

Spelling	Phoneme Correspondence	
	Tense V plus Glide	Lax
a	/ey/	/æ/
	sane	sanity
	mate	mat
	ration	rattle
e	/iy/	/ɛ/
	athlete	athletic
	mete	met
	penal	pennant
i	/ɑy/	/ɪ/
	rise	risen
	malign	malignant
	site	sit
o	/ow/	/ɑ/
	cone	conic
	robe	rob
	posy	possible
u	/uw/	/ʌ/
	induce	induction
	rude	rudder
	lucre	luxury

Notes: 1. Generally, the tense vowel with a glide is pronounced
when it is in the context of the following:
   a. A single consonant grapheme followed by another
   vowel (penal, rise, cone, rude, etc.).
   b. A single consonant grapheme followed by a liquid (**l**
   or **r**) and then a vowel (ladle, zebra, noble, microbe).
2. Generally, the lax vowel is pronounced when it is in the
context of the following:

       a. A compound grapheme or a cluster of consonants
        (ba**dg**e, sa**ddl**e, e**x**it, ante**nn**a, chi**ck**en, epi**st**le,
        po**ck**et, co**gn**ate, lu**x**ury, su**pp**er).
       b. A consonant at the end of a word (sa**t**, e**bb**, hi**tch**, so**d**,
        ru**g**).
   3. When a vowel is followed by /r/, the vowel is often dis-
     torted from its principle pronunciation. In the word **bird**
     or **girl**, we might expect [ɪ], yet the /r/ seems to over-
     power or even replace the vowel. We might expect [ʌ] in
     fur, **hurry**, or **urn**, yet again we see that the vowel has
     been replaced by an [ɾ]. When an [ɾ] replaces a vowel
     phone, it is called a syllabic r or [ɾ̩], pronounced like
     [əɾ].

o   When **o** (expected to be pronounced /ɑ/) is followed by a final **-ll**
    and a medial or final **l** plus a consonant, it is pronounced /o/:
    bold, polka, folk, jolt, molt, scold, told, yolk, and troll. In the
    following words, we do find the expected pronunciation: pollen,
    trolley.

i   before a final **-nd**, **-ld**, and **gn/gm** ⇒ /ɑy/, instead of /ɪ/: behind,
    mind, child, mild, align, sign, and paradigm.

i   before **-gh-** ⇒ /ay/. The **-gh-** is not pronounced. Examples follow:
    light, bright, sigh, and so forth. Note these other correspon-
    dences that hold before **-gh-**:

        ai before **-gh-** ⇒ /ey/ as in straight.

        au before **-gh-** ⇒ /æ/ as in laugh, draught (gh ⇒ /f/).

        au before **-gh-** ⇒ /ɔ/ as in caught, daughter, naughty,
         taught, and so forth.

        ei before **-gh-** ⇒ /ey/ as in sleigh, freight, neighbor.

        ei before **-gh-** ⇒ /ɑy/ as in height.

        ou before **-gh-** ⇒ /ʌ/ as in enough, rough, tough.

        ou before **-gh-** ⇒ /o/ as in dough, furlough, thorough,
         though.

        ou before **-gh-** ⇒ /u/ as in through.

        ou before **-gh-** ⇒ /aw/ as in bough.

        ou before **-gh-** ⇒ /ɔ/ or /ɑ/ as in bought, ought, cough,
         fought, trough.

ai/ay ⇒ /ey/ as in bait, day, player, wait,

   OR   /ɑy/ in aisle, bayou, cayenne,

        ɛ/ in again, said, against,

        / æ / in plaid.

au/aw ⇒ /ɔ/ or /ɑ/ in audience, claw, cause,

   OR   /e/ in gauge,

        /æ/ in aunt, laugh,

        /o/ in chauffer, chauvinist, mauve (from French),

        /ɑw/ in sauerkraut, umlaut (from German).

ea ⇒ /iy/ as in breach, reach, teach,

   OR   /e/ in break, great, reach, teach,

        /ɛ/ before -l, in health, realm, wealth, before -sure, in measure, treasure, pleasure, and in the following frequent words:

bread	spread	endeavor	pheasant
breadth	thread	feather	sweat
dead	tread	weather	sweater
dread	treadle	heaven	threat
head	breast	heavy	treachery
instead	breath	leather	weapon
meadow	deaf	leaven	ready
death	peasant		

ee ⇒ / iy / as in bleed, eel, absentee,

   OR   /ɪ / as in been, breeches, creek,

        /ey/ as in matinee, melee.

ei/ey ⇒ /ey/ as in obey, reign, veil,

      OR /ɑy/ as in eye, fahrenheit, geyser, height, stein, walleye,

          /iy/ as in caffein, ceiling, conceit, deceive, either, key, leisure, neither, seize,

          /ɛ/ as in heifer.

eu/ew ⇒ /yu/ as in ewe, eucharist, neutron, pewter.

          /ow/ as in sew.

ie ⇒ /ɑy/ (in final position in monosyllable words): die, lie, pie, tie.

          /iy/ in final position in polysyllabic words): calorie, collie, eerie, movie and in medial position: achieve, diesel, niece, yield,

      OR /ey/ in lingerie,

          /ɪ/ in sieve,

          / ɛ / in friend.

Note: allied, applied, dried, and so forth, are ally + ed, apply + ed, dry + ed;. bodied, candied, studied are body + ed, candy + ed, study + ed.

oa ⇒ / ow / as in approach, boast, goal, shoal,

      OR / ɔ / or /ɑ/ as in broad.

oi/oy ⇒ /oy/ as in boy, join, loiter, oyster,

      OR /ɑy/ as in coyote,

          /iy/ as in chamois,

          / ə/ as mademoiselle, porpoise, tortoise.

oo ⇒ /uw/ as in boot, broom, proof, tycoon, pooh,

      OR / ʌ/ as blood, blood,

          /ow/ as in brooch,

/ ʊ/ as in book, foot, look, shook, wood, brook, forsook, mistook, soot, wool, cook, good, nook, stood, crook, hook, rook, took.

ou/ow ⟹   /ɑw/ as in abound, crown, mountain, owl, allow, brow, cow, endow, how, now, plow, sow, prow, thou, vow.

/ow/ as in arrow, bow, glow, pillow, mow, sow.

/ʌ/ as in double, trouble, country, enough, young, couple, touch, cousin, rough, tough, boulevard, could, should, would.

/ ɔ/ or /a/ as in cough, trough.

/ow/ as in boulder, bowl, cantaloup, mould, owe, own, poultice, shoulder, soul, thorough.

/uw/ as in bayou, cougar, group, caribou, routine, troubadour, rendezvous, soup, uncouth, boudoir, coupon, rouge, souvenir, vermouth, ghoul, route, toucan.

ui   ⟹   /uw/ bruise, nuisance, pursuit, suitor,

OR /ɪ/ as in biscuit, build, circuit.

THE USE OF GRAPHEMES AS MARKERS

So far the major and minor uses of consonant and vowel graphemes have more or less directly represented phonemes. We turn now to discuss the use of graphemes, not to represent phonemes, but rather to give information about other grapheme to phoneme correspondences elsewhere in the word. These markers give information about the way that other graphemes in the word are to be interpreted and pronounced.

1. The final **e** generally indicates the pronunciation of the previous vowel.

Tense vowel or diphthong:	Lax vowel
mate	mat
mete	met
site	sit
note	not
cute	cut

2. The final **e** sometimes indicates the pronunciation of the previous consonant as in the word peace. The final **e** in peace indicates both the pronunciation of the previous vowel as /iy/, and that the **c** corresponds to its "soft" alternative pronunciation: /s/ and not /k/. This principle is the same in words like bath and bathe, where the final **e** in the verb marks not only the vowel, but also the voiced pronunciation of the **th**, or /ð /. The final **e** in age or college indicates the "soft" or affricate pronunciation of **g**, /dʒ/.

3. The **u** in guest marks that the **g** is a "hard" (or stopped) /g/ and not its soft (or affricate) alternative: / dʒ/ guess, guide, guest, guise, catalogue, guilt, plague, guild. (Note that catalogue has an alternative catalog, because it is clear that the final **g** would be hard. This alternative is not available for plague (i.e., plag) because the vowel sound would be distorted. The final **e** maintains the tense pronunciation of the vowel as /ey/.)

4. Geminated consonants mark the preceding vowel as lax; examples follow: anal/annals, fetal/fetter, hypo/hippo, rotor/rotter, super/supper.

5. Suffixing:
Final **e**, when it marks the preceding **c** or **g** as soft (fricative /s/ or affricate /dʒ/) or hard (stop /k/ or /g/) is dropped when followed by a suffix that achieves the same purpose. For example, where the final **e** marks the **c** as /s/, it can be dropped when adding -ing, because the **i** in the suffix also marks the **c** as soft, but it must be retained in the word noticeable because the following **a** would make the pronunciation of the **c** "harden" to /k/ if the word were spelled "*noticable." (The asterisk marks a word that is incorrect.)

When a suffix like -ing is added to a word with a final "hard" **c** as in traffic, to make the word trafficking, note that a **k** must be inserted so that the hardness of the **c** is retained. Other words like this follow: picnic: picnicking, panic, panicky, shellac, and shellacked.

6. Graphemes inserted to make words consistent with English spelling patterns. Some of these spelling patterns appear to have arisen because of legibility problems when manuscripts were handwritten, so they are very old patterns.
    a. The final **u** is not allowed, so **e** is inserted in continue and blue, but note that this final **e** is dropped when suffixes are added because the **u** is no longer final: argue, arguing. Similar words follow: glue, plague.
    b. The final **v** is not allowed generally, so an **e** is inserted at the end: love, glove, have. (Note that these appear to be counterexamples to the tense vowel and final **e** rule, but they are mandated by spelling patterns which do not allow a final **v**.
    c. Some common words would have consisted of two letters and in general, two letter words are not allowed, so an extra **e** has been added: see, doe, toe, rye, axe, foe, hoe, sloe. (Note that many of these words have **o**, so the final **e** also serves to mark the vowel as tense.)
    d. Final **dg** is not allowed, so an **e** is inserted in words like edge, hedge, badge. (Note that these appear to be counterexamples to the use of final **e** as a vowel marker; here it is only used to make the words consistent with spelling patterns.)

7. Some patterns are based on confusions with the addition of suffixes. In some words that would end in **s**, an **e** has been added to avoid the appearance of a plural word. The idea is that "moos" looks like a plural of "moo," so **e** is added to form moose. Similar cases follow: goose, mouse, hearse, house, praise, raise, noise, poise. There are some adjectives and verbs that also avoid a final **s**: collapse, eclipse, dense, sense, else, false, coarse.

Exceptions follow: summons, lens, and words ending in ous. (Note that many people misspell the singular lens as lense, supported by the plural lenses, so it is in the process possibly of becoming a regular spelling.) Other exceptions are hydraulics, mathematics, mumps, and billiards, which can be either singular or plural. When **s** is preceded by a simple vowel, **e** is not added because the resulting pronunciation might be distorted: us/use, his/rise, locus/recluse, tennis/improvise.

COMMON GRAPHEMIC ALTERNATIONS

Sometimes there is a fairly regular pattern of alternative graphemes used in particular positions in the word:

1. **i** and **y**: Generally **i** occurs in initial or medial position; **y** in final position. However, there are many exceptions; for instance, **y** occurs in medial position in Greek and Latin borrowed words like embryo, asylum, and rhythm. Some exceptions, like rye and bye, have come about because final **es** were added to avoid two letter words. Sometimes earlier scribes substituted medial **y**s for **i**s to make words seem more learned: rhyme instead of the older form: rime on a mistaken analogy with rhythm. Final **i** occurs in a few patterns: plural of Latin words—alumni, fungi, cacti, and stimuli are examples; plural of Italian borrowings—broccoli, confetti, ravioli, macaroni, and spaghetti; other borrowed words—alkali, potpourri (Fr), anti (Gr.), ski (Norwegian), chili (Mexican Spanish), khaki (Urdu), mufti (Arabic), and yogi (Hindustani); apparently the spelling with **i** was kept to maintain their appearance as foreign. Taxi is an American clipped word from taximeter.

   In suffixes—when words end in **ie**, **e** is dropped and the **i** changes to **y** to add the suffix -ing, presumably to avoid the two **ii**s that would result: die/dying (not diing), tie/tying (not tiing).

   When a suffix is added to a base word ending in **y**, icy, the **y** is changed to **i**, iciest, mercy, and merciless. These then follow the consistent pattern where **i** occurs medially. Similarly, consider day/daily, say/said, or lay/laid.

2. **u** and **w**: **u** appears instead of **w** in **gu**, **su**, **qu**, **nu**, **pu**, and **cu**. **w** occurs elsewhere (except for suave, suede, and suite).
   gu: anguish, distinguish, extinguish, jaguar, language, languid, linguistics.
   su: persuade, assuage.
   pu: pueblo.
   nu: ennui.
   cu: cuisine.

   Another pattern (but with many exceptions) is that with **a**, **e**, and **o**; the **w** variant occurs before another vowel and in morpheme final position, when the **u** occurs elsewhere:
   au: auction, audit, applaud, fault, trauma.
   aw: awe, draw, gnaw, saw, straw, thaw.

eu: eulogy, eucharist, feud, neuter, pneumatic, rheumatism.
ew: ewe, brewer, flew, threw.
ou: ounce, oust, out, compound, trousers.
ow: coward, however, power, allow, cow, vow.

Exceptions follow:

aw before a consonant: awkward, awl, awning, dawn, scrawl, spawn.

ew in medial position before a consonant: newt, pewter, lewd, shrewd.

ow in initial and medial position before a consonant: owl, own, crowd, drowse, fowl, town.

ou in final position: bayou, caribou, bijou (Fr), and you, thou.

u in final position is generally avoided (mentioned earlier), but in these words borrowed mainly from Fr: beau, bureau, chateau, plateau, trousseau, adieu, lieu, menu, tabu. Flu is a clipped form of influenza; presumably the **e** was not added to maintain the connection with influenza and avoid confusion with "flue."

ous becomes **os** before **ity**: viscous—viscosity, curious—curiosity, generous—generosity, monstrous—monstrosity.

Appendix B

ENGLISH PHONEMES AND THEIR PRINCIPAL SPELLINGS

This information is adapted from *Word Recognition: The Why and How* (pp. 20–28), by P. Groff and D. Seymour, 1987, Springfield, IL: Thomas, and used by permission of the author.

CHART OF ENGLISH CONSONANT PHONEMES AND THEIR PRINCIPAL SPELLINGS

In this table, we find the consonant phonemes in English, their most common graphemic representations, and the percentage of occurrence of the major relations associating a particular phoneme with a grapheme.

Phonemic Symbol	Most Frequent Spellings	Frequency	Other Spellings
b	**b**at	97	e**bb**
p	**p**at	96	ha**pp**y
d	**d**ot	98	a**dd**
t	**t**ap	98	pu**tt**
g	**g**ot	88	e**gg**, e**x**act, ro**gue**
k	**c**at	73	ba**ck**, s**ch**ool, e**x**it, oc**c**upy
	keep	13	

Phonemic Symbol	Most Frequent Spellings	Frequency	Other Spellings
tʃ	chap	55	watch
	culture	31	
dʒ	gem	66	budget, educate
	jet	22	
v	vat	99.5	
f	fat	78	phone, off
ð	the	100	
θ	thin	100	
z	as	64	buzz, dessert
	zap	23	
s	sat	73	pass, scent
	cent	17	
ʒ	fusion	82	regime
ʃ	action	53	social, mission, pension, ocean, chef
	shut	26	
h	hit	98	who
m	man	94	mummy
n	not	97	inn
ŋ	sing	59	
	bank	41	
l	lap	91	all, able
r	run	97	purr
y	senior	55	
	yet	44	
w	wet	92	liquid

CHART OF SIMPLE ENGLISH VOWEL PHONEMES
AND THEIR PRINCIPAL SPELLINGS

Phonemic Symbol	Most Frequent Spellings	Frequency	Other Spellings
I	it	66	give, senate, and before r, hero, hear
	myth	23	deer, here, pier, souvenir, fierce, weird
æ	at	96	bade
ʊ	put	54	could, woman, sure
	foot	31	
ʌ	up	86	oven, touch, come, budge
ɛ	bed	91	head, edge, millionaire
	vary	29	
	hair	23	
	there	15	
i	be	70	eve, elite, ski, chief, baby
	eat	10	
	feel	10	
e	angel	45	aid, way
	ate	35	
u	boot	38	you, threw, true, choose, lose, fruit
	truth	21	
	who	8	
	rude	8	
o	both	38	oak, own
	code	14	
ɑ	odd	79	dodge, are, heart
	arm		
ɔ	all	n.a.	faucet, dawn, ought, caught, broad

CHART OF ENGLISH DIPHTHONGS AND THEIR
PRINCIPLE SPELLINGS

Phonemic Symbol	Most Frequent Spellings	Frequency	Other Spellings
ay	find	37	night, pie, dye
	ice	37	
	by	14	
oy	boil	62	
	boy	32	
aw	out	56	
	how	29	

Workbook Supplement

EXERCISE 1: PHONETIC DESCRIPTIONS AND SYMBOLS

A. Match the term with the definition or example that best fits it:

a. voiceless   c. interdental   e. phoneme
b. voiced   d. bilabial

1. When the vocal cords vibrate during speech.

2. A sound produced by putting the tip of the tongue between the two teeth.

3. A meaning-distinguishing sound in a language.

4. When the air passes through the vocal tract without making the vocal cords vibrate.

5. A sound produced with the two lips pursed together.

a. minimal pair   c. liquids   e. labiodental
b. allophones   d. nasals

6. Math–match.

7. Phonetic variants used to realize a single phoneme.

8. /l, r/.

9. A sound produced with the lower lip pressed against the upper teeth.

10. A sound produced when some of the air escapes through the nose.

a. alveolar   c. fricative   e. glide
b. phone   d. affricate

11. When the air flow is constricted by two articulators, causing friction.

12. /f, s, v, z/ are examples of this type of sound.

13. /y, w/ are examples of this type of sound.

14. /t, d/, s/ are examples of this type of sound.

15. A sound produced when the air flow is stopped and then released with a puff of friction.

B. Write the phonetic symbol and the full description for the final sounds in these words:

16. wax   18. pressed   20. dear   22. allow

17. swish   19. edge   21. candy   23. laugh

C. Write the following words in phonetic transcription to indicate the way you say them. Compare your answers to other students' answers. Are there any differences in the transcriptions?

24. penny   27. orange   30. fish   33. Think

25. petty   28. cot   31. jungle   34. pleasure

26. wash   29. caught   32. raisin   35. other

EXERCISE 2: SIMPLE VOWELS

A. Get a lollipop and put it in your mouth. Go over the chart of English vowels and say each cue word. Notice how the lollipop moves as your tongue moves.

B. Say the following sets of words. Are the vowels the same or different the way you say them? Select the phonetic symbol from the previous chart that represents the sound of the vowels as you say them.

WORDS		SAME/DIFFERENT	PHONETIC SYMBOLS
No. 1	No. 2		
tan	ton	**different**	æ
tin	ten		
teen	tune		
Dane	tone		
dune	done		
Tom	tome		
Don	Dawn		
cut	cat		
cot	caught		
coot	coat		
cane	can		

C. Compare your answers with your classmates. Do you find any variation in the pronunciation of some words?

EXERCISE 3: PHONOLOGICAL PROCESSES IN ENGLISH (PART 1)

A. There are three true diphthongs that occur in English: /oy/, /aw/, and /ay/. Identify the diphthongs in the following words: house, fight, kite, white, poison, toy, flounce, and about.

B. The glides /y/ and /w/ usually occur with some of the simple vowel phonemes in English (the tense vowels) when they are pronounced.
   a. Transcribe the vowels in the following words using a diphthong (tense vowel plus [y] or [w]): bead, bade, leap, lay, booed, bode, school, poll. Write these vowels in the middle of [ ], because they are "phones" and not "phonemes." Which vowels take [y] and which take [w]?
   b. Spanish does not have these diphthongized vowels. Speakers of English who learn Spanish often have trouble "removing" the diphthongs from their speech, so they can get rid of their accent. Say these words in Spanish. If there is a Spanish speaker in the class, compare the way you say the following words: amigo, taco, No fumar, and Que.

c. Here is another characteristic of English phonology that transfers to Spanish and results in a typical accent. Consider the fact that voiceless consonants are aspirated when they are syllable initial in English. The English speaker says "taco" with an aspirated /t/ and /k/, but the Spanish speaker does not. (The /t/ in Spanish is dental, not alveolar.)

English speaker [tʰɑhkow]   Spanish speaker /tɑko/

How might the English speaker pronounce the following words in learning Spanish? Write the transcriptions between [ ] because they are phonetic and not phonemic:

pato   patio   Que tal?   tengo

d. What difficulties might the Spanish speaker have in learning to pronounce English?

EXERCISE 4: PHONETIC TRANSCRIPTION EXERCISES

Transcribe the following words using phonetic symbols. Use the following procedure:

1. Say the word as naturally as possible. Don't distort your pronunciation.

2. Find the phonetic symbol that represents your pronunciation of each phoneme in the word.

3. Don't forget to put them in [ ].

4. Indicate diphthongization of tense vowels and aspiration of syllable initial voiceless stops.

A. breath, breathe, egg, edge, ache, axe, cloth, clothe, clothes, khaki, bureau, buy, trace, traceable, guest, write, ride, writer, rider. (Note: use [D] to indicate the "flapped t" sound that occurs between two vowels in "writer.")

B. champagne, canyon, weave, web, deceive, deception, worth, worthy, through, throw, birth, thyme, then, these, those, aisle, chrome.

C. fifth, twelfth, north, northern, thief, thieves, cats, dogs, houses, louse, lousy, sugar, creature, create, simmer, singer, sinner, thing, thin.

D. lingerie, matinee, heaven, ghoul, kaleidoscope, plait, again, behind, consign, waggle, wander, sergeant, delirium, irrigate, beware, spur, cure.

EXERCISE 5: PHONEMES AND ALLOPHONES

Phonemes are symbols that stand for abstract mental images of sounds, like /t/, /l/, and /o/. Phones are symbols that represent concrete sounds as we might hear them or say them. There are more phones needed to represent speech than phonemes. All the phones that have a relation to a certain phoneme are called allophones. For example, all voiceless stops have at least two allophones, the "regular" pronunciation as in [p] and [k] and the aspirated pronunciation that occurs at the beginning of syllables: [pʰ] and [kʰ]. When the occurrence of one allophone is predictable when compared to the other, as in this case, we call this *complementary distribution*.

Complementary distribution means that the allophones are "distributed" as complements (in the mathematical sense of the word) to each other. In one situation, one will occur and in the rest, another will occur. We can write this as follows: At the beginning of syllables, the aspirated allophone will occur. Elsewhere, the unaspirated allophone will occur. They are in complementary distribution.

A. In the case of /t/, which has several allophones ([t], [tʰ], [D], [ʔ]), which of these are in complementary distribution?
Write the distribution for [t], [tʰ].
Is this a case of complementary distribution?
Write the distribution for [t] and [D].
Is this a case of complementary distribution?

Examine the following data to see if the distribution of [t] and [ʔ] is predictable:

[k ɪ t]   [k ɪ ʔ]   [b æ t]   [b æ ʔ],
and in some dialects: [bʌDər]   [bʌʔər].
Is this a case of complementary distribution?

If two allophones occur in the same environments in words unpredictably, they are in random distribution or *free variation*. Are [t] and [ʔ] in complementary distribution or free variation?

B. Are these vowels in complementary distribution or free variation (: indicates extra lengthening of the vowel.)? Explain why or why not.
bead   [biy:d]   beat   [biyt]

mowed	[mow:d]	moat	[mowt]
snag	[snæ:g]	snack	[snæ:k]
lube	[luw:b]	loop	[luwp]

EXERCISE 6: PHONEMIC TRANSCRIPTION

A. Using what you have learned about phonemes and allophones, identify which of these are phonemic transcriptions by putting / / around them and which are phonetic transcriptions by putting [ ] around them. Identify the word. There may be some ambiguity in some answers; if so, point them out.

tʰiy:m	tim			
ret	red	rey:Dər	redər	retər
mid	mit	miy:d	miytʰ	miyʔ

B. Write the following words in phonetic and phonemic transcription. Note that aspiration can occur in syllable–initial consonant clusters with voiceless stops, such as pl, pr, kr, kl, and tr.

bleed
bleat
clothe
crude
clad
clatter
critter

C. How important is the phonemic transcription to our ideas of what ESL learners should know for various skills? How important is the phonetic transcription to our ideas of what ESL learners should know for various skills?

EXERCISE 7: PHONOLOGICAL PROCESSES (PART 2)

So far we have talked about several phonological processes that occur in English and in this exercise we will learn about a few more. One general process is called *assimilation*. We say that assimilation has taken place when two sounds which are near each other become more similar to each other in terms of voicing, place, or manner of articulation.

A. Here are some examples of assimilation. Identify whether they seem to be assimilating in voicing or place of articulation.

   a. i<u>n</u>put   [impʊt]
   b. i<u>n</u>come   [iŋkʌm]

c. escape**d**   [ɛskeypt]

d. Cho**m**sky   [tʃampskiy]

B. A special type of assimilation is called *palatalization*, in which a stop or fricative becomes palatalized in some environments. Explain where the palatalization occurs in each word set. Do you see some generalizations in this process?

a. innate   native   nature
b. press   depression   depressive
c. definition   define   definite
d. cult   culture   cultural
e. permit   permissive   permission
f. rate   ratio   ration
g. provide   proviso   provision
h. act   actual   action

C. Another phonological process is called *velar softening*, in which /k/ and /g/ become "softened" to /s/ or /dʒ/. Pick out where the velar softening has occurred in these word sets. Then make any generalizations you can about the process.

a. analog   analogy
b. electric   electrician   electricity
c. colleague   collegial   college
d. mag- (bound root)   magic
e. log- (bound root)   logic   (socio)logy
f. automatic   automation   automaticity

D. *Vowel reduction* occurs when vowels are so lacking in stress that they are pronounced as a schwa [ə]. Where has vowel reduction occurred?

a. parade   [pəreyd]
b. laboratory   [læbrətɔriy]
c. telegraph   [t ɛləgræf]
d. telegraphy   [t ɛlɛgrəfiy]
e. police   [pəliys]

EXERCISE 8: MORPHOPHONOLOGICAL PROCESSES AND SPELLING PATTERNS

If English writing were truly alphabetic, the changes that occur in the pronunciation of word derived by adding suffixes, as shown in the last exercise, would mean that words like **native**, **nation**, and **national**, would not look the same. In a consistent alphabetic writing system, where one symbol would represent one sound, it is possible that native would be written naitiv, nation would be written naishun, and national would be written nashunl. However, English has taken another course. English writing has another principle which governs these cases: the morphemic principle. This principle states that morphemes will maintain their visual appearance no matter how their pronunciations change because of phonological processes like assimilation, palatalization, vowel reduction, and so on. Although this principle doesn't always hold, it has a strong consistency.

Given the morphemic principle, we are still faced with a quandary. Which of the pronunciations of a morpheme is basic? Which is the one to represent consistently, if there are alternatives? Certain procedures have evolved in answer to this question. We try to maintain the spelling of the tense vowel or diphthong, the "hardest" consonant, and include graphemes that are pronounced in some words but are silent in other words.

1. To write a morpheme consistently in spite of variations in pronunciation, the spelling that represents a tense vowel or diphthong is basic. Similarly, always represent the original vowel although it may be "reduced" to [ə] with a change of stress.
   Examples: **pro̲test—pro̲testant**
   [protɛst] [pratəstənt]
   because /o/ is tense and /a/ is lax.

   sacrifi̲ce—sacrifi̲cial
   [sækrɪfays] [sækrɪfɪʃḷ]

2. We assume that stops are "harder" than fricatives and fricatives are harder than affricates. Choose the stop rather than the fricative, and the fricative rather than the affricate to represent in the spelling.
   Examples: **analog̲—analogy**
   [ænəlɔg] [ænælədʒi]
   because /g/ is a stop and /dʒ/ is an affricate.

   physic̲— physici̲st—physici̲an
   [fɪzɪks]   [fɪzɪsɪst]   [fɪzɪʃʌn]
   because the letter **c** represents the stop /k/ and the other alternatives are fricative [s] or affricate [ʃ].

   refrigerate̲—refrigerati̲on
   [rəfrɪdʒəret] [rəfrɪdʒəreʃʌn]
   because /t/ is a stop and /ʃ/ is an affricate.

   depres̲s̲—depres̲s̲ion
   [dəprɛs] [dəprɛʃʌn]
   because /s/ is a fricative and /ʃ/ is an affricate.

B. Choose the most complete spelling, that is, the spelling that includes all sounds although they may be silent in some words.

Examples: **paradigm—paradigmatic**
because the /g/ is pronounced in **paradigmatic**, it must be written in the word **paradigm** to preserve the most complete representation of the morpheme.

iamb—iambic
because the /b/ is pronounced in **iambic**, it must be written in **iamb**.

Exercises

A. Match the justification (tense vowel or diphthong, stop>fricative> affricate, or most complete spelling) with the pronunciation and spelling difficulty in the following word sets. Some words may have more than one justification.
a. domestic—domesticity
b. phlegm—phlegmatic
c. severe—severity
d. define—definite
e. electric—electricity
f. confess—confession
g. bomb—bombard
h. signature—sign

B. Find two original examples for each of the morphemic spelling principles.

C. English writing has been called *morphophonemic*. What does this mean?

D. These are counterexamples to the morphemic principle. Explain how they are exceptions.
a. goose—gosling
b. maintain—maintenance
c. pronounce—pronunciation

EXERCISE 9: GRAPHEMES: PROBABILITIES
AND RIMES

In teaching reading, teachers sometimes distinguish between words that follow spelling patterns and those that don't. Words that have irregular spellings are called *sight words* and they are commonly taught as whole words that must be memorized. Here are some words from common sight word lists. Divide them into categories of (a) true sight words, (b) words that are probably not true sight words based on the probabilities, (c) words that could be taught as a common rime pattern, or (d) words that could be taught as compound words.

above	dead	head	neighbor	soldier	wolf
across	deaf	heart	neither	some	woman
again	debt	heaven	night	someone	women
aisle	desire	heavy	none	something	won
answer	do	here	ocean	sometime	would
anxious	does	high	of	son	wrong
any	done	idea	office	soul	you
bear	don't	Indian	often	special	young
beautiful	double	instead	oh	spread	your
because	doubt	isle	once	square	
been	dove	key	one	steak	
behind	dozen	kind	onion	straight	
believe	early	knee	only	sure	
bind	earn	knew	other	sword	
both	eight	knife	ought	their	
bough	enough	know	patient	there	
bread	eye	language	piece	they	
break	father	laugh	pretty	though	
bright	fence	laughed	pull	thought	
brought	field	leather	purpose	to	
build	fight	library	push	together	
built	find	light	put	ton	
bury	folks	lion	quiet	tongue	
busy	four	live	ranger	too	
buy	freight	lived	ready	touch	
calf	friend	love	really	two	
captain	front	machine	right	use	
caught	garage	many	rough	usual	
chief	get	measure	said	vein	
child	ghost	might	says	very	
clothes	give	mild	school	view	
colt	gloves	million	science	was	
coming	gone	mind	scissors	wash	
cough	great	minute	sew	weather	

could	guard	mischief	shoe	were
couple	guess	mother	should	what
cousin	guest	move	sign	who
cruel	guide	Mr.	snow	wild
curve	have	Mrs.	soften	wind

EXERCISE 10: ONSETS AND RIMES

One strategy that appears to develop in English-speaking readers is that of reasoning by analogy to try to pronounce a new word found in reading. If you can pronounce a new word, even imperfectly, it helps you decide if you know the word in your productive oral vocabulary or if you have heard the word in your receptive vocabulary. If so, you may already have a lexical entry for the word in your mental lexicon to which you can attach additional information about the visual image of the word or about the meaning as encountered in the reading. If, after trying to figure out the pronunciation, you still don't know what the word is, you can begin to form a new lexical entry with the visual and auditory image you have formed in response to the unknown word and you can start making connections to meaning from the information in the passage. An additional strategy, then, is to guess the meaning from context.

A. (a.) Separate these words into their component onsets and rimes and find word that are likely to be known to ESL readers that can serve for reasoning by analogy. (b.) Then list context clues that assist in forming a meaning. (c.) Write any additional information that you might tell students to help them with this word and with other words in general. (d.) Does the onset or rime strategy seem to help with this word? Follow the following example:

1. (From label) Apply *deodorant* topically under arms for all-day protection.
   a. deodorant   Syllables: de - o - der - ant
   Onsets and rimes: Analogies:
   d / e   me
   / o   no
   d / er   her
   / ant   plant
   b. Context clues: something you can apply; you apply it under your arms; it protects you.
   c. -ant as a suffix is usually unstressed and pronounced [-ənt].
   d. yes.

2. Before 1965, no financial *transactions* were possible for women without their husband's consent.

3. Newspapers used to carry *sex-segregated* help-wanted ads.

4. Few women held *prominent* positions in medicine, law, or politics.

5. No women *anchored* the news programs on television.

EXERCISE 11: INFLECTIONAL MORPHEMES

English does not use inflectional morphology very much. Following are the inflectional morphemes:

Nouns: -s marks the regular plural—He needed two book**s**.

          -s marks the possessive form (especially of animate things)—The dog**'s** dish is empty.

Verbs: -s marks the third person singular present tense—He want**s** the newspaper.

          -ed marks the past tense for regular verbs—He want**ed** the newspaper.

          -ed marks the past participle for regular verbs—He has stud**ied** in Canada for years.

          An allomorph, -en, marks the past participle for many irregular verbs—He has spok**en** French since then.

          -ing marks the present participle for all verbs—He is learn**ing** Japanese.

Adjectives & Adverbs: -er marks the comparative form—He has bought the new**er** car.

          -est marks the superlative form—He can't afford the new**est** car.

   a. Examine the following data about the plural -s suffix (morpheme) and answer the questions that follow:

decks	maps	boxes	cats	dogs
ditches	fads	tabs	hills	rivers
dishes	buses	cuffs	coves	combs

1. How many spellings are there for this morpheme?

2. What three pronunciations are there for this morpheme? (These are called *allomorphs*. Can you define this term?)

3. List the words in three columns based on the pronunciation of the suffix. List both the singular and plural words.

4. Can you identify the phonetic property shared by the final sounds of each of the singular words in each columns?

5. If I said there was a phonological process called *Voicing Assimilation*, would that help explain what is going on here?

6. If I said there was a phonological process called *Dissimilation*, would that help explain some of what is going on there?

7. Does this example follow the morphemic principle of English writing, that morphemes are written the same no matter how they change in pronunciation?

Using these sets of data, answer the same set of questions:

b. Dave's	Bill's	Fred's	Ross's	Jack's
Max's	Matt's	Jeff's	Doug's	Mr. Birch's
Jeb's	Rap's	Mary's	Jennifer's	Maria's
c. leaves	dents	relaxes	spends	traps
confesses	clutches	robs	sniffs	speaks
logs	spills	plays	draws	naps
d. waited	needed	learned	saved	sniffed
snored	mapped	cracked	noted	rubbed
fogged	spilled	played	wanted	escused

How much of this is useful to teach your typical ESL and EFL student?

EXERCISE 12: DERIVATIONAL MORPHEMES

A. Identify the following as a derivational morpheme or as a bound root: comment*ary*, re*ceive*, *pro*-war, pro*gress*, *non*standard, *sub*processor, process*or*, pro*cess*,*pro*cess. What does each morpheme mean?

B. Divide these words into their component morphemes: moccasin, money, monoxide, morpheme, mortgaged, mousetrap, muffler, multiple, multivariable, mustache, mythology. You may need a dictionary.

C. Look back at the definitions of inflectional morphemes and derivational morphemes and try to classify each of the following examples as one or the other. Note the context in which the word appears. Make a note of your difficulties.

   a. Jennifer is tall**er** than Jane.   Jennifer is a basketball play**er**.
   b. She is play**ing** basketball right now.   Play**ing** is her main activity.
   c. She expect**ed** to win the game.   Her expect**ed** win did not happen.

D. How can you explain these different forms of the morpheme "-in"?

a. illegal	c. improbable	e. inconceivable (in rapid speech)
b. irrelevant	d. inefficient	f. intangible

References

Abu-Rabia, S. (1997). Verbal and working memory skills of bilingual Hebrew–English speaking children. *International Journal of Psycholinguistics, 1*, pp. 25–40.

Adams, M. (1990). *Beginning to read: Thinking and learning about print.* Cambridge, MA: MIT Press.

Aebersold, J., & Field, M. L. (1997). *From reader to reading teacher: Issues and strategies for second language classrooms.* Cambridge, England: Cambridge University Press.

Aidinis, A., & Nunes, T. (1998). The role of different levels of phonological awareness in the development of reading and spelling in Greek. *Reading and Writing. 14*(1–2), 145–177.

Alderson, J. C., & Urquhart, A. H. (1984). *Reading in a Foreign Language.* London: Longman.

Baddeley, A., Gathercole, S., & Papagno, C. (1998). The phonological loop as a language learning device. *Psychological Review, 105,* 1158–1173.

Bauer, T. (1996). Arabic writing. In P. Daniels & W. Bright (Eds.), *The world's writing systems* (pp. 559–564). New York: Oxford University Press.

Been, S. (1979). Reading in the Foreign Language Teaching Program. In R. Mackay, B. Barkman, & R. Jordan (Eds.) *Reading in a second language: Hypotheses, organization, and practice* (pp. 91–102). Rowley, MA: Newbury House.

Ben-Dror, I., Frost, R., & Bentin, S. (1995). Orthographic representation and phonemic segmentation in skilled readers: A cross-language comparison. *Psychological Science, 6,* 176–181.

Bensoussan, M., & Laufer, B. (1984). Lexical Guessing in context in EFL reading comprehension. *Journal of Research in Reading, 7,* 15–31.

Bentin, S., & Frost, R. (1995). Morphological factors in visual word identification in Hebrew. In L. Feldman (Ed.), *Morphological aspects of language processing* (pp. 271–292). Hillsdale, NJ: Lawrence Erlbaum Associates.

187

Berndt, R. S., Reggia, J. A., & Mitchum, C. C. (1987). Empirically derived probabilities for grapheme-to-phoneme correspondences in English. *Behavior Research Methods, Instruments, & Computers, 19*, 1–9.

Bernhardt, E. (1991). *Reading development in a second language: Theoretical, empirical, and classroom perspectives.* Norwood, NJ: Ablex.

Bradley, L., & Bryant, P. E. (1983). Categorizing sounds and learning to read—A causal connection. *Nature, 303,* 3.

Braten, I., Lie, A., & Andreassen, R. (1998). Explaining individual differences in reading: On the orthographic component of word recognition. *Scandinavian Journal of Educational Research, 42,* 389–399.

Bryant, P., Nunes, T., & Bindman, M. (1999). Morphemes and spelling. In T. Nunes (Ed.), *Learning to read: An integrated view from research and practice* (pp. 15–42). Dordrecht, The Netherlands: Kluwer.

Byrne, B. (1998). *The foundation of literacy: The child's acquisition of the alphabetic principle.* East Sussex, England: Psychology Press.

Caramazza, A., Laudanna, A., & Romani, C. (1988). Lexical access and inflectional morphology. *Cognition, 28,* 297–322.

Carney, E. (1994). *A survey of English spelling.* London: Routledge & Kegan Paul.

Carrell, P. (1993). Introduction: Interactive approaches to second language reading. In P. Carrell, J. Devine, & D. Eskey (Eds.), *Interactive approaches to second language reading* (pp. 1–7). Cambridge, England: Cambridge University Press.

Carroll, S. (1992). *On Cognates Second Language Research, 8,* 93–119.

Chall, J. (1983). *Stages of reading development.* New York: McGraw-Hill.

Cheung, H. (1996). Nonword span as a unique predictor of second language vocabulary learning. *Developmental Psychology, 32,* 867–873.

Chikamatsu, N. (1996). The effects of L1 orthography on L2 word recognition. *Studies in Second Language Acquisition, 18,* 403–432.

Chitiri, H., & Willows, D. (1994). Word recognition in two languages and orthographies: English and Greek. *Memory and Cognition, 22,* 313–325.

Clarke, M., & Silberstein, S. (1979). Toward a realization of psycho-linguistic principles in the ESL reading class. In R. Mackay, B. Barkman, & R. Jordan (Eds.), *Reading in a second language: Hypotheses, organization, and practice* (pp. 48–65). Rowley, MA: Newbury House.

Clymer, T. (1963). The utility of phonic generalizations in the primary grades. *Reading Teacher, 16,* 252–258.

Coady, J. (1979). A psycholinguistic model of the ESL reader. In R. Mackay, B. Barkman, & R. Jordan (Eds.), *Reading in a second language: Hypotheses, organization, and practice* (pp. 5–12). Rowley, MA: Newbury House.

Comrie, B. (1981). *Language universals and linguistic typology.* Chicago: University of Chicago Press.

Crowder, R., & Wagner, R. (1992). *The psychology of reading.* Oxford, England: Oxford University Press.

Day, R. R., & Bamford, J. (1998). *Extensive reading in the second language classroom.* Cambridge, England: Cambridge University Press.

Derwing, B., Smith, M., & Weibe, G., (1995). On the role of spelling in morpheme recognition: Experimental studies with children and adults. In L. Feldman (Ed.), *Morphological aspects of language processing* (pp. 3–27). Hillsdale, NJ: Lawrence Erlbaum Associates.

Dewey, D. (1970). *Relative frequency of English spellings*. New York: Teachers College Press.

Downer, M. Viewer's Guide Teaching Word Identification a video in the series Teaching Reading: Strategies from successful classrooms (a six-part national training series). Produced by the Center for the Study of Reading. Champaign, IL: University of Illinois–Urbana.

Ehri, L. (1998). Grapheme-phoneme knowledge is essential for learning to read words in English. In J. Metsala & L. Ehri (Eds.), *Word recognition in beginning literacy* (pp. 3–40). Mahwah, NJ: Lawrence Erlbaum Associates.

Ellis, N., & Beaton, A. (1993). Psycholinguistic determinants of foreign language vocabulary learning. *Language Learning, 43,* 559–617.

Eskey, D. (1979). A model program for teaching advanced reading to students of English as a foreign language. In R. Mackay, B. Barkman, & R. Jordan (Eds.), *Reading in a second language: Hypotheses, organization, and practice* (pp. 66–78). Rowley, MA: Newbury House.

Eskey, D. (1993). Holding in the bottom: An interactive approach to the language problems of second language readers. In P. Carrell, J. Devine, & D. Eskey (Eds.), *Interactive approaches to second language reading* (pp. 93–100). Cambridge, England: Cambridge University Press.

Fowler, A. E., & Liberman, I. Y. (1995). The role of phonology and orthography in morphological awareness. In L. Feldman (Ed.), *Morphological aspects of language processing* (pp. 157–188). Hillsdale, NJ: Lawrence Erlbaum Associates.

Freeman, D., & Freeman, Y. (1999). The California Reading Initiative: a formula for failure for bilingual students. *Language Arts, 76*(3), 241–248.

Garnham, A., Oakhill, J., Ehrlich, M., & Carreiras, M. (1995). Representations and processes in the interpretation of pronouns: New evidence from Spanish and French. *Journal of Memory and Language, 34,* 41–62.

Gaskill, W. (1979). The teaching of intermediate reading in the ESL classroom. In M. Celce-Murcia & L. McIntosh (Eds.), *Teaching English as a second or foreign language* (pp. 144–154). Rowley, MA: Newbury House.

Gaskins, I. (1997). Teaching the delayed reader: The Benchmark School model. In J. Flood, S. B. Heath, & D. Lapp (Eds.), *Handbook of research on teaching literacy through the communicative and visual arts* (pp. 657–677). A project of the International Reading Association, New York: Macmillan Library reference USA.

Gathercole, S. E., Willis, C., Emslie, H., & Baddeley, A. D. (1991). The influences of number of syllables and wordlikeness on children's repetition of nonwords. *Applied Psycholinguistics, 12,* 349–367.

Geva, E. (1999). Issues in the development of second language reading: Implications for instruction and assessment. In T. Nunes (Ed.), *Learning to read: An integrated view from research and practice* (pp. 343–367). Dordrecht, The Netherlands: Kluwer.

Goerwitz, R. (1996). The Jewish scripts. In P. Daniels & W. Bright (Eds.), *The world's writing systems* (pp. 487–498). New York: Oxford University Press.

Goodman, K. S. (1967). Reading: A psycholinguistic guessing game. *Journal of the Reading Specialist, 6*, 126–35.

Goodman, K. (1968). The Psycholinguistic nature of the reading process. In K. Goodman (Ed.), *The Psycholinguistic nature of the reading process*. Detroit, MI: Wayne State University Press.

Goodman, K. (1973). On the psycholinguistic method of teaching reading. In F. Smith (Ed.), *Psycholinguistics and Reading* (pp. 158–176). New York: Holt, Rinehart, and Winston.

Goswami, U. (1998). The role of analogies in the development of word recognition. In J. Metsala & L. Ehri, (Eds.), *Word recognition in beginning literacy* (pp. 41–63). Mahwah, NJ: Lawrence Erlbaum Associates.

Groff, P., & Seymour, D. (1987). *Word recognition: The why and how.* Springfield, IL: Thomas.

Gunning, T. (1988). *Teaching phonics and other word attack skills.* Springfield, IL: Thomas.

Hatch, E. (1979). Reading a second language. In M. Celce-Murcia, & L. McIntosh (Eds.), *Teaching English as a second or foreign language* (pp. 129–134). Rowley, MA: Newbury House.

Henderson, L. (1982). *Orthography and word recognition in reading.* London: Academic.

Henderson, L. (1984b). Writing systems and reading processes. In L. Henderson (Ed.), *Orthographies and reading: Perspectives from cognitive psychology, neuropsychology and linguistics* (pp.11–24). Hillsdale, NJ: Lawrence Erlbaum Associates.

Jarvella, R. J., Job, R., Sandstrom, G., & Schreuder, R. (1987). Morphological constraints on word recognition. In A. Allport, D. G. Mackay, W. Prinz, & E. Scheerer (Eds.), *Language perception and production: Relationships between listening, speaking, reading, and writing* (pp. 245–265). London: Academic Press.

Kanda, Shunho. The Yomiuri Weekly, 59, 41, September 24, 2000, page 37.

Kang, H., & Simpson. G. (1996). Development of semantic and phonological priming in a shallow orthography. *Developmental Psychology, 32*, 860–866.

King, R. (1996). Korean writing. In P. Daniels & W. Bright (Eds.), *The world's writing systems* (pp. 218–227). New York: Oxford University Press.

Koda, K. (1993). Transferred L1 strategies and L2 syntactic structure in L2 sentence comprehension. *Modern Language Journal, 77*, 490–500.

Koda, K. (1995). Cognitive consequences of L1 and L2 orthographies. In I. Taylor & D. Olson (Eds.), *Scripts and literacy* (pp. 311–326). Dordrecht, The Netherlands: Kluwer.

Lennon, P. (1996). Getting "easy" verbs wrong at the advanced level. *IRAL, 34*, 23–36.

Leong, C., & Tamaoka, K. (1995). Use of phonological information in processing kanji and katakana by skilled and less skilled Japanese readers. *Reading and Writing, 7*, 377–393.

Levin, I., Ravid, D., & Rapaport, S. (1999). Developing morphological awareness. In T. Nunes (Ed.), *Learning to read: An integrated view from research and practice* (pp. 77–105). Dordrecht, The Netherlands: Kluwer.

Lewis, M. (1993). *The lexical approach: The state of ELT and a way forward.* Hove, UK: Language Teaching Publications.

Lewis, M. (1997). *Implementing the lexical approach: Putting theory into practice.* Hove, UK: Language Teaching Publications.

Lukatela, G., Gligorijevic, B., Kostic, A., & Turvey, M. (1980). Representation of inflected nouns in the internal lexicon. *Memory and Language, 8,* 415–423.

Mair, V. (1996) Modern Chinese writing. In P. Daniels & W. Bright (Eds.), *The world's writing systems* (pp. 200–208). New York: Oxford University Press.

Meara, P. (1983). Word associations in a foreign language. *Nottingham Linguistic Circular, 11,* 29–38.

Medsker, L., & Liebowitz, J. (1994). *Design and development of expert systems and neural networks.* New York: Macmillan.

Merritt, R. (1999). Technology: Introduction, Encarta 99 Encyclopedia, CD-ROM.

Millward, C. M. (1996). *A biography of the English language.* Fort Worth, TX: Harcourt Brace.

Moats, L. (1995). The missing foundation in teacher education. *American Educator, 19-2,* 43–51.

Morais, J., Cary, L., Alegria, J., & Bertelson, P. (1979). Does awareness of speech as a sequence of phonemes arise spontaneously? *Cognition, 7,* 323–331.

Morton, J., & Sasanuma, S. (1984). Lexical Access in Japanese. In L. Henderson, *Orthographies and reading: Perspectives from cognitive psychology, neuropsychology and linguistics* (pp. 25–42). Hillsdale, NJ: Lawrence Erlbaum Associates.

Muljani, D., Koda, K., & Moates, D. (1998). The development of word recognition in a second language. *Applied Psycholinguistics, 19,* 99–113.

Naeslund, J. C., & Schneider, W. (1996). Kindergarten letter knowledge, phonological skills, and memory processes: Relative effects on early literacy. *Journal of Experimental Child Psychology, 62,* 30–59.

Napoli, D. (1996). *Linguistics: An introduction.* New York: Oxford University Press.

Navon, D., & Shimron, J. (1984). Reading Hebrew: How necessary is the graphemic representation of vowels? In Henderson, L.

Nunes, T. (1999). *Learning to read: An integrated view from research and practice.* Dordrecht, The Netherlands: Kluwer.

Oney, B., Peters, M., & Katz, L. (1997). Phonological processing in printed word recognition: Effects of age and writing system. *Scientific Studies of Reading, 1,* 65–83.

Osburne, A., & Mulling, S. (2001). Use of morphological analysis by Spanish L1 ESOL learners. *International Review of Applied Linguistics, 39,* 153–159.

Osburne, A., & Mulling, S. (1998). Vocabulary recognition in Spanish-speaking learners of English as a second language. In A. Osburne &

S. Mulling (Eds.), *Writing together: A project for team research* (pp. 12–28). Ann Arbor: University of Michigan Press.

Oz, A. (1989). *Knowing a Woman* (in Hebrew). Jerusalem: Keter Publishing House.

Papagno, C., & Vallar, G. (1992). Phonological short-term memory and the learning of novel words: The effects of phonological similarity and item length. *Quarterly Journal of Experimental Psychology, 44*, 47–67.

Park, K. (1998). *Kwangsoo's thoughts* (in Korean, p. 94). Seoul, Korea: Sodam Publisher.

Rachlin, H. (1989). *Judgment, decision, and choice: A cognitive/behavioral synthesis*. New York: Freeman.

Ryan, A., & Meara, P. (1991). The case of the invisible vowels: Arabic speakers reading English words. *Reading in a Foreign Language, 7*, 531–540.

Saito, S. (1995). Effects of pronounceability and articulatory suppression on phonological learning. *Perceptual and Motor Skills, 81*, 651–657.

Sakuma, N., Sasanuma, S., Tatsumi, I., & Masaki, S. (1998). Orthography and phonology in reading Japanese kanji words. *Memory and Cognition, 26*, 75–87.

Sasanuma, S. (1984). Can surface dyslexia occur in Japanese? In Henderson, L.

Schmitt, N., & Meara, P. (1997). Researching vocabulary through a word knowledge framework. *Studies in Second Language Acquisition, 19*, 17–36.

Schreuder, R., & Baayen, R. (1995). Modeling morphological processing. In L. Feldman (Ed.), *Morphological aspects of language processing* (pp. 131–154). Hillsdale, NJ: Lawrence Erlbaum Associates.

Schreuder, R., Grendel, M., Poulisse, N., Roelofs, A., & van de Voort, M. (1990). Lexical processing, morphological complexity and reading. In D. A. Balota, B. Flores d'Arcais, & K. Rayner (Eds.), *Comprehension processes in reading* (pp. 125–142). Hillsdale, NJ: Lawrence Erlbaum Associates.

Seidenberg, M. (1990). Lexical access: Another theoretical soupstone? In D. Balota, G. Flores D'Arcais, & K. Rayner (Eds.), *Comprehension processes in reading* (pp. 000–000). Hillsdale, NJ: Lawrence Erlbaum Associates.

Service, E., & Kohonen, V. (1995). Is the relation between phonological memory and foreign language learning accounted for by vocabulary acquisition? *Applied Psycholinguistics, 16*, 155–172.

Seymour, P. (1997). Foundations of orthographic development. In C. Perfetti, L. Reiben, & M. Fayol (Eds.), *Learning to spell: Research, theory, and practice across languages* (pp. 319–337). Mahwah, NJ: Lawrence Erlbaum Associates.

Shimron, J., & Sivan, T. (1994). Reading proficiency and orthography: Evidence from Hebrew and English. *Language Learning, 44*, 5–27.

Singleton, D. (1997). Learning and processing L2 vocabulary. *Language Teaching 30*, 213–225.

Smith, F. (1971). *Understanding reading: A psycholinguistic analysis of reading and learning to read*. New York: Holt, Rinehart & Winston.

Smith, J. (1996). Japanese writing. In P. Daniels & W. Bright (Eds.), *The world's writing systems* (pp. 209–217). New York: Oxford University Press.

Stanovich, K. (1991). Changing models of reading and reading acquisition. In L. Reiben & C. A. Perfetti (Eds.), *Learning to read: Basic research and its implications* (pp. 19–31). Hillsdale, NJ: Lawrence Erlbaum Associates.

Taft, M., & Zhu, X. (1995). The representation of bound morphemes in the lexicon: A Chinese study. In L. Feldman (Ed.), *Morphological aspects of language processing* (pp. 293–316). Hillsdale, NJ: Lawrence Erlbaum Associates.

Taylor, I., & Olson, D. (1995a). An introduction to reading the world's scripts. In I. Taylor & D. Olson (Eds.), *Scripts and literacy* (pp. 000–000). Dordrecht, The Netherlands: Kluwer.

Taylor, I., & Taylor, M. M. (1983). *The psychology of reading*. New York: Academic.

Tierney, R. J., & Readence, J. (2000). *Reading strategies and practices*. Boston: Allyn & Bacon.

Tseng, O., & Hung, D. (1981). Linguistic determinism: A written language perspective. In O. Tseng & H. Singer (Eds.), *Perception of print: Reading research in experimental psychology* (pp. 000–000). Hillsdale, NJ: Lawrence Erlbaum Associates.

Treiman, R. (1992). The role of intrasyllabic units in learning to read and spell. In P. B. Gough, L. C. Ehri, & R. Treiman (Eds.), *Reading acquisition* (pp. 65–106). Hillsdale, NJ: Lawrence Erlbaum Associates.

Tyler, A., & Nagy, W. (1990). Use of derivational morphology during reading. *Cognition, 36,* 17–34.

Underwood, G., & Batt, V. (1996). *Reading and understanding*. Cambridge, MA: Blackwell.

Urquhart, S., & Weir, C. (1998). *Reading in a second language*. London: Longman.

Venezky, R. (1970). *The structure of English orthography*. The Hague, Netherlands: Mouton.

Walker, L. J. (1983). Word identification strategies in reading in a foreign language. *Foreign Language Annals, 16,* 293–229.

Wallace, C. (1992). *Reading*. Oxford, England: Oxford University Press.

Wang, W. (1973). The Chinese language. *Scientific American, 228,* 55–56.

Weaver, C. (1994). *Reading process and practice*. Portsmouth, NH: Heinemann.

von Winterfeldt, D., & Edwards, D. (1986). Cambridge, England: Cambridge University Press.

Ying, H. (1996). Multiple constraints on processing ambiguous sentences: Evidence from adult L2 learners. *Language Learning, 46,* 681–711.

Author Index

Subject Index

199